Foundation of Information Technology

Foundation of INFORMATION TECHNOLOGY

Shalini Gupta

ANMOL PUBLICATIONS PVT. LTD.
NEW DELHI-110 002 (INDIA)

ANMOL PUBLICATIONS PVT. LTD.
Regd. Office: 4360/4, Ansari Road, Daryaganj,
New Delhi-110002 (India)
Tel.: 23278000, 23261597, 23286875, 23255577
Fax: 91-11-23280289
Email: anmolpub@gmail.com
Visit us at: www.anmolpublications.com

Branch Office: No. 1015, Ist Main Road, BSK IIIrd Stage
IIIrd Phase, IIIrd Block, Bengaluru-560 085 (India)
Tel.: 080-41723429 • Fax: 080-26723604
Email: anmolpublicationsbangalore@gmail.com

Foundation of Information Technology

First Edition, 2011

PRINTED IN INDIA

Printed at Tarun Offset, Delhi

Contents

Preface

The development of the modern day computer was the result of advances in technologies and man's need to quantify. Papyrus helped early man to record language and numbers. The abacus was one of the first counting machines. Some of the earlier mechanical counting machines lacked the technology to make the design work.

The electronic computers were given this name because they performed the work that had previously been assigned to people. "Computer" was originally a job title: it was used to describe those human beings whose job it was to perform the repetitive calculations required to compute such things as navigational tables, tide charts, and planetary positions for astronomical almanacs.

Imagine you had a job where hour after hour, day after day, you were to do nothing but compute multiplications. Boredom would quickly set in, leading to carelessness, leading to mistakes. And even on your best days you wouldn't be producing answers very fast.

Author

1

Introduction

OVERVIEW

To accomplish its various tasks, the computer is made of different parts, each serving a particular purpose in conjunction with other parts.

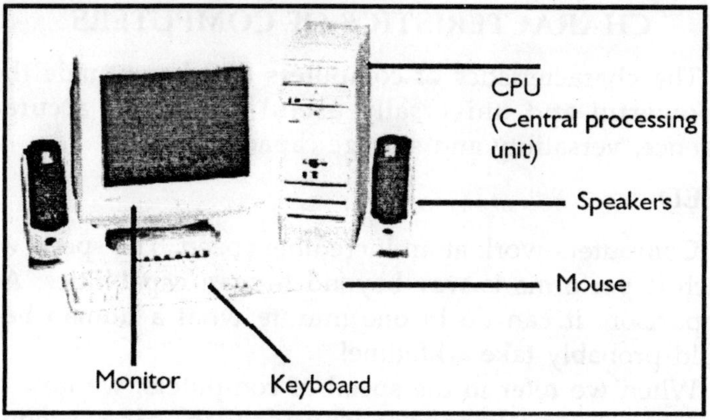

The "computer" is an ensemble of different machines that you will be using to get your job done. A computer is primarily made of the Central Processing Unit (usually referred to as the computer), the monitor, the keyboard, and the mouse.

Other pieces of hardware, commonly referred to as peripherals, can enhance or improve your experience with the computer. To use the computer, you must first turn it on. To do this, the first thing you should find is the power switch that is used to put the unit on. Nowadays, it is usually located in front of the computer. Pushing it would start the computer. The computer works by receiving and giving instructions (in future lessons, we will learn that an instruction or a group of instructions is actually called a programme).

For example, when you press the power button, you give the instruction to the electricity to "wake" up the computer. This instruction causes the computer to start giving its own instructions to internal parts.

One of the instructions is called BIOS (it stands for Basic Input/Output System). Depending on the computer you are using, when it comes up, it may directly display the desktop or it may ask you to log in.

Because there are so many scenarios, we cannot review all of them. If you are using Microsoft Windows 95, 98, Millennium, or XP, the desktop may display once the computer is ready.

CHARACTERISTICS OF COMPUTERS

The characteristics of computers that have made them so powerful and universally useful are speed, accuracy, diligence, versatility and storage capacity.

SPEED

Computers work at an incredible speed. The speed with which it performs is way beyond human capabilities. As a comparison, it can do in one minute what a human being would probably take a lifetime!

When we refer to the speed of computers, we now talk in terms of milliseconds (hundredth of a second), microseconds (millionth of a second), nanoseconds (billionth of a second), and even picoseconds (trillionth of a second). A powerful computer is capable of performing about 3-4 million simple instructions per second.

ACCURACY

In addition to being fast, computers are also accurate. Errors that may occur can almost always be attributed to human error (inaccurate data, poorly designed system or faulty instructions/programmes written by the programmer) rather than technological weaknesses.

DILIGENCE

Unlike human beings, computers are highly consistent. They do not suffer from human traits of boredom and tiredness resulting in lack of concentration.

Computers, therefore, score high over human beings in performing voluminous and repetitive jobs.

VERSATILITY

Computers are versatile machines and are capable of performing any task as long as it can be broken down into a series of logical steps.

This means that their capability is, once again, limited only by human intelligence. As is evident, in today's fast developing technology-world, it is almost inconceivable to find an area where computers are not being used.

STORAGE CAPACITY

Today's computers can store volumes of data. Unlike human memory where unimportant information is relegated to the back of the mind and forgotten as time progresses, a piece of information once recorded (or stored) in the computer, can never be forgotten and can be retrieved almost instantaneously.

COMPONENTS OF COMPUTER

A *computer* is a device capable of performing computations and making logical decisions at speeds millions and even billions of times faster than human beings can. For example, many of today's personal computers can perform hundreds of millions of additions per second.

Computers process data under the control of sets of instructions called *computer programmes*. These computer programmes guide the computer through orderly sets of actions specified by people called computer programmers. A computer is comprised of various devices that are referred to as *hardware*. The computer programmes that run on a computer are referred to as *software*.

COMPUTER HARDWARE

Almost every computer may be seen as being divided into six logical units. Figure illustrates the main computer components.

Input Unit

This unit obtains information from various input devices and places this information at the disposal of the other units so that the information may be processed. The information is entered into computers today through keyboards and mouse devices.

Output Unit

This unit takes information that has been processed by the computer and places it on various output devices to make information available for use outside the computer. Most output from computer today is displayed on screens, printed on paper, or used to control other devices.

Memory Unit

The memory unit stores information. Each computer contains memory of two main types: *RAM* and *ROM*. *RAM* is volatile. Your programme and data are stored in RAM when you are using the computer.

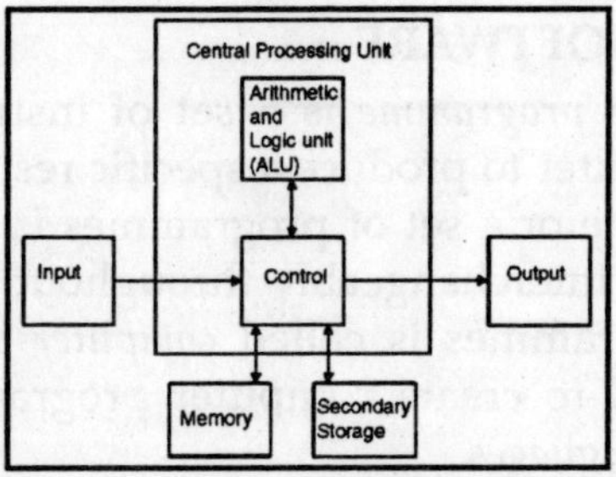

Fig. Basic Hardware Units of a Computer

ROM contains fundamental instructions that cannot be lost or changed by the user. ROM is non-volatile.

Arithmetic and Logic Unit: The ALU performs all the arithmetic and logic operations. Ex: addition, subtraction, comparison, etc.

Central Processing Unit (CPU): The unit supervises the overall operation of the computer. The CPU tells the input unit when information should be read into the memory unit, tell the ALU when information from the memory should be used in calculations and tells the output unit when to send information from the memory unit to certain output devices.

Secondary Storage: Secondary storage devices are used to be permanent storage area for programmes and data. Virtually all secondary storage is now done on magnetic tapes, magnetic disks and CD-ROMs. A magnetic hard disk consists of either a single rigid platter or several platters that spin together on a common spindle. A movable access arm positions the read and write mechanisms over, but not quite touching, the recordable surfaces. Such a configuration is shown in Figure.

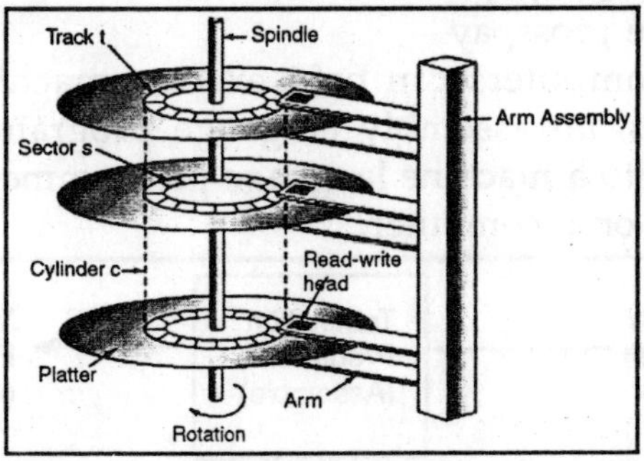

Fig. The Internal Structure of a Magnetic hard Disk Drive

COMPUTER SOFTWARE

A *computer programme* is a set of instructions used to operate a computer to produce a specific result. Another term for a programme or a set of programmes is *software,* and we use both terms interchangeably throughout the text. Writing computer programmes is called *computer programming.*The languages used to create computer programmes are called *programming languages.*

Machine and Assembly Languages

Machine languages are the lowest level of computer languages. Programmes written in machine language consist of entirely of 1s and 0s.

Programmes in machine language can control directly to the computer's hardware.

00101010 000000000001 000000000010
10011001 000000000010 000000000011

A machine language instruction consists of two parts: an instruction part and an address part.

The *instruction part* (opcode) is the leftmost group of bits in the instruction and tells the computer the operation to be performed. The *address part* specifies the memory address of the data to be used in the instruction.

Assembly languages perform the same tasks as machine languages, but use symbolic names for opcodes and operands instead of 1s and 0s.

- Load basepay
- Add overpay
- Store grosspay

Since computers can only execute machine language programmes, an assembly language programme must be translated into a machine language programme before it can be executed on a computer.

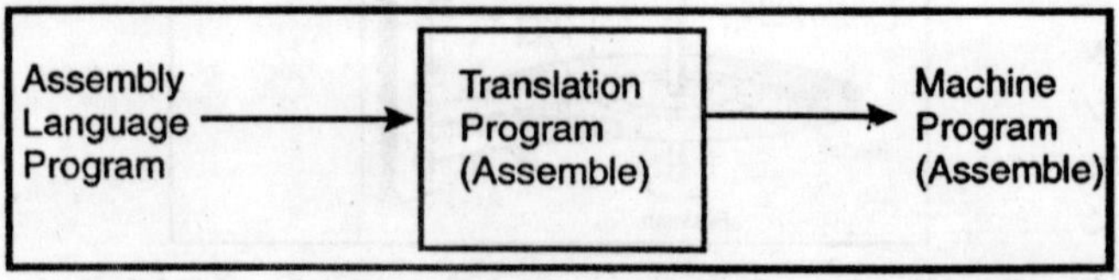

Fig. Assembly Translation

Machine languages and assembly languages are called low-level languages since they are closest to computer hardware.

High-level Programming Languages: High-level programming languages create computer programmes using instructions that much easier to understand than machine or assembly language instructions.

Programmes written in a high-level language must be translated into a low level language using a programme called a*compiler*. A compiler translates programming code into a low-level format. High-level languages allow programmers to write instructions that look like every English sentences and commonly used mathematical notations.

Each line in a high-level language programme is called a *statement*.

Ex: Result = (First + Second)*Third.

Once a programme is written in a high-level language, it must also be translated into the machine language of the computer on which it will be run. This translation can be accomplished in two ways.

When each statement in a high-level source programme is translated individually and executed immediately upon translation, the programming language used is called an *interpreted language,* and the programme doing the translation is called an *interpreter*.

When all of the statements in a high-level source programme are translated as a complete unit before any one statement is executed, the programming language used is called is called a *compiled language*. In this case, the programme doing the translation is called a *compiler*.

Application and System Software

Two types of computer programmes are: application software and system software.

Application software consists of those programmes written to perform particular tasks required by the users.

System software is the collection of programmes that must be available to any computer system for it to operate.

The most important system software is the *operating system*. Examples of some well-known operating systems include MS-DOS, UNIX, and MS WINDOWS. Many operating systems allow user to run multiple programmes. Such operating systems are called *multitasking systems*.

OPERATIONS OF COMPUTER

INPUT

Home computers are microcomputers. Input is supplied to the microcomputer with the use of a keyboard, a mouse, or another input device. These input devices may be called peripheral devices.

PROCESSING

Processing is done inside the computer in an area called the central processing unit (CPU). Processing is the conversion of input to output.

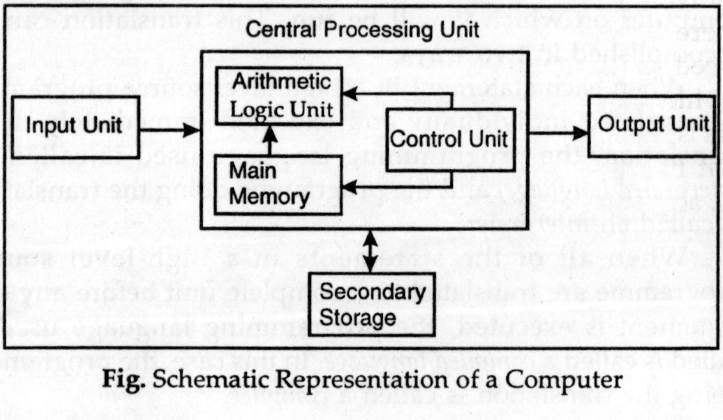

Fig. Schematic Representation of a Computer

STORAGE

Storage refers to holding information somewhere. RAM, Random Access Memory, is short-term memory. It is volatile memory because the memory is automatically "erased" when the power is turned off or interrupted. The RAM memory is located inside the computer case on the motherboard. A motherboard is not the keyboard. The keyboard is what you type with. A motherboard holds RAM memory, electronic circuits and other computer parts including the central processing unit. ROM, Read-Only-Memory, is not volatile meaning the memory is still there when power is interrupted or turned off. When the computer is turned back on again, ROM memory is still in storage on the internal hard disk.

OUTPUT

Output is the result of a computer process. Output may be viewed on a monitor screen, heard through speakers, printed on printers, and so forth. Output devices may be considered hardware and are also considered to be peripheral devices.

TYPES OF COMPUTERS

THE DESKTOP

A computer is referred to as "desktop" when it is relatively small enough to be positioned on top of a table where a person is working. Such a computer can also be placed on the floor or somewhere under, or aside of, the table, in which case the monitor would be placed on top of the table. This is the most common type of computers used in the office or at home. A desktop computer is made of different parts that are connected with cables.

THE LAPTOP

A computer is called laptop when it combines the CPU,

the monitor, the keyboard, and the mouse in one unit to be so small that you can carry it on your laps when traveling or commuting. A laptop is also called a notebook. Other parts, such as an external mouse, an external keyboard, a monitor, or peripherals such as a printer or a projector, can be connected to the laptop. A laptop is only physically smaller than a desktop but, everything considered, it can do anything that a desktop can do.

THE SERVER

A server is a computer that holds information that other computers, called workstations, can retrieve. Such workstations are connected to the server using various means. This means that they could be connected using cable, wireless connection, etc.

Only computers that maintain a type of connection with the server can get the information that is stored in the server. Normally, although not particularly recommended, any computer, including a desktop or even a laptop can be used as a server, as long as it can do the job required.

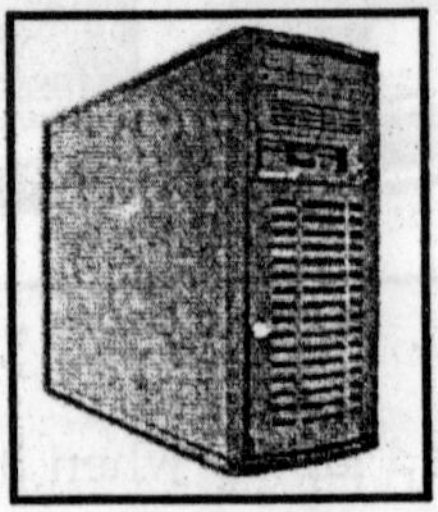

Any type of computer, including a desktop, a laptop, a CD or DVD machine, etc can be connected to a server. The person who sets up a server also defines the types of connections it is made for.

THE MAINFRAME

A mainframe is a computer, usually physically big, that does almost all the jobs for other types of computers that are connected to it.

This is a broad definition but other aspects are involved. Like a server, the programme that runs in the mainframe defines its role.

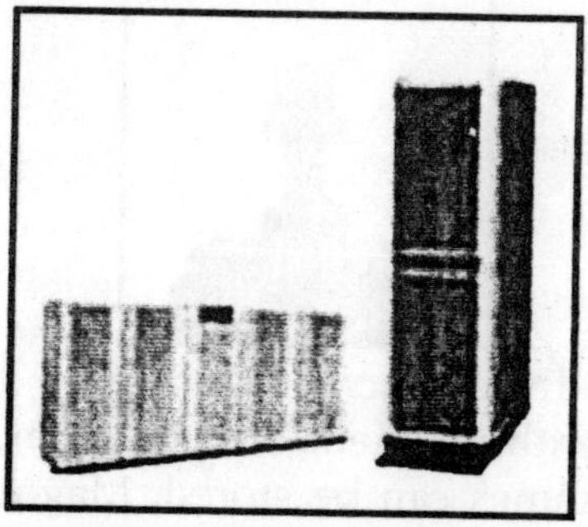

GENRATIONS OF COMPUTER

The history of computer development is often referred to in reference to the different generations of computing devices. A generation refers to the state of improvement in the development of a product. This term is also used in the different advancements of computer technology. With each new generation, the circuitry has gotten smaller and more advanced than the previous generation before it. As a result of the miniaturization, speed, power, and memory of computers has proportionally increased. Each generation of computer is characterized by major technological development that fundamentally changed the way computers operate, resulting in increasingly smaller, cheaper, more powerful and more efficient and reliable devices. Read about each generation and the developments that led to the current devices that we use today.

FIRST GENERATION

The first computers used vacuum tubes for circuitry and magnetic drums for memory, and were often enormous, taking up entire rooms.

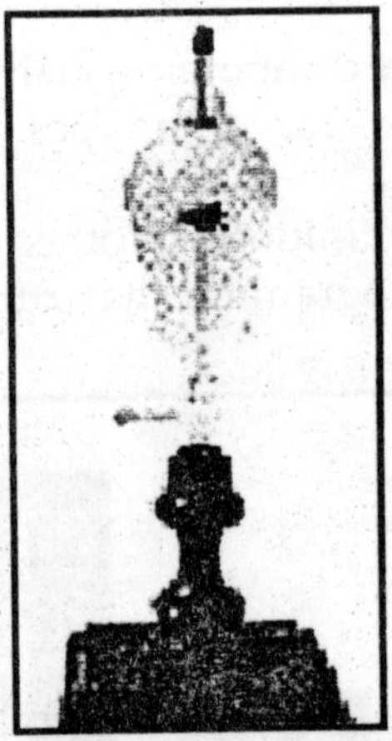

A magnetic drum, also referred to as drum, is a metal cylinder coated with magnetic iron-oxide material on which data and programmes can be stored. Magnetic drums were once use das a primary storage device but have since been implemented as auxiliary storage devices.

The tracks on a magnetic drum are assigned to channels located around the circumference of the drum, forming adjacent circular bands that wind around the drum. A single drum can have up to 200 tracks. As the drum rotates at a speed of up to 3,000 rpm, the device's read/write heads deposit magnetized spots on the drum during the write operation and sense these spots during a read operation.

This action is similar to that of a magnetic tape or disk drive. They were very expensive to operate and in addition to using a great deal of electricity, generated a lot of heat, which was often the cause of malfunctions. First generation computers relied on machine language to perform operations, and they could only solve one problem at a time.

Machine languages are the only languages understood by computers. While easily understood by computers, machine languages are almost impossible for humans to use because they consist entirely of numbers. Programmers, therefore, use either a high-level programming language or an assembly language.

An assembly language contains the same instructions as a machine language, but the instructions and variables have names instead of being just numbers. Programmes written in high-level languages retranslated into assembly language or machine language by a compiler. Assembly language programmes retranslated into machine language by a programme called an assembler.

Every CPU has its own unique machine language. Programmes must be rewritten or recompiled, therefore, to run on different types of computers. Input was based on punched cards and paper tape, and output was displayed on printouts. The UNIVAC and ENIAC computers are examples of first-generation computing devices.

Acronym for Electronic Numerical Integrator And Computer, the world's first operational electronic digital computer, developed by Army Ordnance to compute World War II ballistic firing tables. The ENIAC, weighing 30 tons, using 200 kilowatts of electric power and consisting of 18,000 vacuum tubes,1,500 relays, and hundreds of thousands of resistors, capacitors, and inductors, was completed in 1945. In addition to ballistics, the ENIAC's field of application included weather prediction, atomic-energy calculations, cosmic-ray studies, thermal ignition, random-number studies, wind-tunnel design, and other scientific uses.

SECOND GENERATION

Transistors replaced vacuum tubes and ushered in the second generation of computers. Transistor is a device composed of semiconductor material that amplifies a signal or opens or closes a circuit. Invented in 1947at Bell Labs, transistors have become the key ingredient of all digital circuits, including computers. Today's microprocessors contain tens of millions of microscopic transistors.

Prior to the invention of transistors, digital circuits were composed of vacuum tubes, which had many disadvantages. They were much larger, required more energy, dissipated more heat, and were more prone to failures. It's safe to say that without the invention of transistors, computing as we know it today would not be possible.

The transistor was invented in 1947 but did not see widespread use in computers until the late 50s. The transistor was far superior to the vacuum tube, allowing computers to become smaller, faster, cheaper, more energy-efficient and more reliable than their first-generation predecessors. Second-generation computers still relied on punched cards for input and printouts for output.

Second-generation computers moved from cryptic binary machine language to symbolic, or assembly, languages, which allowed programmers to specify instructions in words. High-level programming languages were also being developed at this time, such as early versions of COBOL and FORTRAN. These were also the first computers that stored their instructions in their memory, which moved from a magnetic drum to magnetic core technology.

THIRD GENERATION

The development of the integrated circuit was the hallmark of the third generation of computers. Transistors were miniaturized and placed on silicon chips, called semiconductors, which drastically increased the speed and efficiency of computers.

A nonmetallic chemical element in the carbon family of elements. Silicon - atomic symbol "Si" - is the second most abundant element in the earth's crust, surpassed only by oxygen. Silicon does not occur uncombined in nature. When silicon combines with other elements, such as iron, aluminum or potassium, a silicate is formed. Compounds of silicon also occur in the atmosphere, natural waters,many plants and in the bodies of some animals.

Silicon is the basic material used to make computer chips, transistors, silicon diodes and other electronic circuits and switching devices because its atomic structure makes the element an ideal semiconductor. Silicon is commonly doped, or mixed, with other elements, such as boron, phosphorous and arsenic, to alter its conductive properties.

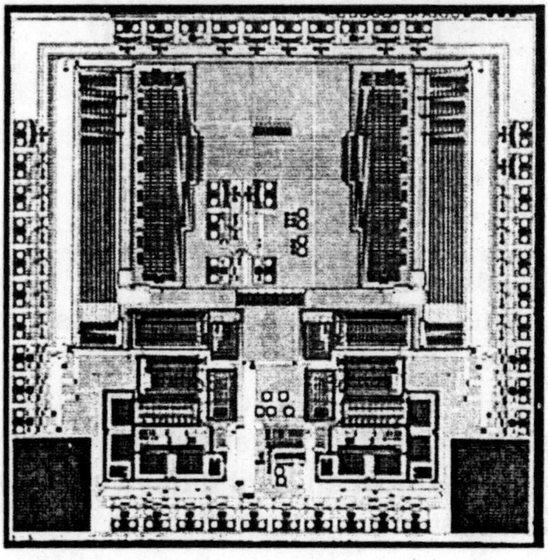

A chip is a small piece of semi conducting material (usually silicon) on which an integrated circuit is embedded. A typical chip is less than ¼-square inches and can contain millions of electronic components (transistors). Computers consist of many chips placed on electronic boards called printed circuit boards. There are different types of chips. For example, CPU chips (also called microprocessors) contain an entire processing unit, whereas memory chips contain blank memory. Semiconductor is a material that is neither a good conductor of electricity (like copper) nor a good insulator (like rubber). The most common semiconductor materials are silicon and germanium. These materials are then doped to create an excess or lack of electrons.

Computer chips, both for CPU and memory, are composed of semiconductor materials. Semiconductors make it possible to miniaturize electronic components, such as transistors. Not only does miniaturization mean that the components take up less space, it also means that they are faster and require less energy.

FOURTH GENERATION

The microprocessor brought the fourth generation of computers, as thousands of integrated circuits we rebuilt onto a single silicon chip.

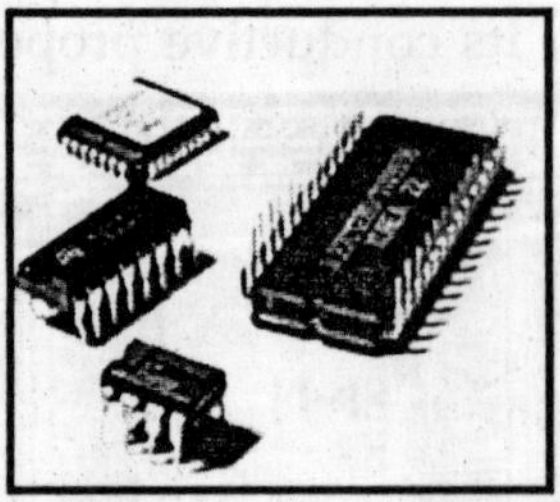

A silicon chip that contains a CPU. In the world of personal computers,the terms microprocessor and CPU are used interchangeably.

At the heart of all personal computers and most workstations sits a microprocessor. Microprocessors also control the logic of almost all digital devices, from clock radios to fuel-injection systems for automobiles.

Three basic characteristics differentiate microprocessors:

- *Instruction set*: The set of instructions that the microprocessor can execute.
- *Bandwidth*: The number of bits processed in a single instruction.
- *Clock speed*: Given in megahertz (MHz), the clock speed determines how many instructions per second the processor can execute.

In both cases, the higher the value, the more powerful the CPU. For example, a 32-bit microprocessor that runs at 50MHz is more powerful than a 16-bitmicroprocessor that runs at 25MHz.

Abbreviation of central processing unit, and pronounced as separate letters. The CPU is the brains of the computer. Sometimes referred to simply as the processor or central processor, the CPU is where most calculations take place. In terms of computing power,the CPU is the most important element of a computer system. On large machines, CPUs require one or more printed circuit boards. On personal computers and small workstations, the CPU is housed in a single chip called a microprocessor.

Two typical components of a CPU are:

- The arithmetic logic unit (ALU), which performs arithmetic and logical operations.
- The control unit, which extracts instructions from memory and decodes and executes them, calling on the ALU when necessary.

In 1981 IBM introduced its first computer for the home user, and in 1984 Apple introduced the Macintosh. Microprocessors also moved out of the realm of desktop computers and into many areas of life as more and more everyday products began to use microprocessors.

FIFTH GENERATION

Fifth generation computing devices, based on artificial intelligence, are still in development, though there are some applications, such as voice recognition, that are being used today.

Artificial Intelligence is the branch of computer science concerned with making computers behave like humans.

Artificial intelligence includes:

- *Games playing*: programming computers to play games such as chess and checkers
- *Expert systems*: programming computers to make decisions in real-life situations (for example, some expert systems help doctors diagnose diseases based on symptoms)
- *Natural language*: programming computers to understand natural human languages
- *Neural networks*: Systems that simulate intelligence by attempting to reproduce the types of physical connections that occur in animal brains
- *Robotics*: Programming computers to see and hear and react to other sensory stimuli

Currently, no computers exhibit full artificial intelligence (that is, are able to simulate human behaviour). The greatest advances have occurred in the field of games playing. The best computer chess programmes are now capable of beating humans. In May,1997, an IBM super-computer called Deep Blue defeated world chess champion Gary Kasparov in a chess match. In the area of robotics, computers are now widely used in assembly plants, but they are capable only of very limited tasks. Robots have great difficulty identifying objects based on appearance or feel, and they still move and handle objects clumsily.

Natural-language processing offers the greatest potential rewards because it would allow people to interact with computers without needing any specialized knowledge. You could simply walk up to a computer and talk to it. Unfortunately, programming computers to understand natural languages has proved to be more difficult than originally thought.

There are also voice recognition systems that can convert spoken sounds into written words, but they do not understand what they are writing; they simply take dictation. Even these systems are quite limited — you must speak slowly and distinctly.

In the early 1980s, expert systems were believed to represent the future of artificial intelligence and of computers in general. To date, however, they have not lived up to expectations. Many expert systems help human experts in such fields as medicine and engineering, but they are very expensive to produce and are helpful only in special situations.

Voice Recognition

The field of computer science that deals with designing computer systems that can recognize spoken words. Note that voice recognition implies only that the computer can take dictation, not that it understands what is being said. Comprehending human languages falls under a different field of computer science called natural language processing. A number of voice recognition systems are available on the market. The most powerful can recognize thousands of words. However, they generally require an extended training session during which the computer system becomes accustomed to a particular voice and accent. Such systems are said to be speaker dependent. Many systems also require that the speaker speak slowly and distinctly and separate each word with a short pause. These systems are called discrete speech systems. Recently, great strides have been made in continuous speech systems — voice recognition systems that allow you to speak naturally. There are now several continuous-speech systems available for personal computers.

Most computers have just one CPU, but some models have several. There are even computers with thousands of CPUs. With single-CPU computers, it is possible to perform parallel processing by connecting the computers in a network. However, this type of parallel processing requires very sophisticated software called distributed processing software. Note that parallel processing differs from multitasking, in which a single CPU executes several programmes at once.

Parallel processing is also called parallel computing. Quantum computation and molecular and nano-technology will radically change the face of computers in years to come. First proposed in the 1970s, quantum computing relies on quantum physics by taking advantage of certain quantum physics properties of atoms or nuclei that allow them to work together as quantum bits, or qubits, to be the computer's processor and memory.

While traditional computers encode information into bits using binary numbers, either a 0or 1, and can only do calculations on one set of numbers at once, quantum computers encode information as a series of quantum-mechanical states such as spin directions of electrons or polarization orientations of a photon that might represent a 1 or a 0, might represent a combination of the two or might represent a number expressing that the state of the qubit is somewhere between 1 and 0, or a superposition of many different numbers at once. A quantum computer can doan arbitrary reversible classical computation on all the numbers simultaneously, which a binary system cannot do, and also has some ability to produce interference between various different numbers. By doing a computation on many different numbers at once,then interfering the results to get a single answer, a quantum computer has the potential to be much more powerful than a classical computer of the same size.In using only a single processing unit, a quantum computer can naturally perform myriad operations in parallel. Quantum computing is not well suited for tasks such as word processing and e-mail, but it is ideal for tasks such as cryptography and modeling and indexing very large databases. Nanotechnology is a field of science whose goal is to control individual atoms and molecules to create computer chips and other devices that are thousands of times smaller than current technologies permit. Current manufacturing processes use lithography to imprint circuits on semiconductor materials.

While lithography has improved dramatically over the last two decades — to the point where some manufacturing plants can produce circuits smaller than one micron(1,000 nanometers) — it still deals with aggregates of millions of atoms. It is widely believed that lithography is quickly approaching its physical limits. To continue reducing the size of semiconductors, new technologies that juggle individual atoms will be necessary. This is the realm of nanotechnology.

COMPUTER ARCHITECTURE

To understand digital signal processing systems, we must understand a little about how computers compute. The modern definition of a *computer* is an electronic device that performs calculations on data, presenting the results to humans or other computers in a variety of ways.

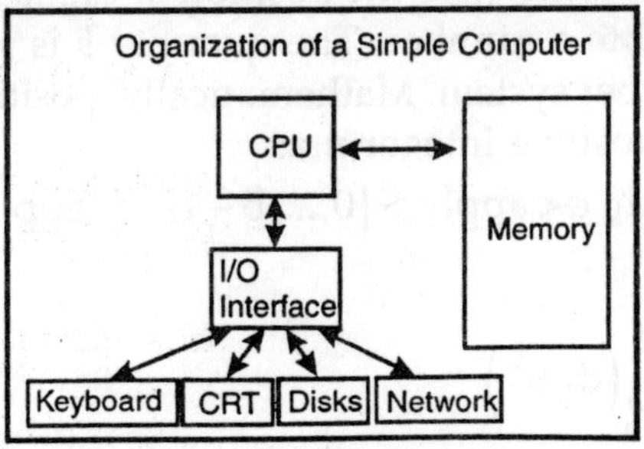

Fig. Generic Computer Hardware Organization.

The generic computer contains *input* devices (keyboard, mouse, A/D (analog-to-digital) converter, etc.), a *computational unit,* and output devices (monitors, printers, D/A converters). The computational unit is the computer's heart, and usually consists of a *central processing unit* (CPU), a *memory,* and an input/output (I/O) interface. What I/O devices might be present on a given computer vary greatly.

A simple computer operates fundamentally in discrete time: Computers are *clocked* devices, in which computational steps occur periodically according to ticks of a clock. This description belies clock speed: When you say "I have a 1 GHz computer," you mean that your computer takes 1 nanosecond to perform each step. That is incredibly fast! A "step" does not, unfortunately, necessarily mean a computation like an addition; computers break such computations down into several stages, which means that the clock speed need not express the computational speed. *Computers perform integer (discrete-valued) computations*: Computer calculations can be numeric, logical, or symbolic. Each computer instruction that performs an elementary numeric calculation — an addition, a multiplication, or a division — does so only for integers. The sum or product of two integers is also an integer, but the quotient of two integers is likely to not be an integer.

REPRESENTING NUMBERS

Focusing on numbers, all numbers can represented by the *positional notation system.* 2 The *b*-ary positional representation system uses the position of digits ranging from 0 to *b*-1 to denote a number. The quantity *b* is known as the *base* of the number system. Mathematically, positional systems represent the positive integer *n* as

$$\forall d_k, d_k \in \lt apply \gt \{0,\ldots,b-1\}. \lt /apply \gt :$$

(

$$n = \sum_{k=0}^{\infty} \left(d_k b^k \right)$$

)

and we succinctly express *n* in base-*b* as $n_b = d_N d_{N''1} \ldots d_0$. The number 25 in base 10 equals $2 \times 10^1 + 5 \times 10^0$, so that the*digits* representing this number are $d_0=5$, $d_1=2$, and all other d_k equal zero. This same number in *binary* (base 2) equals 11001 ($1 \times 2^4 + 1 \times 2^3 + 0 \times 2^2 + 0 \times 2^1 + 1 \times 2^0$) and 19 in hexadecimal (base 16). Fractions between zero and one are represented the same way.

$$\forall d_k, d_k \in <\text{apply}> \{0,\ldots,b-1\}.</\text{apply}>:$$

(

$$f = \sum_{k=-\infty}^{-1} \left(d_k b^k \right)$$

)

All numbers can be represented by their sign, integer and fractional parts. Complex numbers can be thought of as two real numbers that obey special rules to manipulate them.

Humans use base 10, commonly assumed to be due to us having ten fingers. Digital computers use the base 2 or *binary* number representation, each digit of which is known as a *bit* (*b*inary dig*it*).

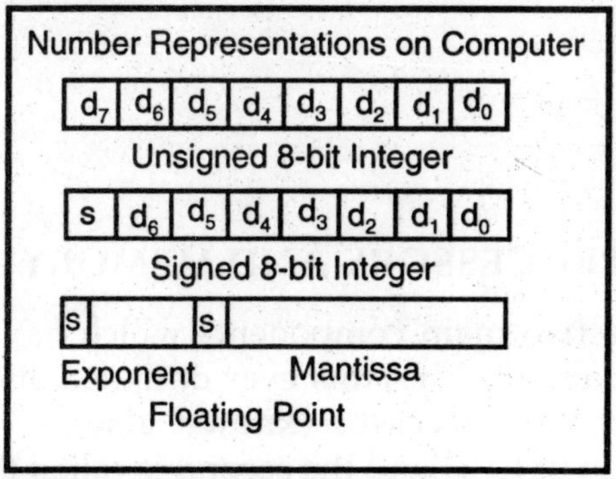

Fig. Numbers Represented in binary.

Here, each bit is represented as a voltage that is either "high" or "low," thereby representing "1" or "0," respectively. To represent signed values, we tack on a special bit—the *sign bit*—to express the sign. The computer's memory consists of an ordered sequence of *bytes*, a collection of eight bits. A byte can therefore represent an unsigned number ranging from 0 to255. If we take one of the bits and make it the sign bit, we can make the same byte to represent numbers ranging from "128to 127. But a computer cannot represent *all* possible real numbers. The fault is not with the binary number system; rather having only a finite number of bytes is the problem. While a gigabyte of memory may seem to be a lot, it takes an infinite number of bits to represent ð. Since we want to store many numbers in a computer's memory, we are restricted to those that have a *finite*binary representation. Large integers can be represented by an ordered sequence of bytes. Common lengths, usually expressed in terms of the number of bits, are 16, 32, and 64.

COMPUTER ARITHMETIC AND LOGIC

The binary addition and multiplication tables are:

(
0 + 0 = 0
0 + 1= 1
1 + 1 = 10
1 + 0 = 1
0 × 0 = 0
0 × 1 = 0
1 × 1 = 1
1 × 0 = 0
)

PROCESSORS AND MEMORY

There are two main components which have been part of nearly all computer systems ever designed and built. The first is called the processor (known also as the Central Processing Unit or CPU)and the second is called the memory. The processor is the part of a computer system which does the actual computing. That is, the part which adds, subtracts, multiplies and divides. Most processors can also compare values and perform conditional actions as a result of such comparisons. Many processors have instructions which perform various types of conversions between different representations of data. The processor itself is divided into three components that carry out the various functions that the computer is capable of performing. The first component of the processor is the controller. The controller acts as a foreman that oversees the tasks of the processor.

Another component of the processor is the Arithmetic-Logic Unit (ALU). This unit is the part of the processor which performs the mathematical computations and logical tasks that we expect a computer to be able to do. Addition, subtraction, comparison, etc., are all carried out by the ALU.

A computer memory system is accessed (or read) by specifying the location (called an address) of the memory cell. The memory system then responds by producing a copy of the contents of that cell. The original value of the cell is not changed by this process. This is sometimes called a non-destructive read.

The processor and memory unit are wired together wiring connections called buses. A *bus* is a low resistance connection consisting of 1 or more wires. There are three such connections. The first, called the address bus, is used by the processor to tell the memory system the number or location of the memory cell the processor wishes to access. The second bus is used to send data out to the memory. The third bus is used to transmit data and instructions to the processor.

A typical computer might be organized as indicated in the following diagram:

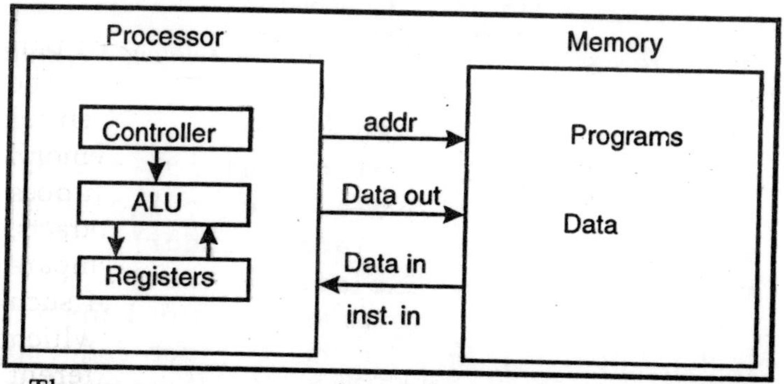

The processor contains a few memory cells, called registers, which are used for efficient temporary storage:

PROCESSOR REGISTERS

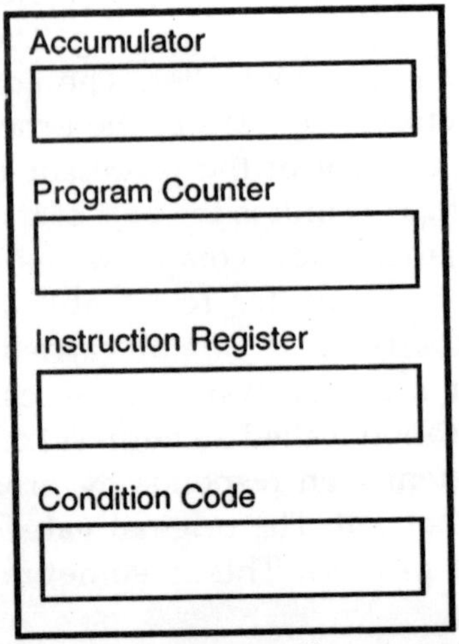

The Contents of a memory cell or a register is simply a number. For purposes of illustration, suppose that each memory cell is large enough to hold numbers up to 4 decimal digits in size. If a memory cell holds an an instruction, use the first two decimal digits represent the operation and the remaining digits to represent the adderess or location of the instruction operand.

INSTRUCTION FORMAT

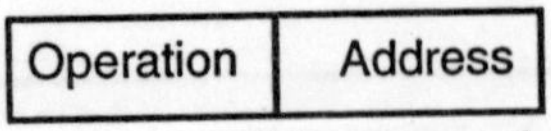

Using this scheme, we could set up the following operation codes:

Operation	Code	Function
add	01	c(acc)=c(acc)+c(addr)
sub	02	c(acc)=c(acc)-c(addr)
load	03	c(acc)=c(addr)
store	04	c(addr)=c(acc)

These codes do not correspond to any known real computer, but rather, they are the operation codes for a hypothetical model computer which we will use to illustrate important aspects of computer organization.

SIMPLE PROGRAMMES

Perhaps the shortest useful programme we might write would move a value from one memory cell to another.

This could be modeled by the J expression:

```
q =: r
```

To accomplish this task, it is necessary to first load the value of r into the accumulator and then store the accumulator in the memory cell q.

```
load    r
store   q
```

Consider a programme which computes the following expression:

```
c =:    a + b
load    a
add     b
store   c
```

It is possible to write a programme which will automatically translate from the J version of this programme to the symbolic form of the machine instructions shown above.

Such a programme, which translates from the J notation, c =: a + b to the machine language:

```
load    a
add     b
store   c
```

is called a J compiler.

The programme must be stored in memory before it may be executed. Since we don't know exactly where in memory we wish to put either the programme or the data items a, b or c, we can only partially translate the programme into machine readable form as:

```
op location
03 a
01 b
04 c
```

The memory system is a collection of memory cells, each having a number or address.

The following diagram illustrates the organization of memory:

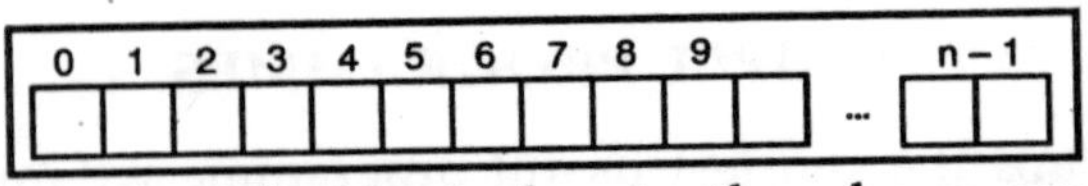

Suppose we decide to locate the above programme beginning in memory cell 4. Since the programme takes 3 cells we might put the data in the first free cell after the last instruction in the programme which means that we could define:

```
Symbol   Location
a  7
b  8
c  9
```

The final translated programme then looks like:

MACHINE LANGUAGE PROGRAMME

```
location operation   address
04        03          07
05        01          08
06        04          09
```

A programme which translates from the symbolic form for a programme:

```
load     a
add      b
store    c
```

to the machine language form is called a symbolic assembler, or simply an assembler.

HOW COMPUTER EXECUTES A PROGRAMME

We next focus on how a computer executes such a programme. *Recall the organization of the processor*:

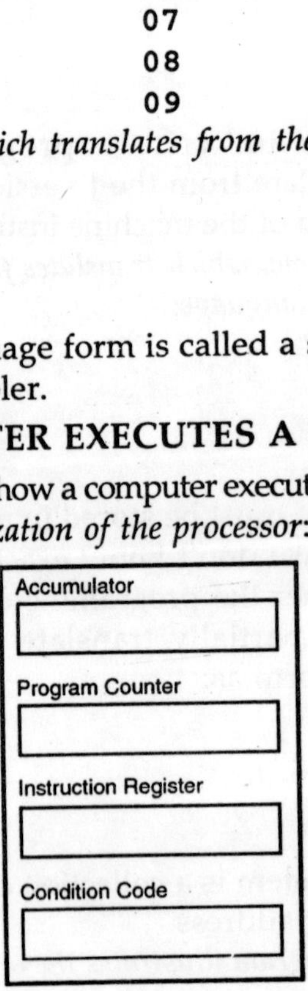

The programme counter register always contains the location of the next instruction to be processed. To get started executing this programme we somehow have to set the contents of the programme counter (pc) to 4 because this is the location of the first instruction of our programme. The following flow chart best explains how the processor executes a programme.

PROCESSOR FLOW CHART

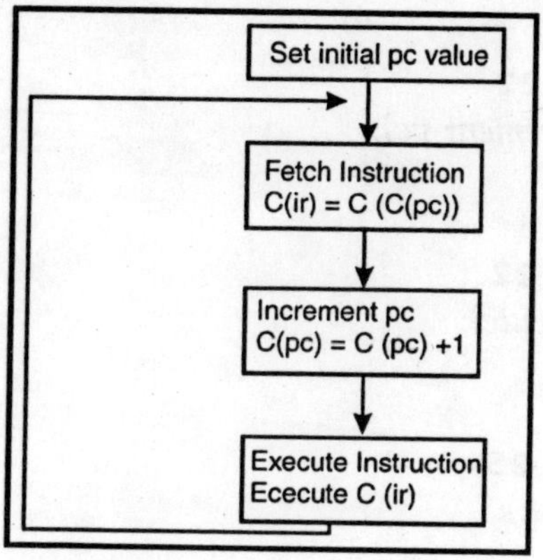

EXECUTING A PROGRAMME

To illustrate the various steps in the processor flow chart we give the following trace of the execution of Programme.

Step 0 Set initial value for the pc:

```
pc 04
ir ?
acc      ?
```

Step 1 *(fetch)*:

```
pc 04
ir 0307
ac ?
```

Step 2 *(increment pc)*:

```
pc 05
ir 0307
ac ?
```

Step 3 *(execute)*:

```
pc 05
ir 0307
ac 22     (here we are supposing
                that C(07) has been set
                      to 22 somehow and also
                            suppose C(08) has
   been                           set to 3)
```

Step 4 (fetch):

```
pc 05
ir 0108
acc      22
```

Step 5 (increment pc):

```
pc 0666
ir 0108
acc      22
```

Step 6 (execute):

```
pc 06
ir 0108
acc      25
```

Step 7 (fetch):

```
pc 06
ir 0409
acc      25
```

Step 8 (increment pc):

```
pc 07
ir 0409
acc      25
```

Step 9 (execute):

```
pc 07
ir 0409
acc      25    (contents of 09 changed to 25)
```

Step 10 (fetch):

```
pc 07
ir 0022
acc      25
```

Step 11 (increment pc):

```
pc 08
```

```
ir 0022
acc     25
```

Step 12 *(execute)*:

```
pc 08
ir 0022
acc     25
```

This means we need some kind of more elaborate setup for placing programmes in memory and starting and stopping programmes. These are some of the tasks performed by a computer operating system.

STORAGE DEVICES

A device capable of storing data. The term usually refers to mass storage devices, such as disk and tape drives. In a computer, storage is the place where data is held in an electromagnetic or optical form for access by a computer processor. Computer data storage; often called storage or memory refer to computer components, devices and recording media that retain digital data used for computing for some interval of time. Knowing what kinds of storage devices are available can keep you from using up too much space on your computer's hard drive. They can also help keep your computer's hard drive from crashing, along with keeping it running at top speed. As we see in modern day computers, storage devices can be found in many forms. Storage devices can be classified based on many criterions. Of them, the very basic is as we learned in schools ie; Primary storage and Secondary storage. Storage devices can be further classified based on the memory technology that they use, based on its data volatility etc.

The following list gives a few classifications of memory devices:

- Primary and Secondary and Tertiary Storage
- Volatile and non-volatile storage
- Read only and Writable storage
- Random Access and Sequential Access storage
- Magnetic storage
- Optical storage
- Semiconductor storage

Let us see in detail about each type of storage devices.

Primary and Secondary and Tertiary Storage

In simple words, primary storage is the storage device that is directly connected to the CPU and store data temporarily during execution. *i.e.* CPU can directly access primary storage and stores instruction and data for execution/ processing. The most popular example of this kind of memory is the RAM (Random Access Memory) that we use in modern day computers. CPU registers, Caches and other memories connected to the CPU local bus falls in this category. Primary storage devices are comparatively faster than all other kinds of memory types.

Usually primary storage devices are considered to be directly connected to the processor. But in reality, modern computers employ components like Virtual Memory Manager, DRAM controllers etc.. in between processor and the memory but the notion of 'Direct connection' is still valid since these components are transparent to the processor. Volatile memories are usually used as primary storage. The picture below shows a RAM module.

Fig. RAM Module, Example for Primary Storage Device.

On the contrary, Secondary storage may not be directly accessible by the processor. And is usually used for more permenent storage of data. This requires secondary storage devices to be non-volatile. Secondary storage devices are connected to storage controllers and the CPU is required to talk to the controllers in order to access information from secondary devices.

The most popular example of secondary device is the Hard disk. CD ROM, DVD ROM, USB mass storage devices, Floppy etc.. are also falls in this category. Secondary storage devices are also called Mass Storage Devices since the capacity of these devices are comparatively large. The picture below illustrates the classification of different types of Storage Devices as described above.

Primary Storage		
Directly accessible from CPU		
Ram	Regster	Cache
Secondary Storage		
Accessible through special hardware		
Hard disk	Flash	Floppy
Tertiary Storage		
Accessible through mechanical means		
Tape libraries	Optical jukebox	

Volatile and Non-volatile Storage

As the name implies, volatile memory looses its contents when power supply is withdrawn. So usually Volatile memories are used for temporary storage of data. In some exceptional cases, volatile memory devices are used along with long life batteries to make semi-permenent storage devices. Compared with non-volatile storage, Volatile storage devices are faster while both reading and writing data. This makes these kinds of memories very suitable to be used as main memories of computers. In fact, the memories we use in computers (RAM) are volatile devices.

Volatile Storage		
Data is lost when power is withdrawn		
Ram	Register	Cache
Non-Volatile Storage		
Maintains data even after power cycle		
Hard disk	Flash	Floppy

Non-volatile storage devices retain the contents even in absence of active power source. This makes non-volatile devices suitable for long term permenent data storage. Non-volatile devices usually available in large capacities. Hard

Disks, CD ROM, Floppy disks, Flash, ROM etc.. are examples of non-volatile memory devices. Non-volatile storage devices are slower when compared to volatile storage devices. But some non-volatile can faster during read operation and slower during write operation. Semiconductor non-volatile memory devices fall in this category.

Read only and Writable Storage

Read only storage devices only allows contents to be read from and doesn't allow the contents to be modified. Meanwhile, Writable storage devices allow both content retrieval as well as content modification. Read only devices are usually used for long term permanent storage where modification of data is not necessary.

CD ROM, DVD etc are examples of Read Only Storage devices. Some Read Only Storage devices comes with factory programmed data which you can only read but not modify. There is another class of devices called Write Once Read Multiple (WORM) devices which allows us to write data to it one and only one time and allows any number of subsequent reads. CD-R and DVD-R are technically comes under this category.

Read only Storage		
Data can't be written to the Device		
Rom	CD-R	EEPROM
Read/write storage		
Data can be written to the Device		
Hard disk	Flash	Ram

Random Access and Sequential Access storage

Random Access storage devices allow retrieval of content from any location in the same amount of time. *i.e.* Latency (The time taken to access a particular location in storage) is independent of content's location. RAM used in computers is an example of Random Access Memory. In sequential access storage devices, data can be accessed in sequential manner only. And the time taken to read from a particular location will be dependant on the location last accessed. Example of a sequential access device is the Tape storage device. Sequential access devices are usually used for backup purpose only, where frequent access of information is not required.

Random access storage		
Access any location randomly		
Ram	Flash	EEPROM
Sequential access storage		
Access data sequentially		
Tape		

Magnetic Storage

Magnetic storage devices store information in the form of magnetic field on magnetically coated surface. Magnetic storage devices fall in the category of non-volatile devices. This makes magnetic storage devices to be useful for long term data storage. Hard disks, Floppy disks and tape devices are examples of magnetic storage devices. Data is written to magnetic media with the help of electromagnetic heads.

The same head is usually used also for retrieval of data. Though magnetic storage medias can hold large amount of data, these are considered to be bulky and not usable for mobile applications. But technological advancements made it possible to create large capacity magnetic storage devices with small size. An example for this is Apple's ipod classic which is available with a built in hard disk with a capacity as large as 160 GB for music/video storage.

Magnetic storage	
Data is recorded on magnetic media	
Hard disk	Floppy

Optical Storage

Optical storage devices store data on reflective polycarbonate discs in the form of pits and bumps. Data is recorded on the disc by pointing modulated laser beam on to the rotating disc. This makes a series of tiny pits which doesn't reflect light and bumps that reflect light. For reading the data, a low power laser beam is focused to the track and the reflected beam is directed to a photo diode.

Optical storage	
Data is recorded on optical media	
CD	DVD

Semiconductor Storage

Semiconductor storage devices store data in tiny memory cells made of very small transistors and capacitors made of semiconductor materials such as silicon. Each cell can hold one bit of information and an array of cells stores large chunk of information. Semiconductor storage devices can be volatile and non-volatile.

RAM is an example of volatile semiconductor storage device. EEPROM and FASH are examples of non-volatile semiconductor storage devices. FLASH devices are gaining popularity over conventional secondary storage devices like hard disks. There are a large number of products in the market now which uses FLASH devices exclusively as secondary storage (Eg. MP3 players, Mobile Phones etc...).

Random access storage		
Access any location randomly		
Ram	Flash	Eprom

Part1 of this series of articles end here. This article is expected to give you very basic information of storage device classifications and technologies. For more advanced information please read the other articles in this series.

COMMON STORAGE DEVICES

- Floppy Disks
- Zip Disks
- CD + RW
- CD + R

- DVD + RW
- DVD + R
- Removable Hard Drive
- Internet Hard Drive
- Flash
- PC Cards
- Smart Cards
- Storage Tapes
- Memory Sticks
- Smart Media

Floppy Disk

They are plastic square disks, usually with a silver or black sliding piece going across the top. These disks come in a variety of colours and they hold about 144 million bytes. (Bytes are characters, symbols and letters).

Zip Disk

They look like a floppy disk, but they are a little thicker. This disk also comes in a variety of colours and holds about 200 MB of data.

CD + RW Disc (Compact Disc Rewriteable)

This disc looks like a regular CD. The only difference is that you can write on this disc and erase it as many times as you want. It works just like a floppy disk or a zip disk. A CD + RW disc holds about 650 MB.

CD + R Disc (Compact Disc Recordable)

This one is a CD that you can record on. It's mostly used to record audio and once it's been written on, you cannot rewrite or erase anything off of it. This compact disc comes in different sizes, but they are usually silver in colour. (Some CDs are black in colour and they actually don't get as many scratches on them as the silver ones do. They are also a lot less fragile).

A DVD – R Disc (Digital Video Recordable)

These discs hold the space of about 4.7 GB and are used to record movies on.

Removable Hard Drive

This is a disk drive in which a plastic or metal case surrounds the hard drive. It can be inserted and removed just like a floppy disk. It holds about 2 GB of data.

Internet Hard Drive

This one is a service on the Internet that provides storage space to computer users. This service offers about 25 MB of space, but it could be more, depending on the service type.

Flash Drive

This a storage device that comes in many colours and

has a stick shape to it. They are very small in size, but they can hold anywhere between 256 MB and 3 GB of material on them.

PC Card

This is a thin credit card size device that fits into a PC card slot, usually on a notebook computer. This card simply adds storage to most notebooks.

Smart Cards

These are the size of an ATM card. When inserted into a smart card reader, they can read and update data for you.

Storage Tape

This one is a magnetically coated ribbon of plastic, capable of storing large amounts of data at a very low cost. Usually, storage tapes are a little bigger than audio tapes.

Older computers used tape and tape drives, but even today, some people still back their systems up with storage tape.

These tapes hold between 20 GB to about 110 GB of data. An external tape drive can be purchased separately as well, but those are even harder to find.

Miniature Mobile Storage Media

This is used mostly with handheld computers and digital cameras.

Memory Stick

This is a rectangular shaped disk that is used mostly with digital cameras and notebook computers. They hold approximately 128 MB as well.

Micro Drive

This is a square disk that has 1 GB of space and is used with digital cameras and handheld computers.

Smart Media Disc

This is a square disk that has 2 MB to about 128 MB of space on it. It's used with digital cameras, handheld computers and photo printers.

INPUT UNITS

OVERVIEW

The aim of the Input Unit is to provide an efficient service regarding crime and accident recording. The Unit provides advice and support to Police Officers regarding the creation, update and amendment of our crime reporting system and also the creation of accident reports. Input staff has responsibility for the initial investigation into minor, historic, and non-urgent crime complaints.

INPUT: GETTING DATA FROM THE USER TO COMPUTER

Some input data can go directly to the computer for processing. Input in this category includes bar codes, speech that enters the computer through a microphone, and data entered by means of a device that converts motions to on-screen action.

Some input data, however, goes through a good deal of intermediate handling, such as when it is copied from a source document and translated to a medium that a machine can read, such as a magnetic disk. In either case the task is to gather data to be processed by the computer ‹sometimes called raw data and convert it into some form the computer can understand.

Keyboard

A keyboard is usually part of a personal computer or part of a terminal that is connected to a computer somewhere else.

Alphanumeric keypad: It consists of keys for English alphabets, 0 to 9 numbers, and special characters like +/* () etc.

Function Keys: There are twelve function keys labeled F1, F2, F3, ..., F12. The functions assigned to these keys differ from one software package to another. These keys are also user programmable keys.

Special-function keys: These keys have special functions assigned to them and can be used only for those specific purposes. Functions of some of the important keys are defined below.

Enter: It is similar to the 'return' key of the typewriter and is used to execute a command or programme.

Spacebar: It is used to enter a space at the current cursor location.

Backspace: This key is used to move the cursor one position to the left and also delete the character in that position.

Delete: It is used to delete the character at the cursor position.

Insert: Insert key is used to toggle between insert and overwrite mode during data entry.

Shift: This key is used to type capital letters when pressed along with an alphabet key. Also used to type the special characters located on the upper-side of a key that has two characters defined on the same key.

Caps lock: Cap Lock is used to toggle between the capital lock feature. When 'on', it locks the alphanumeric keypad for capital letters input only.

Tab: Tab is used to move the cursor to the next tab position defined in the document. Also, it is used to insert indentation into a document.

Ctrl: Control key is used in conjunction with other keys to provide additional functionality on the keyboard.

Alt: Also like the control key, Alt key is always used in combination with other keys to perform specific tasks.

Esc: This key is usually used to negate a command. Also used to cancel or abort executing programmes.

Numeric keypad: Numeric keypad is located on the right side of the keyboard and consists of keys having numbers (0 to 9) and mathematical operators (+ - */) defined on them. This keypad is provided to support quick entry for numeric data.

Cursor movement keys: These are arrow keys and are used to move the cursor in the direction indicated by the arrow (up, down, left, right).

Mouse

A mouse is an input device with a ball on its underside that is rolled on a flat surface, usually the desk on which the computer sits.

The rolling movement causes a corresponding movement on the screen. Moving the mouse allows you to reposition the pointer, or cursor, an indicator on the screen that shows where the next interaction with the computer can take place. The cursor can also be moved by pressing various keyboard keys.

Mouse Actions

Left click: Used to select an item.

Double click: Used to start a programme or open a file.

Right click: Usually used to display a set of commands.

Drag and drop: It allows you to select and move an item from one location to another. To achieve this place the cursor over an item on the screen, click the left mouse button and while holding the button down move the cursor to where you want to place the item, and then release it.

Trackball

A variation on the mouse is the trackball. You may have used a trackball to play a video game. The trackball is like an upside-down mouse-you roll the ball directly with your hand. The popularity of the trackball surged with the advent of laptop computers, when traveling users found them- selves without a flat surface on which to roll the traditional mouse.

Source Data Automation: Collecting Data Where It Starts

Efficient data input means reducing the number of intermediate steps required between the origination of data and its processing.

This is best accomplished by source data automation ‹the use of special equipment to collect data at the source, as a by-product of the activity that generates the data, and send it directly to the computer.

Recall, for example, the supermarket bar code, which can be used to send data about the product directly to the computer.

Magnetic-Ink Character Recognition

Abbreviated MICR, magnetic-ink character recognition is a method of machine-reading characters made of magnetized particles. The most common example of magnetic characters is the array of numbers across the bottom of your personal check.

Most magnetic-ink characters are preprinted on your check. If you compare a check you wrote that has been cashed and cleared by the bank with those that are still unused in your checkbook, you will note that the amount of the cashed check has been reproduced in magnetic characters in the lower-right corner. These characters were added by a person at the bank by using a MICR inscriber.

Scanner

Fig. Flatbed Scanner

An inexpensive way to get entire documents, pictures, and anything on a flat Surface into a computer is by using a scanner. Scanners use optical recognition systems that have a light beam to scan input data to convert it into electrical signals, which are sent to the computer for processing.

Optical recognition is by far the most common type of source input, appearing in a variety of ways: optical marks, optical characters, bar codes, handwritten characters, and images. Scanners use *Optical Character Recognition* software, described below, to translate text on scanned documents into text that is suitable for word processors and other computer applications.

Optical Mark Recognition

Abbreviated OMR, optical mark recognition is sometimes called mark sensing, because a machine senses marks on a piece of paper. As a student, you may immediately recognize this approach as the technique used to score certain tests. Using a pencil, you make a mark in a specified box or space that corresponds to what you think is the answer. The answer sheet is then graded by a device that uses a light beam to recognize the marks and convert them to computer-recognizable electrical signals.

Optical Character Recognition

Abbreviated OCR, optical character recognition devices also use a light source to read special characters and convert them into electrical signals to be sent to the central processing unit. The characters-letters, numbers, and special symbols-can be read by both humans and machines. They are often found on sales tags on store merchandise. A standard typeface for optical characters, called OCR-A, has been established by the American National Standards Institute.

The handheld wand reader is a popular input device for reading OCR-A. There is an increasing use of wands in libraries, hospitals, and factories, as well as in retail stores. In retail stores the wand reader is connected to a point-of-sale (POS) terminal. This terminal is somewhat like a cash register, but it performs many more functions. When a clerk passes the wand reader over the price tag, the computer uses the input merchandise number to retrieve a description (and possibly the price, if not on the tag) of the item. A small printer produces a customer receipt that shows the item description and price.

The computer calculates the subtotal, the sales tax (if any), and the total. This information is displayed on the screen and printed on the receipt; notice that both screen and printer are output, so the POS terminal is a complex machine that performs both input and output functions. The raw purchase data becomes valuable information when it is summarized by the computer system.

This information can be used by the accounting department to keep track of how much money is taken in each day, by buyers to determine what merchandise should be reordered, and by the marketing department to analyse the effectiveness of their ad campaigns.

Bar Codes

Each product on the store shelf has its own unique number, which is part of the Universal Product Code (UPC). This code number is represented on the product label by a pattern of vertical marks, or bars, called bar codes. (UPC, by the way, is an agreed-upon standard within the supermarket industry; other kinds of bar codes exist. You need only look as far as the back cover of this book to see an example of another kind of bar code.) These zebra stripes can be sensed and read by a bar code reader, a photo- electric device that reads the code by means of reflected light. As with the wand reader in a retail store, the bar code reader in a bookstore or grocery store is part of a point-of-sale terminal. When you buy, say, a can of corn at the supermarket, the checker moves it past the bar code reader. The bar code merely identifies the product to the store's computer; the code does not contain the price, which may vary.

Handwritten Characters

Machines that can read handwritten characters are yet another means of reducing the number of intermediate steps between capturing data and processing it. In many instances it is preferable to write the data and immediately have it usable for processing rather than having data entry operators key it in later.

Imaging

In a process called imaging, a scanner converts a drawing, a picture, or any document into computer-recognizable form by shining a light on the image and sensing the intensity of the reflection at each point of the image. Scanners come in both handheld and desktop models. The electronic version of the image can then be stored, probably on disk, and reproduced on screen when needed.

Businesses find imaging particularly useful for documents, since they can view an exact replica of the original document at any time. If a text image is run through an optical character recognition (OCR) programme, then all words and numbers can be manipulated by word processing and other software.

The Internal Revenue Service, using imaging and also OCR software that can recognize characters from the image, is now scanning 17,000 tax returns per hour, a significant improvement over hand processing. Another way to keep photos computer accessible is to have film that was shot with a conventional camera processed onto optical disk instead of prints or slides. Professional photo agencies keep thousands of images on file, ready to be leased for a fee. Typically, a couple of dozen thumbnail-size images can be displayed on the screen at one time; a particular image can be enlarged to full-screen size with a click of a mouse button.

Data Collection Devices

Another source of direct data entry is a data collection device, which may be located in a warehouse or factory or wherever the activity that is generating the data is located. As we noted earlier in the chapter, for example, factory employees can use a plastic card to punch job data directly into a computerized time clock. This process eliminates intermediate steps and ensures that the data will be more accurate.

Data collection devices must be sturdy, trouble-free, and easy to use because they are often located in dusty, humid, or hot or cold locations. They are used by people such as warehouse workers, packers, forklift operators, and others whose primary work is not clerical. Examples of remote data collection devices are machines for taking inventory, reading shipping labels, and recording job costs.

Voice Input

Does your computer have ears? Speaking to a computer, known as voice input or speech recognition, is another form of source input. Speech recognition devices accept the spoken word through a microphone and convert it into binary code (0s and 1s) that can be understood by the computer. Originally, typical users were those with "busy hands," or hands too dirty for the keyboard, or with no access to a keyboard.

Most speech recognition systems are speaker-dependent; that is, they must be separately trained for each individual user. The speech recognition system "learns" the voice of the user, who speaks isolated words repeatedly. The voiced words the system "knows" are then recognizable in the future. Speech recognition systems that are limited to isolated words are called discrete word systems, and users must pause between words. Experts have tagged speech recognition as one of the most difficult things for a computer to do. Eventually, continuous word systems will be able to interpret sustained speech, so users can speak normally; so far, such systems are limited by vocabulary to a single subject, such as insurance or the weather. A key advantage of delivering input to a computer in a normal speaking pattern is ease of use.

Touch Screens

One way of getting input directly from the source is to have a human simply point to a selection. The edges of the monitor of a touch screen emit horizontal and vertical beams of light that criss-cross the screen. When a finger touches the screen, the interrupted light beams can pinpoint the location selected on the screen. Kiosks in public places such as malls offer a variety of services via touch screens.

Looking

Delivering input to a computer by simply looking at the computer would seem to be the ultimate in capturing data at the source. The principles are reminiscent of making a screen selection by touching the screen with the finger. Electrodes attached to the skin around the eyes respond to movement of the eye muscles, which produce tiny electric signals when they contract. The signals are read by the computer system, which determines the location on the screen where the user is looking.

OUTPUT: INFORMATION

As we have seen, computer output takes the form of screen or printer output. Other forms of output include voice, microfilm, and various forms of graphics output. A computer system often is designed to produce several kinds of output. An example is a travel agency that uses a computer system. If a customer asks about airline connections to Toronto, Calgary, and Vancouver, say, the travel agent will probably make a few queries to the system to receive on-screen output indicating availability on the various flights. After the reservations have been confirmed, the agent can ask for printed output that includes the tickets, the traveller's itinerary, and the invoice.

Computer Screen Technology

A user's first interaction with a computer screen may be the screen response to the user's input. When data is entered, it appears on the screen. Furthermore, the computer response to that data-the output-also appears on the screen. Computer screens come in many varieties, but the most common kind is the cathode ray tube (CRT). Most CRT screens use a technology called raster-scan technology. The backing of the screen display has a phosphorous coating, which will glow whenever it is hit by a beam of electrons. But the light does not stay lit very long, so the image must be refreshed often. If the screen is not refreshed often enough, the fading screen image appears to flicker.

A computer display screen that can be used for graphics is divided into dots that are called addressable, because they can be addressed individually by the graphics software. Each dot can be illuminated individually on the screen. Each dot is potentially a picture element, or pixel. The resolution of the screen, its clarity, is directly related to the number of pixels on the screen:

There have been several colour screen standards, relating particularly to resolution. The first colour display was CGA (colour graphics adapter), which had low resolution by today's standards (320x200 pixels). This was followed by the sharper EGA (enhanced graphics adapter), featuring 640x350 pixels. Today, VGA and SVGA are common standards. VGA (video graphics array) has 640x480 pixels. SVGA (super VGA) offers 800x600 pixels or 1024x768 pixels, by far the superior clarity.

Types of Screens

Cathode ray tube monitors that display text and graphics are in common use today. Although most CRTs are colour, some screens are monochrome, meaning only one colour, usually green, appears on a dark background. Another type of screen technology is the liquid crystal display (LCD), a flat display often seen on watches and calculators. LCD screens are used on laptop computers.

Terminals

A screen may be the monitor of a self-contained personal computer, or it may be part of a terminal that is one of many terminals attached to a large computer. A terminal consists of an input device, an output device, and a communications link to the main computer. Most commonly, a terminal has a keyboard for an input device and a screen for an output device, although there are many variations on this theme.

Printers

A printer is a device that produces printed paper output, known in the computer industry as hard copy because it is tangible and permanent (unlike soft copy, which is displayed on a screen). Some printers produce only letters and numbers, whereas others can also produce graphics. Letters and numbers are formed by a printer either as solid characters or as dot-matrix characters. Dot-matrix printers create characters in the same way that individual lights in a pattern spell out words on a basketball scoreboard.

Dot-matrix printers construct a character by activating a matrix of pins that produce the shape of the character. A traditional matrix is 5 × 7-that is, five dots wide and seven dots high. These printers are sometimes called 9-pin printers, because they have two extra vertical dots for descenders on the lowercase letters g, j, p, and y. The 24-pin dot-matrix printer, which uses a series of overlapping dots, dominates the dot-matrix market. There are two ways of printing an image on paper: the impact method and the non-impact method. Let us take a closer look at the difference.

Impact Printers

The term impact refers to the fact that impact printers

use some sort of physical contact with the paper to produce an image, physically striking paper, ribbon, and print hammer together. The impact may be produced by a print hammer character, like that of a typewriter key striking a ribbon against the paper, or by a print hammer hitting paper and ribbon against a character.

A dot-matrix printer is one example of an impact printer. High- quality impact printers print only one character at a time. However, users who are more concerned about high volume than high quality usually use line printers - impact printers that print an entire line at a time.

Organizations that use mainframe and minicomputers usually have several line printers. Such organizations are likely to print hearty reports, perhaps relating to payroll or costs, for internal use.

Non-impact Printers

A non-impact printer places an image on a page without physically touching the page. The major technologies competing in the non-impact market are laser and ink-jet. Laser printers use a light beam to help transfer images to paper, producing extremely high-quality results. Laser printers print a page at a time at impressive speeds. Large organizations use laser printers to produce high-volume customer-oriented reports. At the personal computer end, low-end black and white laser printers can now be purchased for a few hundred dollars. However, colour laser jet printers are more expensive.

Ink-jet printers, by spraying ink from multiple jet nozzles, can print both black and white and in several different colours of ink to produce excellent graphics. As good as they are, colour printers are not perfect. The colour you see on your computer screen is not necessarily the colour you will see on the printed output.

Nor is it likely to be the colour you would see on a four-colour offset printing press. Nevertheless, with low-end printers now under $250, they may be a bargain for users who want their own colour output capability.

Voice Output

We have already examined voice input in some detail. As you will see in this section, however, computers are frequently like people in the sense that they find it easier to talk than to listen. Speech synthesis is the process of enabling machines to talk to people is much easier than speech recognition.They are the product of voice synthesizers (also called voice-output devices or audio-response units), which convert data in main storage to vocalized sounds understandable to humans.

There are two basic approaches to getting a computer to talk. The first is synthesis by analysis, in which the device analyses the input of an actual human voice speaking words, stores and processes the spoken sounds, and reproduces them as needed. The process of storing words is similar to the digitizing process we discussed earlier when considering voice input. In essence, synthesis by analysis uses the computer as a digital tape recorder.

The second approach to synthesizing speech is synthesis by rule, in which the device applies a complex set of linguistic rules to create artificial speech. Synthesis based on the human voice has the advantage of sounding more natural, but it is limited to the number of words stored in the computer. Voice output has become common in such places as airline and bus terminals, banks, and brokerage houses. It is typically used when an inquiry is followed by a short reply (such as a bank balance or flight time).

Music Output

Personal computer users have occasionally sent primitive musical messages, feeble tones that wheezed from the tiny internal speaker. Many users remain at this level, but a significant change is in progress.

2

Digital Logic

SIGNED NUMBERS

Binary representations of positive can be understood in the same way as their decimal counterparts. For example

$$86_{10} = 1*64 + 0*32 + 1*16 + 0*8 + 1*4 + 1*2 + 0*1$$

or

$$86_{10} = 1*\ 2^6 + 0*\ 2^5 + 1*\ 2^4 + 0*\ 2^3 + 1*\ 2^2 + 1*\ 2^1 + 0*\ 2^0$$

or

$$86_{10} = 1010110_{\ 2}$$

The subscript 2 denotes a binary number. Each digit in a binary number is called a bit. The number 1010110 is represented by 7 bits. Any number can be broken down this way, by finding all of the powers of 2 that add up to the number in question (in this case 2^6, 2^4, 2^2 and 2^1). You can see this is exactly analagous to the decimal deconstruction of the number 125 that was done earlier. Likewise we can make a similar set of observations:

- To multiply a number by 2 you can simply shift it to the left by one digit, and fill in the rightmost digit with a 0. To divide a number by 2, simply shift the number to the right by one digit.
- To see how many digits a number needs, you can simply take the logarithm (base 2) of the number, and add 1 to it. The integer part of the result is the number of digits. For instance,

$$\log_2(86)+1=7.426.$$

The integer part of that is 7, so 7 digits are needed.

- With n digits, 2^n unique numbers (from 0 to 2^n-1)

can be represented. If n=8, 256 (=2^8) numbers can be represented 0-255.

It is often convenient to handle groups of bits, rather than individually. The most common grouping is 8 bits, which forms a byte. A single byte can represent 256 (2^8) numbers. Memory capacity is usually referred to in bytes. Two bytes is usually called a word, or short word (though word-length depends on the application). A two-byte word is also the size that is usually used to represent integers in programming languages. A long word is usually twice as long as a word. A less common unit is the nibble which is 4 bits, or half of a byte.

It is cumbersome for humans to deal with writing, reading and remembering individual bits, because it takes many of them to represent even fairly small numbers. A number of different ways have been developed to make the handling of binary data easier for us. The most common is hexadecimal. In hexadecimal notation, 4 bits (a nibble) are represented by a single digit. There is obviously a problem with this since 4 bits gives 16 possible combinations, and there are only 10 unique decimal digits, 0 to 9. This is solved by using the first 6 letters (A..F) of the alphabet as numbers. The table shows the relationship between decimal, hexadecimal and binary.

Decimal	Hexadecimal	Binary
0	0	0000
1	1	0001
2	2	0010
3	3	0011
4	4	0100
5	5	0101
6	6	0110
7	7	0111
8	8	1000
9	9	1001
10	A	1010
11	B	1011
12	C	1100

13	D	1101
14	E	1110
15	F	1111

There are some significant advantages to using hexadecimal when dealing with electronic representations of numbers (if people had 16 fingers, we wouldn't be saddled with the awkward decimal system). Using hexadecimal makes it very easy to convert back and forth from binary because each hexadecimal digit corresponds to exactly 4 bits ($\log_2(16) = 4$) and each byte is two hexadecimal digit.

In contrast, a decimal digit corresponds to $\log_2(10) = 3.322$ bits and a byte is 2.408 decimal digits. Clearly hexadecimal is better suited to the task of representing binary numbers than is decimal.

As an example, the number $CA3_{16} = 1100\ 1010\ 0011_2$ ($1100_2 = C_{16}$, $1010_2 = A_{16}$, $0011_2 = 3_{16}$). It is convenient to write the binary number with spaces after every fourth bit to make it easier to read. Converting back and forth to decimal is more difficult, but can be done in the same way as before.

$$3235_{10} = C_{16}*256 + A_{16}*16 + 3_{16}*1 = C_{16}*16^2 + A_{16}*16^1 + 3_{16}*16^0$$

or

$$3235_{10} = 12*256 + 10*16 + 3*1 = 12*16^2 + 10*16^1 + 3*16^0$$

Octal notation is yet another compact method for writing binary numbers. There are 8 octal characters, 0...7. Obviously this can be represented by exactly 3 bits. Two octal digits can represent numbers up to 64, and three octal digits up to 512. A byte requires 2.667 octal digits. Octal used to be quiete common, it was the primary way of doing low level I/O on some old DEC computers. It is much less common today but is still used occasionally (*e.g.*, to set read, write and execute permissions on Unix systems)

In summary:

Bit: a single binary digit, either zero or one.

Byte: 8 bits, can represent positive numbers from 0 to 255.

Hexadecimal: A representation of 4 bits by a single digit 0..9,A..F. In this way a byte can be represented by two hexadecimal digits *long word*: A long word is usually twice as long as a word.

Nibble: 4 bits, half of a byte.

Octal: A representation of 3 bits by a single digit 0..7. This is used much less commonly than it once was (early DEC computers used octal for much of their I/O)

Word: Usually 16 bits, or two bytes. But a word can be almost any size, depending on the application being considered — 32 and 64 bits are common sizes

SIGNED BINARY INTEGERS

It was noted previously that we will not be using a minus sign (-) to represent negative numbers. We would like to represent our binary numbers with only two symbols, 0 and 1. There are a few ways to represent negative binary numbers. The simplest of these methods is called ones complement, where the sign of a binary number is changed by simply toggling each bit (0's become 1's and vice-versa). This has some difficulties, among them the fact that zero can be represented in two different ways (for an eight bit number these would be 0000 0000 and 1111 1111)., we will use a method called two's complement notation which avoids the pitfalls of one's complement, but which is a bit more complicated.

To form a two's complement number that is negative you simply take the corresponding positive number, invert all the bits, and add 1. The example below illustrated this by forming the number negative 35 as a two's complement integer:

$35_{10} = 0010\ 0011_2$

invert $\rightarrow 1101\ 1100_2$

add 1 $\rightarrow 1101\ 1101_2$

So 1101 1101 is our two's complement representation of -35. We can check this by adding up the contributions from the individual bits

$1101\ 1101_2 = -128 + 64 + 0 + 16 + 8 + 4 + 0 + 1 = -35.$

The same procedure (invert and add 1) is used to convert the negative number to its positive equivalent. If we want to know what what number is represented by 1111 1101, we apply the procedure again

$1111\ 1101_2$
invert $\rightarrow$ $0000\ 0010_2$
add 1 $\rightarrow$ $0000\ 0011_2$

Since 0000 0011 represents the number 3, we know that 1111 1101 represents the number –3.

POSITIVE BINARY FRACTIONS

The representation of unsigned binary fractions proceeds in exactly the same way as decimal fractions. For example

$$0.625_{10} = 1*0.5 + 0*0.25 + 1*0.125 = 1*\ 2^{-1} + 0*\ 2^{-2} + 1*\ 2^{-3} = 0.101_2$$

Each place to the right of the decimal point represents a negative power of 2, just as for decimals they represent a negative power of 10. Likewise, if there are m bits to the right of a decimal, the precision of the number is 2^{-m} (versus 10^{-m} for decimal). Though it is possible to represent numbers greater than one by having digits to the left of the decimal place we will restrict ourselves to numbers less than one. These are commonly used by Digital Signal Processors.

The largest number that can be represented by such a representation is $1\text{-}2^{-m}$, the smallest number is 2^{-m}. For a fraction with 15 bits of resolution this gives a range of approximately 0.99997 to 3.05E-5.

Note that this representationis easily extended to represent all positive numbers by having the digits to the left of the decimal point represent the integer part, and the digits to the right representing the fractional part. Thus

$$6.625_{10} = 110.101_2$$

SIGNED BINARY FRACTIONS

Signed binary fractions are formed much like signed integers. We will work with a single digit to the left of the decimal point, and this will represent the number –1 ($= -(2^0)$). The rest of the representation of the fraction remains unchanged.

Therefore this leftmost bit represents a sign bit just as with two's complement integers. If this bit is set, the number is negative, otherwise the number is positive. The largest positive number that can be represented is still $1\text{-}2^{-m}$ but the largest negative number is -1. The resolution is still $1\text{-}2^{-m}$. There is a terminology for naming the resolution of signed fractions. If there are m bits to the right of the decimal point, the number is said to be in Q*m*format. For a 16 bit number (15 bits to the right of the decimal point) this results in Q15 notation.

BINARY CODES

INTRODUCTION

It would be stretching our imagination to suggest that Sir Francis had digital audio on his minde (sic) when he wrote the prophetic words. Nonetheless, this basic idea forms the basis of everything we do in digital computing, digital communications, and digital audio/video. In 1832, Samuel F. B. Morse used the very same idea to propose that telegram *words* be coded into *binary addresses* or *binary codes* that could be transmitted over telegraph lines and decoded at the receiving end to unravel the telegram. Morse abandoned his scheme, illustrated in Figure, as too complicated and, in 1838, proposed his fabled Morse code for coding letters (instead of words) into objects (dots, dashes, spaces) capable of a threefold difference onely (sic).

In this we study three fundamental questions in the construction of binary addresses or binary codes. First, what are plausible schemes for mapping symbols (such as words, letters, computer instructions, voltages, pressures, etc.) into binary codes? Second, what are plausible schemes for coding likely symbols with short binary words and unlikely symbols with long words in order to minimize the number of binary digits (bits) required to represent a message? Third, what are plausible schemes for "coding" binary words into longer binary words that contain "redundant bits" that may be used to detect and correct errors? These are not new questions. They have occupied the minds of many great thinkers. Sir Francis recognized that arbitrary messages had binary representations.

EXPLANATION

It's kind of like the computer is made up of a bunch of lightswitches, and each lightswitch controls just one lightbulb. On or Off. One or Zero. But if you took *all* of those lightbulbs together, and said "Let's make each sequence of On-and-Off represent a different number!" Well then, you could get some pretty large numbers.

There are four different ways we could flip those switches:

Both Off

First Off, Second On

First On, Second Off

Both On

Binary Code takes each of those combinations and assigns a num berto it, like this:

BothOff= 0

First Off, Second On = 1

First On, Second Off = 2

Both On = 3

Intermediate Explanation

Another way of thinking about it is this: let's give each lightbulb a point value. We'll say the first lightbulb is worth two points, and the second one is worth one point.

Now take a look at the combinations:

Both Off = 0 + 0 = 0

First Off, Second On = 0 + 1 = 1

First On, Second Off = 2 + 0 = 2

Both On = 2 + 1 = 3

If we added in another lightbulb, we would make it worth twice as many points as the 2 pointer. Then, if all the bulbs were on, the point value would be 4 + 2 + 1 = 7. And if we added in *another* bulb, we would make it worth 8 points (twice as much as four).

Now if they are all turned on, that's worth 8 + 4 + 2 + 1 = 15. As you can see, it's going to take a lot of lightbulbs to make a really big number! Finally, even though we're giving point values to each of those lightbulbs, when we write them down we still only write them as ones and zeros. One means On, and Zero means Off.

So let's say we had 8 lightbulbs, and they were set up like this:

Off Off On On Off On Off Off.

The point values of those eight bulbs are: 0 + 0 + 32 + 16 + 0 + 4 + 0 + 0 (remember - we only give points if they're turned on!)

And that adds up to 52. So we would say the sequence of bulbs is worth 52. But how do we write it? We write it like this: 00110100

So now we can say 00110100_{binary} = 52.

8421 BCD CODE

In the 8421 Binary Coded Decimal (BCD) representation each decimal digit is converted to its 4-bit pure binary equivalent.

For example: 57_{dec} = 0101 0111_{bcd}

Addition is analogous to decimal addition with normal binary addition taking place from right to left. For example,

6	0110	BCD for 6	42	0100 0010	BCD for 42
+3	0011	BCD for 3	+27	0010 0111	BCD for 27
	1001	BCD for 9		0110 1001	BCD for 69

Where the result of any addition exceeds 9(1001) then six (0110) must be added to the sum to account for the six invalid BCD codes that are available with a 4-bit number. This is illustrated in the example below

8	1001	BCD for 8
+7	0111	BCD for 7
	1111	exceeds 9 (1001) so
	0110	add six (0110)
	0001 0101	BCD for 15

Note that in the last example the 1 that carried forward from the first group of 4 bits has made a new 4-bit number and so represents the "1" in "15". In the examples above the BCD numbers are split at every 4-bit boundary to make reading them easier. This is not necessary when writing a BCD number down. This coding is an example of a binary coded (each decimal number maps to four bits) weighted (each bit represents a number, 1, 2, 4, etc.) code.

4221 BCD CODE

The 4221 BCD code is another binary coded decimal code where each bit is weighted by 4, 2, 2 and 1 respectively. Unlike BCD coding there are no invalid representations. The decimal numbers 0 to 9 have the following 4221 equivalents

Decimal	4221	1's complement
0	0000	1111
1	0001	1110
2	0010	1101
3	0011	1100
4	1000	0111
5	0111	1000
6	1100	0011
7	1101	0010
8	1110	0001
9	1111	0000

the 1's complement of a 4221 representation is important in decimal arithmetic. In forming the code remember the following rules.

- Below decimal 5 use the right-most bit representing 2 first
- Above decimal 5 use the left-most bit representing 2 first
- Decimal 5 = 2+2+1 and not 4+1

GRAY CODE

Gray coding is an important code and is used for its speed, it is also relatively free from errors. In pure binary coding or 8421 BCD then counting from 7 (0111) to 8 (1000) requires 4 bits to be changed simultaneously. If this does not happen then various numbers could be momentarily generated during the transition so creating spurious numbers which could be read. Gray coding avoids this since only one bit changes between subsequent numbers. To construct the code there are two simple rules. First start with all 0s and then proceed by changing the least significant bit (lsb) which will bring about a new state.

The first 16 Gray coded numbers are indicated below.

Decimal	Gray Code
0	0000
1	0001
2	0011
3	0010
4	0110
5	0111
6	0101
7	0100
8	1100
9	1101
10	1111
11	1110
12	1010
13	1011
14	1001
15	1000

To convert a Gray-coded number to binary then follow this method:

- The binary number and the Gray-coded number will have the same number of bits
- The binary MSB (left-hand bit) and Gray code MSB will always be the same
- To get the binary next-to-MSB (*i.e.* next digit to the right) add the binary MSB and the gray code next-to-MSB. Record the sum, ignoring any carry.
- Continue in this manner right through to the end.

Gray coding is a non-BCD, non-weighted reflected binary code.

CYCLIC CODES

Cyclic codes fall under the category of codes called linear codes.

Definition 6 A linear code of dimension k and length n over a field $\mathbb{F}$ is a k-dimensional subspace of $\mathbb{F}^n$. Such a code is called an n,k code. If the minumum distance of the code is d, then the code is called an $[n,k,d]$ code.

The row-space of the following matrix forms a $[7,3,4]$ code.

$$\begin{pmatrix} 1 & 0 & 1 & 1 & 1 & 0 & 0 \\ 0 & 1 & 0 & 1 & 1 & 1 & 0 \\ 0 & 0 & 1 & 0 & 1 & 1 & 1 \end{pmatrix}$$

Notice that there are 4 ones in each row. Any binary n-vector can be thought of as the coeffiecients of an nth degree polynomial in $\mathbb{Z}_2$. Looking at the first row in the matrix we can relate it to the polynomial

$$g(x) = 1 + x^2 + x^3 + x^4$$

in the polynomial ring $\mathbb{Z}_2[x]$. Given a linear code the following proposition is clear.

Proposition 1 Let C be a linear code. Then $d(C)$ equals the smallest Hammming weight of all nonzero code vectors. There are many different varieties of linear codes, such as the well known Hamming codes.

We now want to consider a brand of linear codes called cyclic codes. Then we will define BCH codes, which are a specific type of cyclic code.

Definition 7 A linear code C is called cyclic if

$(c_1, c_2, ..., n_c) \in C$

implies $(c_n, c_1, c-2, ..., n_{n-1}) \in C$

For example, if $(1,1,1,0,1,0)$ is in a cyclic code, then $(0,1,1,1,0,1)$ is also in the code. The definition is recursive and so every cyclic shift of the elements is in the code.

In order to formalize the discussion we can use the following isomorphism

$$(a_0, a_1, ..., a_{n-1}) \in \mathbb{F}_q^n \rightleftharpoons a_0 + a_1 x + ... + a_{n-1} x^{n-1} \in \mathbb{F}_q[x]$$

between the n-dimensional vector space $\mathbb{F}_q^n$ and the residue class of polynomials

$$\mathbb{F}_q[x]/\left(x^n - 1\right)$$

Recall from algebra that

$$\mathbb{F}_q[x]/\left(x^n - 1\right) = \left\{a_0 + a_1x + ... + a_{n-1}x^{n-1} \middle| a_i \in \mathbb{F}_q, 0 \le i \le n\right\}$$

We can now speak of codeword in C as the polynomials

$$c(x) | \mathbb{F}_q[x]/\left(x^n - 1\right),$$

and the following theorem follows

Theorem 2: A linear code C in $\mathbb{F}_q^n$ is a cyclic code iff C is an ideal in

$$\mathbb{F}_q[x]/\left(x^n - 1\right)$$

Proof. $(\Rightarrow)$ If C is an ideal in

$$\mathbb{F}_q[x]/\left(x^n - 1\right) \text{ and } c(x) = c_0 + c_1x + c_{n-1}x^{n-1}$$

is any codeword, then $xc(x)$ is also a codeword. Thus

$$(c_{n-1}, c_0, c - 1, ..., c_{n-2}) \in C \; (\Leftarrow)$$

If C is cyclic, then for every codeword $c(x)$ the word $xc(x)$ is also a codeword. Therefore $x^i c(x)$ is in C for every i, and since C is linear $a(x)c(x)$ is in C for every polynomial $a(x)$. It follows that C is an ideal.

The next theorem states the general structure of cyclic codes.

Theorem 3: Let C be a cyclic code of length n over a finite field $\mathbb{F}$. To each codeword

$$(a_0, a_1, ..., a_n - 1) \in C,$$

associate the polynomial,

$$a_0 + a_1x + ... + a_{n-1}x^{n-1} \text{ in } \mathbb{F}[x]$$

Among all the nonzero polynomials obtained from C in this way, let $g(x)$ have the smallest degree. We may assume that $g(x)$ is monic. This polynomial is called the generating polynomial for C. Then

- $g(x)$ is uniquely determined by C.
- $g(x)$ is a divisor of x^{n-1}.
- C is exactly the set of coefficients of the polynomials of the form $g(x)f(x)$ with $\deg(f) \leq n-1$.
- Write $x^n - 1 = g(x)h(x)$.

Then $m(x) \in \mathbb{F}[x]/(x^n - 1)$ corresponds to an element of C if $h(x)m(x) \equiv 0 \bmod (x^n - 1)$.

Proof:

(1) The codespace is spanned by the rows of a matrix. Because the row space of the matrix is closed under subtraction the difference between any two vectors, or polynomials, in the space is still in the space. So if there was another monic generating polynomial $g_1(x)$ with minimum degree, then $g(x) - g_1(x)$ is also in the space. But this is a contradiction since this new polynomial has smaller degree than both $g(x)$ and $g_1(x)$.

(2) Divide $g(x)$ into $x^n - 1$. By the division algorithm we get,

$$x^n - 1 = g(x)h(x) + r(x) \Rightarrow -r(x) \equiv g(x)h(x) \bmod (x^n - 1)$$

where $\deg r(x) < \deg g(x)$.

But multiplying $g(x)$ by powers of x corresponds to a cyclic shift of the corresponding code vector and multiplication by a polynomial is thus a linear combination of the code vectors in the generating matrix and all of their cyclic shifts. So $r(x)$ is in the code space of C. Since deg,

$$r(x) < \deg g(x) <, \ r(x)$$

must be equal to zero.

Thus $g(x) \mid x^n - 1$. Notice then that $\mathbb{F}[x]/(x^n - 1)$ is not a field since it has zero divisors.

(3) Let $m(x)$ correspond to an element in C. Divide $g(x)$ into $m(x)$ $m(x) = g(x)f(x) + r_1(x)$ with deg $r(x) <$ deg $g(x)$. From (2) we know that $g(x)f(x)$ corresponds to a codeword and by assumption so does $m(x)$. So, since C is closed under subtraction, $m(x) - g(x)f(x)$ mod $(x^n - 1)$ is also a codeword. But this is just $r_1(x)$ and has degree less than $g(x)$. It follows that $r_1(x) \equiv 0$ and $m(x)$ is the product of the generating polynomial with another polynomial. Because each codeword has length n, deg $m(x) \leq n-1$.

so deg $f(x) \leq n - 1 -$ deg $g(x)$. Conversely, we have shown that the product of any two polynomials $g(x)f(x)$ is in C. Thus, these polynomials yield all of the code words of C.

(4) By (2) we can write $x^n - 1 = g(x)h(x)$.

Let $m(x)$ correspond to an element in C. Then by (3) $h(x)m(x) = h(x)g(x)f(x) = (x^n - 1)f(x) \equiv 0$ mod $(x^n - 1)$

Next suppose that $m(x)h(x) \equiv 0$ mod $(x^n - 1)$. Then $m(x)h(x) = (x^n - 1)q(x) = h(x)g(x)q(x)$ for polynomial $q(x)$. We can now divide through by $h(x)$ and get $m(x) = g(x)q(x)$ and so $m(x)$ coresponds to a code word of C.

Remark: There will be a unique polynomial $h(x)$ such that $g(x)h(x) = x^n - 1$. When thinking of the codespace as a product of polynomials with $g(x)$ instead of the row space of a binary matrix, this polynomial $h(x)$ will take the place of the check matrix in the decoding process.

Let $c(x) = b(x)g(x)$ be a codeword then,

$$c(x) = h(x)g(x)h(x) = b(x)(x^n - 1)$$

Then if $m =$ deg $b(x)$ the coeffiecients of the m highest powers match the coeffiecients of the m lowest powers of x in the polynomial $c(x)h(x)$.

Further, if the generating polynomial

$$g(x) = g_0 + g_1 x + \dots + g_{n-k} x^{n-k}$$

has degree $n - k$, then the codewords,

$$g(x), xg(x) + x^2 g(x), \dots + g_{n-k} x^{n-k}$$

form a basis for the codespae C with a generating matrix

$$\begin{pmatrix} g_0 & g_1 & \cdots & g_{n-k} & 0 & 0 & \cdots & 0 \\ 0 & g_1 & \cdots & g_{n-k-1} & g_{n-k} & 0 & \cdots & 0 \\ 0 & 0 & \cdots & & & & \cdots & 0 \\ 0 & 0 & \cdots & & g_0 & g_1 & \cdots & g_{n-k} \end{pmatrix}$$

and we can Realise a code word as an information sequence $(a_0, a-1, \dots a_{k-1})$ times the matrix

$$aG = \left(a_o + a_1 x + \dots + a_{k-1} x^{k-1}\right) g(x) \bmod x^n - 1$$

As stated before, we can treat the polynomial $h(x)$, having the condition that $g(x)h(x) \equiv 0 \bmod x^n - 1$, as the check polynomial of the code C. Knowing that we want $g_0 h_i + g_1 h_{i-1} + \dots + g_{n-k} h_{i-n-k} = 0$ for $i = 0, 1, \dots, n-1$, it follows that the check matrix for the code is,

$$\begin{pmatrix} 0 & 0 & \dots & 0 & h_k & \dots & h_1 & h_0 \\ 0 & 0 & \dots & h_k & \dots & h_1 & h_0 & 0 \\ \vdots & & & & & & & \vdots \\ h_k & \dots & h_1 & h_0 & 0 & \dots & 0 & 0 \end{pmatrix}$$

Lets now consider an example using a 3×7 matrix of 0's and 1's.

$$\begin{pmatrix} 1 & 0 & 1 & 1 & 1 & 0 & 0 \\ 0 & 1 & 0 & 1 & 1 & 1 & 0 \\ 0 & 0 & 1 & 0 & 1 & 1 & 1 \end{pmatrix}$$

Because each of the three rows are linearly independent we know from linear algebra that the row space of the matrix is a 3-dimensional subspace of $\mathbb{F}^7$ where $\mathbb{F}$ is the field $\mathbb{Z}_2$. In fact, since the algorithm is based on left multiplication by a code vector, the row space is the range of the matrix. In essence, because each code vector corresponds to a polynomial, the code space corresponds to cyclic shifts of the coefficients of polynomials, which is just all polynomial products $a(x)g(x)$ where $g(x)$ is the generating polynomial for the code C. It turns out that in this case all the cyclic shifts of the first row vector account for every vector in the row space. Thus we have a cyclic code and the generating polynomial is

$$g(x) = 1 + x^2 + x^3 + x^4$$

which corresponds to the first row of the generating matrix. Also,

$$(x^4 + x^3 + x^2 + 1)(x^3 + x^2 + 1) = x^7 - 1$$

and so the check polynomial is

$$h(x) = x^3 + x^2 + 1$$

and we get the following check matrix

$$H = \begin{pmatrix} 0 & 0 & 0 & 1 & 1 & 0 & 1 \\ 0 & 0 & 1 & 1 & 0 & 1 & 0 \\ 0 & 1 & 1 & 0 & 1 & 0 & 0 \end{pmatrix}$$

Now taking the codeword c_g corresponding to $g(x)$ we get

$$Hc_g = \begin{pmatrix} 0 & 0 & 0 & 1 & 1 & 0 & 1 \\ 0 & 0 & 1 & 1 & 0 & 1 & 0 \\ 0 & 1 & 1 & 0 & 1 & 0 & 0 \end{pmatrix} \begin{pmatrix} 1 \\ 0 \\ 1 \\ 1 \\ 1 \\ 0 \\ 0 \end{pmatrix} = \begin{pmatrix} 0 \\ 0 \\ 0 \\ 0 \\ 0 \\ 0 \\ 0 \end{pmatrix} \bmod 2$$

In fact, for every codeword C in the space C, the product Hc will be the zero vector. This will be an extremely important detail when creating an algorithm for a single-error correcting BCH code

ERROR DETECTING AND CORRECTING CODES

ERROR-CORRECTING CODES

The theory of error detecting and correcting codes is that

branch of engineering and mathematics which deals with the reliable transmission and storage of data. Information media are not 100% reliable in practice, in the sense that noise (any form of interference) frequently causes data to be distorted. To deal with this undesirable but inevitable situation, some form of redundancy is incorporated in the original data. With this redundancy, even if errors are introduced (up to some tolerance level), the original information can be recovered, or at least the presence of errors can be detected.

We saw in class how adding to the original message the parity bit or the arithmetic sum allows the detection of a (certain type of) error. However, that kind of redundancy doesn't allow for the correction of the error. Error-correcting codes do exactly this: they add redundancy to the original message in such a way that it is possible for the receiver to detect the error and correct it, recovering the original message. This is crucial for certain applications where the re-sending of the message is not possible (for example, for interplanetary communications and storage of data).

The crucial problem to be resolved then is how to add this redundancy in order to detect and correct as many errors as possible in the most efficient way. Most of us have used error-correcting codes, perhaps without knowing it. The International Standard Book Number (ISBN) system identifies every book with a ten-digit number, such as 0-226-53420-0. The first nine digits are the actual number but the tenth is added according to a mathematical formula based on the first nine. If a single one of the digits is changed, as in a misprint when ordering a book, a simple check verifies that something is wrong.

Other common numbers with check digits include the Chemical Abstracts Service (CAS) method of identifying chemical compounds and the United States Postal Service (USPS) nine-digit "zip+four" code, which when it is bar-coded includes a tenth check digit hidden to the human eye but visible to the bar code reader. Some high-end computer memory chips, "ECC RAM," use extended nine-bit bytes. The ninth bit, or "check bit," is always set so that the total number of ones in the extended byte is even. (This rule is called a "checksum." Specifically, if the sum of the nine bits is not even, an error has been detected.) This ninth bit is not used or even seen by your software, but the computer hardware itself will signal an error if it ever reads an extended byte that contains an odd number of ones.

All these processes can *detect* a single error within a very short message: nine decimal digits for the ISBN and USPS codes, a varying number of decimal digits for the CAS numbers, eight binary digits for ECC RAM. However, they cannot *correct* any error that is detected. Furthermore, some combinations of two or more errors occurring within the message will not be detected.

Coding Theory

Coding theory deals with ways of extending the check-bit and checksum ideas to enable detection and even correction of large numbers of errors within messages. It builds on some beautiful mathematical ideas that we can hint at here. Let's focus on binary messages, the stuff of which computer communications is built.

The first thing is to break up the message into "words" of fixed size. We will focus on how to correct errors occurring within individual words. If the words are n bits long, then there are 2^n possible messages each word can carry. The set of all such words has an interesting geometry based on the *Hamming distance.* The distance between two words is just the number of places in which they differ.

For example, let's consider the case n=7. The distance between 0100111 and 1100101 is two, because these words differ in the first and sixth places.Words can also be added to each other. This is done by the usual odd-even rules of addition, performed bit by bit. Specifically, 0+0=0, 0+1 = 1, 1+0 = 1, and 1+1 = 0. Thus 0100111 + 1100101 = 1000010.

Suppose you want to send a message in the form of a binary string, *i.e.*, a string of 0's and 1's. Due to noise in the medium over which you are transmitting the message, be it a telephone line, a radio link or the Internet, it is possible that some of the 0's will be received as 1's and vice versa. Let us denote the probability that any one bit is garbled in transmission by p. Typically, p will be small, say about one in a million, but that may still be too large for our purposes. If we are transferring a file that has 10 million bits, the chance that the file is incorrectly received is nearly 90%. How can we improve the reliability of the transmission? The simplest method is to repeat ourselves three times. For example, if we want to send the string 010, we transmit 000111000.

If a single error occurs in transmission, this may be received for instance as 001111000. At the receiver, we use what is called majority decoding. We look at each set of 3 bits and decode it as the bit which occurs most often. Thus, the received message above is correctly decoded as 010 even though an error occured in transmission. In the above example, it could have happened that two errors occured and we received the string 101111000.

This would be decoded as 110, which is different from the original message. This shows that we cannot eliminate errors altogether, we can only make them less likely. To see how much less likely, let us work out the probability that a single bit is incorrectly received. Since each bit is transmitted three times, it has to be incorrectly received at least twice in order for the decoder to get it wrong. The probability of this is $3p^2+p^3$, which, for p equal to one in a million works out to about one in 330 billion. Thus, using the repetition code, a 10 Mbit file can be sent correctly with probability 99.997%. While this coding scheme dramatically reduces the likelihood of errors, it is rather inefficient. Can we do better?

Here's one way, using the famous (7,4) Hamming code. This works with a block of 4 bits at a time rather than with a single bit. Suppose we want to transmit the block 0011. Look at the picture below. We write these bits in the intersections of the circles. Next, we fill in the part of each circle lying outside the intersection using the rule that the total number of 1's contained in each circle should be even. The extra bits are called parity bits — they ensure even parity for the number of 1's in each circle. The message we transmit will consist of all seven bits, in a pre-arranged order so that the receiver can reconstruct the diagram. Suppose now that a single error occurs, so that the receiver gets a 1 in the intersection of the top two circles. The receiver proceeds to work out the parity for each of the circles, and finds that the top two circles both have odd parity (odd number of 1's), while the bottom circle has even parity.

This enables her to conclude that an error has occurred, and that the error is in the bit position common to the top two circles. Therefore, the intended message can be decoded correctly. It is not hard to see that a similar approach works if the error is in some other bit position. However, if there are two errors, then the decoding procedure fails in that it yields a message different from the intended one.

Applications of Error Correcting Codes

The increasing reliance on digital communication and the emergence of the digital computer as an essential tool in a technological society have placed error-correcting codes in a most prominent position. We cite here a few specific applications, in an attempt to indicate their practicality and importance.

Many computers now have error-correcting capabilities built into their random access memories; it is less expensive to compensate for errors through the use of error-correcting codes than to build integrated circuits that are 100% reliable. The single error-correcting Hamming codes, and linear codes in general, are of use here. Disk storage is another area of computing where error-coding is employed. Storage capacity has been greatly increased through the use of disks of higher and higher density. With this increase in density, error probability also increases, and therefore information is now stored on many disks using error-correcting codes.

In 1972, the *Mariner* space probe flew past Mars and transmitted pictures back to earth. The channel for such transmissions is space and the earth's atmosphere. Solar activity and atmospheric conditions can introduce errors into weak signals coming from the spacecraft. In order that most of the pictures sent could be correctly recovered here on earth, the following coding scheme was used. The source alphabet consisted of 64 shades of gray. The source encoder encoded each of these into binary 6-tuples and the channel encoder produced binary 32-tuples. The source decoder could correct up to 7 errors in any 32-tuple. This was done with the Reed-Muller codes.

In 1979, the *Voyager* probes began transmitting Colour pictures of Jupiter. For Colour pictures the source alphabet needed to be much larger and was chosen to have 4096 Colour shades. The source encoder produced binary 12-tuples for each Colour shade and the channel encoder produced 24-tuples (*i.e.* 24 dimensional vectors). This code would correct up to 3 errors in any 24-tuple, and is the Golay code. The increasing popularity of digital audio is due in part to the powerful error-correcting codes that the digitization process facilitates. Information is typically stored on a small aluminized disk as a series of microscopic pits and smooth areas, the pattern representing a sequence of 0's and 1's. A laser beam is used as the playback mechanism to retrieve stored data. Because the data is digital, error correction schemes can be easily incorporated into such a system.

Given an error-coded digital recording, a digital audio system can on playback, correct errors introduced by fingerprints, scratches, or even imperfections originally present in the storage medium. The compact disc system pioneered by Philips Corporation of the Netherlands in cooperation with Sony Corporation of Japan, allowing playback of pre-recorded digital audio disks, is an excellent example of the application of error-correcting codes to digital communication; *crossinterleaved Reed-Solomon* codes are used for error correction in this system.

Digital audio tape (DAT) systems have also been developed, allowing digital recording as well as playback. Error-correcting codes are particularly suited when the transmission channel is noisy. This is the case of wireless communication. Nowadays, all digital wireless communications use error-correcting codes.

Fundamental Concepts

We begin with a few definitions, in order to develop a working vocabulary. Let A be an alphabet of q symbols. For example, A = {a,b,c,...,z) is the standard lower case alphabet for the English language, and A = (0,1) is the binary alphabet.

Definition: A block code of length n containing M codewords over the alphabet A is a set of M n-tuples where each n-tuple takes its components from A. We refer to such a block code as an [n,M]-code over A.

In practice, we most frequently take A to be the binary alphabet. Given a code C of block length n over an alphabet A, those specific n-tuples over A which are in C are referred to as codewords.

Note that while the channel encoder transmits codewords, the n-tuples received by the channel decoder may or may not be codewords, due to the possible occurrence of errors during transmission.

Example: Suppose the information we are to transmit comes from the set of symbols {A, B, C, D}. For practical considerations we associate sequences of 0's and l's with each of these symbols.

A → 00
B → 01
C → 10
D → 11

This is the source encoding.

Now we want to add some redundancy (channel encoding).

A → 00 → 00000
B → 01 → 10110
C → 10 → 01011
D → 11 → 11101

We have just constructed a [5,4]-code over a binary alphabet. That is, we constructed a code with 4 codewords, each being a 5-tuple (block length 5), with each component of the 5-tuple being O or 1. The code is the set of n-tuples produced by the channel encoder (as opposed to the source encoder). The source encoder transforms messages into k-tuples (k=2 in the example above) over the code alphabet A, and the channel encoder assigns to each of these information k-tuples a codeword of length n (n=5 in the example). Since the channel encoder is adding redundancy, we have n > k and hence we have message expansion. While the added redundancy is desirable from the point of view of error control, it decreases the efficiency of the communication channel by reducing its effective capacity. The ratio k to n is a measure of the fraction of information in the channel which is non-redundant.

Definition: The rate of an [n,M]-code which encodes information k-tuples is,

$$R = K/n$$

The rate of the simple code given in example 1 is 2/5. The quantity r = n-k is sometimes called the redundancy of the code.

A fundamental parameter associated with an [n,M]-code C is the Hamming distance for C. Before we can define the Hamming distance for a code, we must define the Hamming distance between two codewords.

Definition: The Hamming distance d(x,y) between two codewords x and y is the number of coordinate positions in which they differ.

Example: Over the alphabet A = (0,1}, the codewords x and y x=(10110) y=(11O11) have Hamming distance d(x,y) =3.

Example: The codewords u and v over the alphabet A = (0,1,2), given by u = (21002) v=(12001) have Hamming distance d(u,v) =3.

Definition: Let C be an [n,M]-code.

The Hamming distance d of the code C is d= min {d(x,y): x,y belong to C, x != y}.

In other words, the Hamming distance of a code is the minimum distance between two distinct codewords, over all pairs of codewords.

Example: Consider C = (c0,c1,c2,c3} where c0=(00000) c1 =(10110) c2= (01011) c3= (11101) This code has distance d = 3. It is the [5,4] code constructed earlier. Suppose we have an [n,M]-code C with distance d. We need to adopt a strategy for the channel decoder (or just decoder). When the decoder receives an n-tuple r it must make some decision.

This decision may be one of:

- No errors have occurred; accept r as a codeword.
- Errors have occurred; correct r to a codeword c.
- Errors have occurred; no correction is possible.

In general, the decoder will not always make the correct decision; for example, consider the possibility of an error pattern occurring which changes a transmitted codeword into another codeword. The goal is that the decoder take the course of action which has the greatest probability of being correct. One usually makes the assumption that errors are introduced by the channel at random, and that the probability of an error in one coordinate is independent of errors in adjacent coordinates. The decoding strategy we shall adopt, called nearest neighbour decoding, can then be specified as follows. Nearest Neighbour Decoding If an n-tuple r is received, and there is a unique codeword c that belongs to C such that d(r,c) is a minimun, then correct r to the c. If no such c exists, report that errors have been detected, but no correction is possible. By nearest neighbour decoding, a received vector is decoded to the codewords"closest" to it, with respect to Hamming distance. The figure below illustrates the concept. The red dots are the codewords, the green ones are the received words that can be corrected to the closest codewords and the blue dot is a received word that is equidistant from 2 codewords and therefore cannot be corrected.

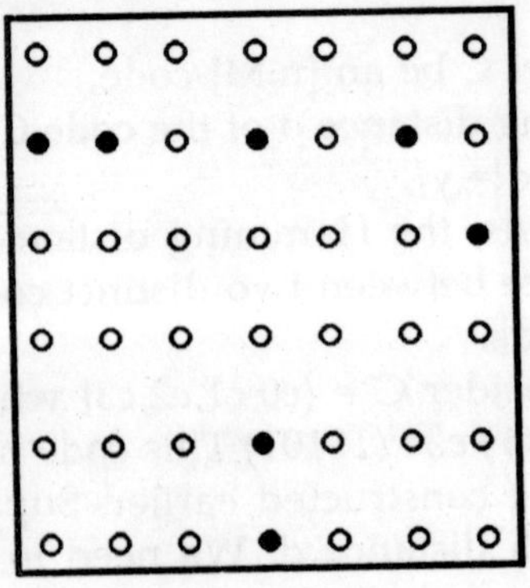

A code is said to correct e errors if a decoder using the above scheme is capable of correcting any pattern of e or fewer errors introduced by the channel. In this case, the decoder can correct any transmitted codeword which has been altered in e or fewer coordinate positions.

Theorem: Let C be an [n,M]-code having distance d = 2e+1. Then C can correct e errors. If used for error detection only, C can detect 2e errors.

Let c be one codeword of C and S be the set of all n-tuples over the alphabet of C and define

S(c) = {x belongs to S: d(x,c) ⇐□ e).

S(c) is called the sphere of radius e about the codeword c. It consists of all n-tuples within distance e of the codeword c, which we think of as being at the Centre of the sphere. In the figure below, the"spheres" arount the codewords of the previous figure.

The radius is in this case is 1.

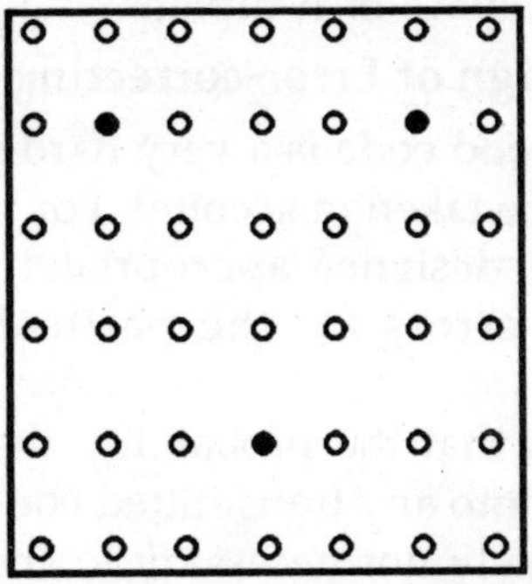

Given 2 codewords, their spheres don't intersect, hence if codeword c is transmitted and t<= e errors are introduced, the received word r is an n-tuple in the sphere S(c) and thus c is the unique codeword closest to r.

The decoder can always correct any error pattern of this type. If we use the code only for error detection, then at least 2e+1 errors must occur in a codeword to carry it into another codeword.

If at least 1 and at most 2e errors are introduced, the received word will never be a codeword and error detection is always possible. The spheres have to be disjoint in order to be able to correct errors. But if a received word happens to be in the space between the spheres, correction is not possible: that space doesn't belong to any sphere, *i.e.* to any codeword: the error is detected but not corrected.

Therefore, we want to find codes such that the the spheres around the codewords are disjoint (to correctly correct the errors) but as close as possible to each other, to correct ALL the errors.

If all the space is taken by the sphere, all the words received will fall into the sphere of a codeword and therefore can be corrected to that codeword. These are the perfect codes. Lets give the formal definition of perfect codes.

Definition: A perfect code is an e-error-correcting [n, M]-code over an alphabet A such that every n-tuple over A is in the sphere of radius e about some codework. In a perfect code of block length n, the sphere of radius e about codeworks are not only disjoint (since the code is e-error-correcting) but exhaust the entire space of n-tuples.

Issues in the Design of Error-correcting Codes

Designing a good code is a very hard problem. Also, lots of factors need to be taken in account. For instance, in practice the code should be designed appropriately depending on the expected rate of errors for the particular channel being employed.

If it is known that the probability that the channel will introduce 2 errors into any transmitted codeword is extremely small, then it is likely not necessary to construct a code that will correct all 2-bit error patterns. A single error correcting code will likely suffice.

Conversely, if double errors are frequent and a single error correcting code is being used, then decoding errors will be frequent. From this brief introduction, a number of questions arise.

- Given n, M and d, can we determine if an [n Al] code with distance d exists?
- Assuming such a code does exist, how would one be constructed in practice?
- How should information k-tuples be associated with

codeword n-tuples to facilitate efficient channel encoding?

- How should channel decoding be performed?

Lets examine the issue of channel decoding in greater detail. When a word is received and it's not a codeword, finding the closest codeword involves computing the distance from the received word to each codeword, requiring M comparisons.

While this might be acceptable for small M, in practice we usually find M quite large. Suppose a code C is used with M = 2^50 codewords, which is not unrealistic. If we could carry out 1 million distance computations per second, it would take around 20 years to make a single correction. Clearly, this is not tolerable and more efficient techniques are required.

Wishing to retain the nearest neighbour decoding strategy, we seek more efficient techniques for its implementation. The theory of error-correcting code is concerned with constructing codes for various values of n, M and d, and the consideration of appropriate encoding and decoding techniques.

Most of the best known codes are algebraic in nature like the linear codes. Linear codes are an important and general class of error-correcting codes. For example, theBCH codes used for CDs are linear codes.

They are heavily mathematical and an appropriate description here is not possible. The next session describes instead the last"discovery" in the theory of error correcting codes, the Turbo codes.

Turbo Codes

In session 3, when we introduced the Nearest Neighbour Decoding, we didn't mention the fact that what the decoding actually does is maximizing the probability P(r|c) that r is received, given that c is sent. *i.e.* choosing the nearest codeword is equivalent to choosing the most likely input message c given the received tuple r. This decoding strategy is known as maximum likelihood decoding

The simplest graphical model:

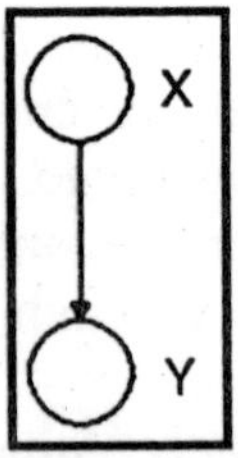

A classical problem of probability estimation is finding the probability distribution P(X|Y) where X and Y are 2 random variables.

The graphical model framework allows for such probability estimations to be calculated in an efficient way. Note that the calculation of P(X|Y) from P(Y|X) and P(X) is just Bayes rule - P(X|Y) = P(Y|X)P(X)/P(Y) - and that graphical model inference algorithms can be viewed as generalizations of Bayes rule to arbitrary graphs.

Lets now see how we can view error correcting codes as graphical models. In the figure below, a convolution code as a graphical model.Let U be the original message, X the encoded message and Y the message received after the noisy channel.

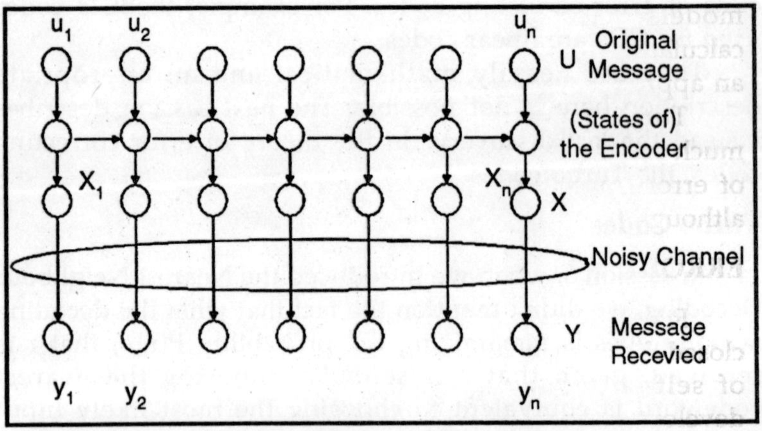

Now, the decoding problem of finding U that maximizes p(U|Y) can be tackled within the framework of graphical models. We have introduced the convolutional codes mainly because the Turbo codes are two convolutional codes put together. The following figure illustrate the graphical representation of a turbo code.

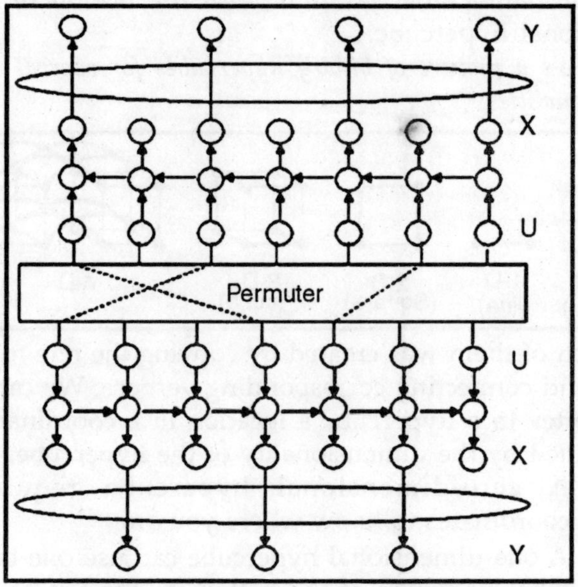

It should be mentioned that general inference in graphical models is NP-hard, and, in particular, exact inference, calculating P(U | Y), for turbo codes is infeasible and therefore an approximate inference algorithm is used.

Turbo codes were discovered very recently. There is much excitement about them. They outperform all other kinds of error-correcting codes in the case of long block lengths, although the reason why they do so is not yet clear.

ERROR DETECTING

R.W. Hamming wrote the paper that both opened and closed this field in 1950. His interest was in providing a means of self-checking in computers, which were just being developed at the time he wrote this. The paper appeared in the Bell System Technical Journal, April, 1950. Definitely worth tracking down in the library and reading.

Bit Strings as Addresses in Binary Hypercubes

The best starting point for understanding ECC codes is to consider bit strings as addresses in a binary hypercube. A hypercube is a generalization of a cube to various dimensions; we're probably most familiar with the notion of a four-dimensional hypercube.

Here's a picture of binary hypercubes for several different dimensionalities:

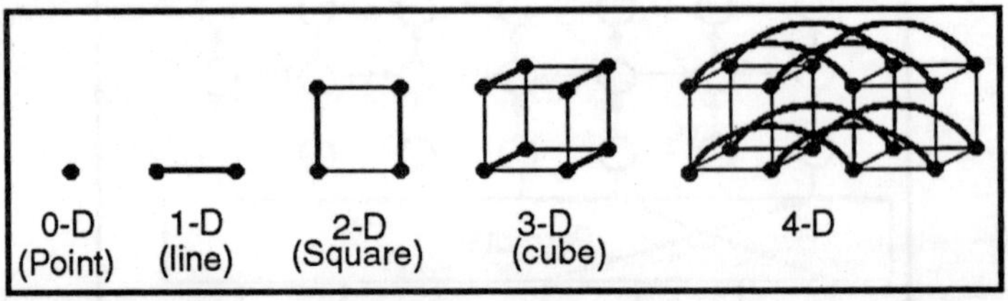

Each of them was created by copying the one to the left twice, and connecting corresponding vertices. We can assign each vertex in a hypercube a location in a coordinate space determined by the dimensionality of the hypercube.

- A zero-dimensional hypercube requires no coordinates to know where you are
- A one-dimensional hypercube can use one bit to tell whether you're at the bottom or the top of the line segment.
- A two-dimensional hypercube can use two bits: first bit is left vs. right, second is inherited from the line.
- A three-dimensional hypercube can use a bit to tell front square from back, and inherit two bits from the square.
- A four-dimensional hypercube can use a bit to tell left cube from right, and inherits three bits from cube.

This can continue through as many dimensions as you want. The Hamming distance between two bit strings is the number of bits you have to change to convert one to the other: this is the same as the number of edges you have to traverse in a binary hypercube to get from one of the vertices to the other. The basic idea of an error correcting code is to use extra bits to increase the dimensionality of the hypercube, and make sure the Hamming distance between any two valid points is greater than one.

- If the Hamming distance between valid strings is only one, a single-bit error results in another valid string. This means we can't detect an error.
- If it's two, then changing one bit results in an invalid string, and can be detected as an error. Unfortunately, changing just one more bit can result in another valid string, which means we can't know which bit was wrong: so we can detect an error but not correct it.
- If the Hamming distance between valid strings is three, then changing one bit leaves us only one bit away from the original error, but two bits away from any other valid string. This means if we have a one-bit error, we can figure out which bit is the error; but if we have a two-bit error, it looks like one bit from the other direction. So we can have single bit correction, but that's all.
- Finally, if the Hamming distance is four, then we can correct a single-bit error and detect a double-bit error. This is frequently referred to as a SECDED (Single Error Correct, Double Error Detect) scheme.

Parity

The simplest case is by adding a parity bit. Suppose we have a three-bit word (so the bit strings define points in a cube). If we add a fourth bit, we can decree that any time we want to switch a bit in the original three-bit string, we also have to switch the parity bit.

If we start with 000 in the left cube, so the full string is 0000, changing any one of the original three bits requires us to change to the other cube: 1001, 1010, and 1100. Now if we change a second bit, we have to move back to the left cube: 0011, 0101, 0110. And if we change the third bit, we move back to the right cube: 0111.

So, there is a Hamming distance of two between any two valid strings. If we get a one-bit error, we know it is an error because it's on one of the invalid vertices. This can be computed by counting the number of 1's, and making sure it's always even (so this is called even parity). We could have selected exactly the opposite set of vertices as the valid ones, which would have given us odd parity. We picked even parity because we'll be using it in the next step.

HAMMING CODES

Several Teletext packets contain information protected by hamming. This is a method for encoding data such that errors in reception can be detected, and if the error is sufficiently small, corrected. Teletext uses two hamming codes. The simpler and more robust version encodes 4 bits of data in one 8-bit byte. This code is used extensively to protect the fields that have meaning to the Teletext system itself. The more efficient code encodes 18 bits of data in three 8-bit bytes. It is used for to protect some of the data fields inside Teletext packets. Both codes are designed such that any one-bit error can be corrected, and any 2-bit error can be detected.

There's an error correction code that separates the bits holding the original value (data bits) from the error correction bits (check bits), and the difference between the calculated and actual error correction bits is the position of the bit that's wrong. It's called a Hamming Code.

8/4 HAMMING

The 8/4 code is quite simple; if the input nibble is the 4-bit value:

```
b3, b2, b1, b0
```

with b3 being the most significant bit, then the output hammed byte is the 8-bit value:

```
b3, b3^b2^b1, b2, !b2^b1^b0, b1, !b3^b1^b0, b0,
!b3^b2^b0
```

where ^ represents bitwise exclusive-or and ! is bitwise not. This code has the property that every value is four bits different from all other such values. A one-bit error is therefore unambiguously correctable, being only one bit away from a valid code. A two-bit error is detectable but not correctable, being equidistant between two valid codes.

24/18 HAMMING

The more efficient 24/18 code is based on the same principle of interleaved check bits and an overall parity bit as the simpler 8/4 code.

Assuming the input bits are:

```
b17, b16, b15, b14, b13, b12, b11, b10, b9, b8,
b7, b6, b5, b4, b3, b2, b1, b0
```

With b17 being the most significant bit, the six hamming check bits are:

```
c0 = ! b17 ^ b15 ^ b13 ^ b11 ^ b10 ^ b8 ^ b6 ^
b4 ^ b3 ^ b1 ^ b0
c1 = ! b17 ^ b16 ^ b13 ^ b12 ^ b10 ^ b9 ^ b6 ^
b5 ^ b3 ^ b2 ^ b0
c2 = ! b17 ^ b16 ^ b15 ^ b14 ^ b10 ^ b9 ^ b8 ^
b7 ^ b3 ^ b2 ^ b1
c3 = ! b10 ^ b9 ^ b8 ^ b7 ^ b6 ^ b5 ^ b4
c4 = ! b17 ^ b16 ^ b15 ^ b14 ^ b13 ^ b12 ^ b11
c5 = b17 ^ b14 ^ b12 ^ b11 ^ b10 ^ b7 ^ b5 ^ b4
^ b2 ^ b1 ^ b0
```

where ^ represents bitwise exclusive-or and ! is bitwise not. c5 can alternatively and equivalently be computed as the odd parity of all the other data and check bits.

The output bytes are then:

```
c3, b3, b2, b1, c2, b0, c1, c0
c4, b10, b9, b8, b7, b6, b5, b4
c5, b17, b16, b15, b14, b13, b12, b11
```

in byte transmission order, with the most significant bit of each byte on the left.

To decode a hammed byte triplet:

```
h7, h6, h5, h4, h3, h2, h1, h0
h15, h14, h13, h12, h11, h10, h9, h8
h23, h22, h21, h20, h19, h18, h17, h16
```

with h0 being the least significant bit of the first byte and h23 being the most significant bit of the third byte, we compute

```
p = h23 ^ h22 ^ h21 ^ h20 ^... ^ h1 ^ h0
c0 = h0 ^ h2 ^ h4 ^ h6 ^ h8 ^ h10 ^ h12 ^ h14
^ h16 ^ h18 ^ h20 ^ h22
```

```
c1 = h1 ^ h2 ^ h5 ^ h6 ^ h9 ^ h10 ^ h13 ^ h14
^ h17 ^ h18 ^ h21 ^ h22
c2 = h3 ^ h4 ^ h5 ^ h6 ^ h11 ^ h12 ^ h13 ^ h14
^ h19 ^ h20 ^ h21 ^ h22
c3 = h7 ^ h8 ^ h9 ^ h10 ^ h11 ^ h12 ^ h13 ^ h14
c4 = h15 ^ h16 ^ h17 ^ h18 ^ h19 ^ h20 ^ h21 ^
h22
```

If the parity, p, is correct (equal to 1) then either 0 or 2 errors occurred. If all the check bits, c0, c1, c2, c3, c4, c5 are correct (equal to 1), then the byte was received intact, (no errors) otherwise it was damaged beyond repair (two errors). If p is 0, then there was a single bit error which can be recovered. For the check bits which are incorrect (equal to 0), add the following powers of two together:

```
if c0 = 0 add 1
if c1 = 0 add 2
if c2 = 0 add 4
if c3 = 0 add 8
if c4 = 0 add 16
```

The sum gives the bit position 1--24 corresponding to h0--h23 which is in error. The erroneous bit should be flipped. Note that there is actually no need to fix errors in bits h23, h15, h7, h3, h1 and h0 since they are not used in the decoded byte. The output data bits, d17--d0 are:

```
h22, h21, h20, h19, h18, h17, h16, h14, h13,
h12,
h11, h10, h9, h8, h6, h5, h4, h2
```

FLOATING POINT REPRESENTATION

There are several ways to represent real numbers on computers. Fixed point places a radix point somewhere in the middle of the digits, and is equivalent to using integers that represent portions of some unit. For example, one might represent 1/100ths of a unit; if you have four decimal digits, you could represent 10.82, or 00.01. Another approach is to use rationals, and represent every number as the ratio of two integers. Floating-point representation - the most common solution - basically represents reals in scientific notation.

Scientific notation represents numbers as a base number and an exponent. For example, 123.456 could be represented as 1.23456×10^2. In hexadecimal, the number 123.abc might be represented as $1.23abc \times 16^2$. Floating-point solves a number of representation problems. Fixed-point has a fixed window of representation, which limits it from representing very large or very small numbers.

Also, fixed-point is prone to a loss of precision when two large numbers are divided. Floating-point, on the other hand, employs a sort of "sliding window" of precision appropriate to the scale of the number. This allows it to represent numbers from 1,000,000,000,000 to 0.0000000000000001 with ease.

Some of the greatest achievements of the 20th century would not have been possible without the floating point capabilities of digital computers. Nevertheless, this subject is not well understood by most programmers and is a regular source of confusion.

Precision vs. accuracy

Precision = tightness of specification. Accuracy = correctness. Do not confuse precision with accuracy. 3.133333333 is an estimate of the mathematical constant À which is specified with 10 decimal digits of precision, but it only has two decimal digits of accuracy. As John von Neumann once said "There's no sense in being precise when you don't even know what you're talking about."

Java typically prints out floating point numbers with 16 or 17 decimal digits of precision, but do not blindly believe that this means there that many digits of accuracy! Calculators typically display 10 digits, but compute with 13 digits of precision. Kahan: the mirror for the Hubble space telescope was ground with great precision, but to the wrong specification.

Hence, it was initially a great failure since it couldn't produce high resolution images as expected. However, it's precision enabled an astronaut to install a corrective lens to counter-balance the error. Currency calculations are often defined in terms of a give precision, *e.g.*, Euro exchange rates must be quoted to 6 digits. Also, in some cases, the floating point formats of different sizes for some machines belonged to different groups. When this happened, all the formats for any one architecture were placed within the discussion of one of the groups of formats included. Particularly unsusual formats discussed below include the single precision floating-point format for the PDP-4, 7, 9 and 15, which can be thought of as a rearranged Group II or Group III format, and the double precision floating-point format of the ICL 1900, which applies the principle of making a double-precision float out of two single-precision floats, usually used with hardware Group I formats, to a base floating-point format which belongs to Group III; this appears to be the result of either successive implementations of the architecture evolving from hardware multiply to full hardware floating-point or the availability of hardware floating-point as an option.

DECIMAL CASES

- 3.141592653589...
- 2.71828...
- 6.023×10^{23} (N_A)
- 6.626×10^{-32} ($\hbar$)

In programming, a floating point number -123.45×10^{-6} is expressed as $-123.45E-6$. In general, a floating-point number can be written as $\pm M \times B^E$

Where,

- M is the fraction mantissa or significand.
- E is the exponent.
- B is the base, in decimal case B = 10.

BINARY CASES

As an example, a 32-bit word is used in MIPS computer to represent a floating-point number:

1 bit..... 8 bits.............. 23 bits representing: $(-1)^S \times M \times 2^E$

- The implied base is 2 (not explicitly shown in the representation).
- The exponent can be represented in signed 2's complement (but also see biased notation later).

- The implied decimal point is between the exponent field E and the significand field M.
- More bits in field E mean larger range of values representable.
- More bits in field M mean higher precision.
- Zero is represented by all bits equal to 0: $0000...000_2$

NORMALIZATION

To efficiently use the bits available for the significand, it is shifted to the left until all leading 0's disappear (as they make no contribution to the precision). The value can be kept unchanged by adjusting the exponent accordingly. Moreover, as the MSB of the significand is always 1, it does not need to be shown explicitly.

The significand could be further shifted to the left by 1 bit to gain one more bit for precision. The first bit 1 before the decimal point is implicit.

The actual value represented is:

$$(-1)^S \times (1.+M) \times 2^E$$

However, to avoid possible confusion, in the following the default normalization does not assume this implicit 1 unless otherwise specified. Zero is represented by all 0's and is not (and cannot be) normalized.

Example

A binary number X = 0.0001101001101 can be represented in 14-bit floating-point form in the following ways (1 sign bit, a 4-bit exponent field and a 9-bit significand field):

- $x = 0.0001101001101 \times 2^0$ $\boxed{0}\boxed{000}\boxed{000110100}$
- $x = 0.001101001101 \times 2^{-1}$ $\boxed{0}\boxed{111}\boxed{001101001}$
- $x = 0.001101001101 \times 2^{-2}$ $\boxed{0}\boxed{1111}\boxed{001101001}$
- $x = 0.1101001101 \times 2^{-3}$ $\boxed{0}\boxed{1101}\boxed{110100110}$
- $x = 1.101001101 \times 2^{-4}$ $\boxed{0}\boxed{1100}\boxed{101001101}$
  with an implied 1.0:

By normalization, highest precision can be achieved.

GATE LEVEL

We now consider the use of K-Maps to simplify expressions that include the"d" or Don't-Care condition often generated when considering digital designs using flip-flops. We give a number of examples related to our previous designs of sequential circuits.

	X = 0	X = 1
Y_1Y_0	J_1	J_1
0 0	0	1
0 1	1	0
1 0	d	d
1 1	d	d

The general rule in considering a simplification with the Don't-Care conditions is to count the number of 0's and number of 1's in the table and to use SOP simplification when the number of 1's is greater and POS simplification when the number of 0's is greater. Again we admit that most students prefer the SOP simplification. With a two-two split, we try SOP simplification.

Y1	Y0	X	J1
0	0	0	0
0	0	1	1
0	1	0	d
0	1	1	d
1	0	0	1
1	0	1	0
1	1	0	d
1	1	1	d

First we should explain the above table in some detail. The first thing to say about it is that we shall see similar tables again when we study flip-flops. For the moment, we call it a"folded over" truth table, equivalent to the full truth table at right. The function to be represented is J1.

Lines 0, 1, 4, and 5 of the truth table seem to be standard, but what of the other rows in which J1 has a value of"d". This indicates that in these rows it is equally acceptable to have J1 = 0 or J1 = 1. We have four"Don't-Cares" or"d" in this table; each can be a 0 or 1 independently of the others - in other words we are not setting the value of d as a variable.

Design with flip-flops is the subject of another course. When attempting a K-Map for SOP simplification, we drop the 0's and plot the 1's and d's. We then attempt to group the 1's into 2-by-1, 2-by-2 groupings, etc. We use the d's as are convenient and have no requirement to cover any or all of them. Note that

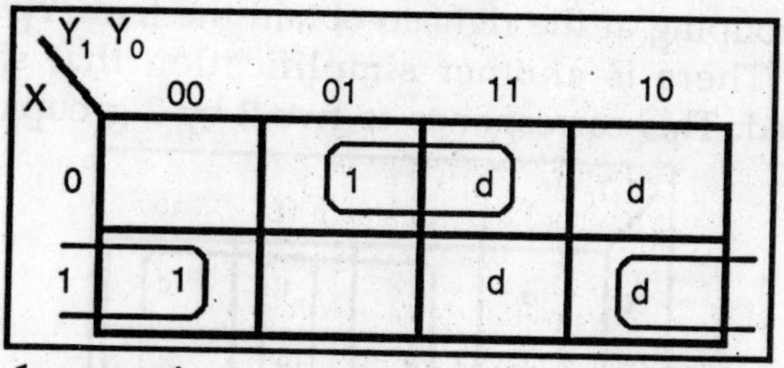

3-by-1 groupings are not valid and that the 2-by-2 grouping of d's does not add anything to the simplification, but only adds an extra useless term.

The terms in the top row, labeled 001 and 011 for $X'Y_1'Y_0$ and $X'Y_1Y_0$, simplify to 0-1 for $X'Y_0$, and the terms in the bottom row, labeled 100 and 110 for $XY_1'Y_0'$ and XY_1Y_0', simplify to 1-0 for XY_0', so the simplified expression is $X' \bullet Y_0 + X \bullet Y_0' = X \oplus Y_0$.

The sample at left, based on an earlier design shows a particularly simple problem. We find that using the d's to combine with the 1's to produce a

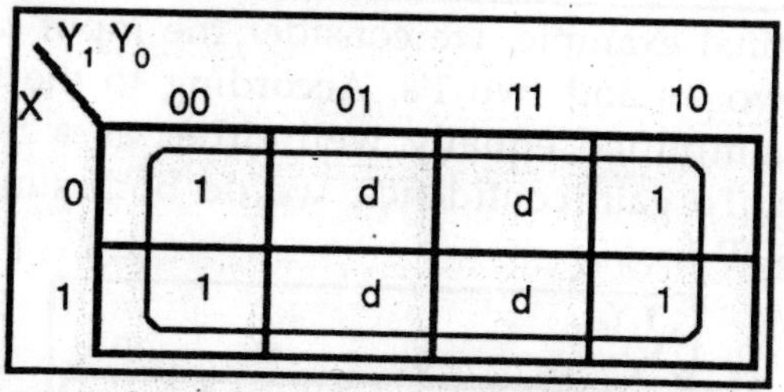

4-by-2 grouping of 1's. Since the entire K-Map is covered, the simplification is F = 1. The K-Map at right corresponds to an input table with one 0 and three 1's. This immediately

suggests a SOP approach to the K-Map; we plot the 1's and d's and drop the 0. The top row corresponds to X'. We then form the,

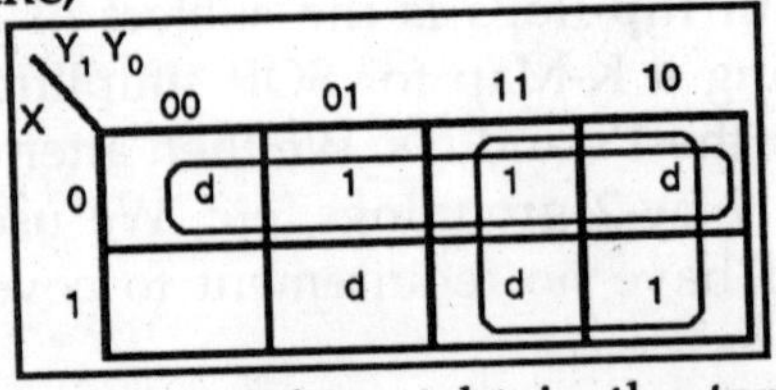

2-by-2 grouping at the right to obtain the term Y_1. Thus F = X' + Y_1. There is another simplification that should be considered. This corresponds to two 2-by-2 groupings.

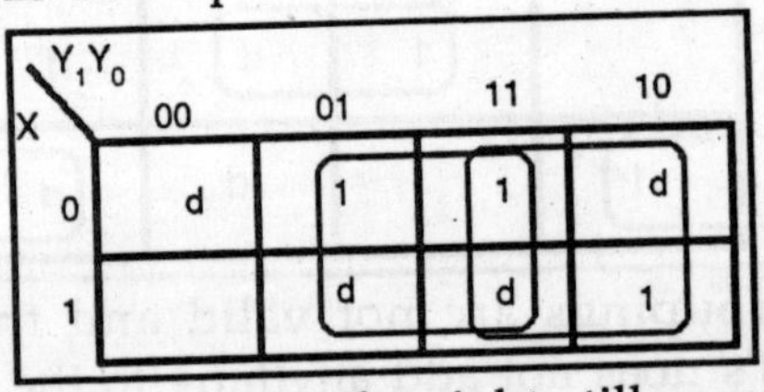

The 2-by-2 grouping at the right still corresponds to Y1. The new 2-by-2 grouping in the middle gives rise to Y0, so we get another simplification F = Y0 + Y1.

	X = 0	X = 1
Y1Y0	K0	K0
0 0	d	d
0 1	d	d
1 0	0	0
1 1	1	1

As a final example, we consider the input table, which contains two 0's and two 1's. According to the theory, this could be simplified equally well either as a SOP or POS expression. To gain confidence, we do both simplifications, with the SOP first.

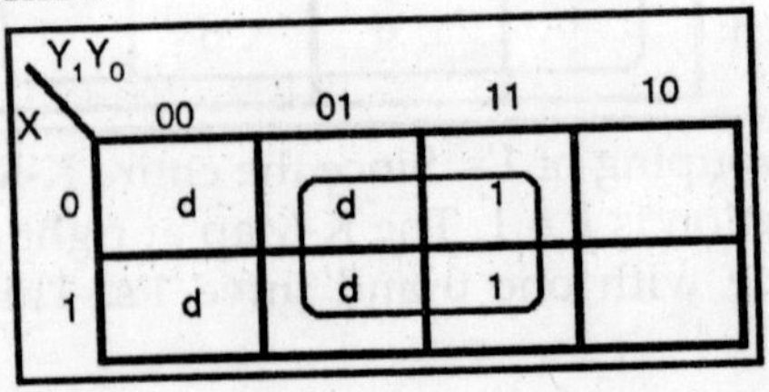

Considered as a SOP problem, we plot the 1's and d's, then form the largest possible group that covers all of the 1's. Note that 3-by-2 is not a valid grouping, so we go with the 2-by-2 grouping. The square corresponds to Y0. The top row simplifies to 0-1 and the bottom to 1-1, thus we have - - 1 or Y0.

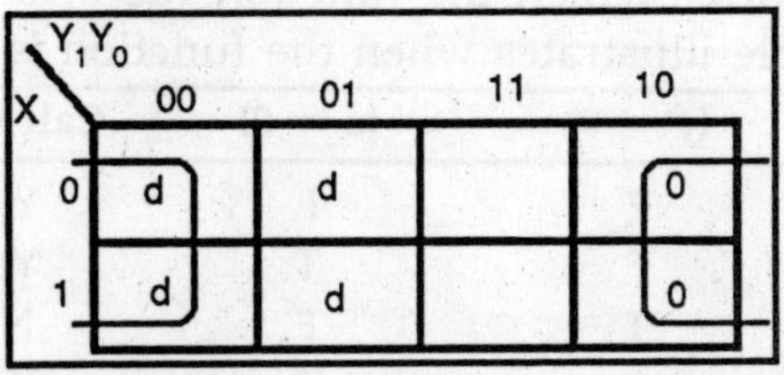

The POS simplification is shown at left. The top row simplifies to 0-0 and the bottom row simplifies to 1-0 so the K-Map simplifies to - - 0. Using the POS copy rule, this translates to Y0, as before. It's a good thing that the two methods agree.

A Diversion: Application of Simplification Techniques to Programming. This next section attempts to apply some of the Boolean simplification techniques to issues sometimes seen in software development, especially C++ programming.

Consider the Boolean expressions in C++ that relate to equality. For variable x, we can have expressions such as (x = 0), (x = 0), and !(x == 0). The last two are logically identical, and all are distinct from the assignment statement (x = 0), which evaluates to False.

In our diversion, we consider three variables: x, y, and z. The only assumption made here is that each of the three is of a type that can validly be compared to 0; assuming that all are integer variables is one valid way to read these examples. Each of the expressions (x == 0), (y == 0), and (z == 0) evaluates to either T (True) or F (False). Consider a function that is to be called conditionally based on the values of three variables: x, y, and z.

We write the Boolean expression as follows

```
if (((x != 0) && (y != 0) && (z != 0) )
|| ((x != 0) && (y != 0) && (z == 0) )
|| ((x != 0) && (y == 0) && (z == 0) )
```

```
|| ((x == 0) && (y != 0) && (z != 0) )
|| ((x == 0) && (y != 0) && (z == 0) )
|| ((x == 0) && (y == 0) && (z == 0) ) ) y =
fzero()
```

We can apply the truth-table approach to analysis of the conditions under which the function fzero is invoked. The following table illustrates when the function is to be called.

(x == 0)	(y == 0)	(z == 0)	Call fzero
F	F	F	Yes
F	F	T	Yes
F	T	F	No
F	T	T	Yes
T	F	F	Yes
T	F	T	Yes
T	T	F	No
T	T	T	Yes

If this looks a bit like a truth table, it is because it is equivalent to a truth table and can be converted to one. Consider the following definitions of Boolean variables A, B, and C.

A = (x = 0)
B = (y = 0)
C = (z = 0)

Consider the expression A = (x == 0) in the C++ programming language. It may seem a bit strange, but is perfectly legitimate. The expression (x == 0) is a Boolean expression - it evaluates to True or False.

The variable A is a Boolean variable, it also takes on one of the Boolean values. In order to translate the table above into a truth table that we recognize, we replace the expressions (x == 0), (y == 0), and (z == 0) by their equivalents - the Boolean variables A, B, and C. We are beginning to construct a Truth Table. In order to apply the truth table approach to this problem, we must define a Boolean function. For our purpose, we define F(A, B, C) as follows.

F(A, B, C) = 1 if fzero is called
= 0 if fzero is not called

Returning to our convention of 0 for False and 1 for True, we have the truth table.

A	B	C	F(A, B, C)
0	0	0	1
0	0	1	1
0	1	0	0
0	1	1	1
1	0	0	1
1	0	1	1
1	1	0	0
1	1	1	1

This is a truth table that we have considered and simplified in an earlier section of the work. Using terminology we have already discussed, we see that this function F(A, B, C) can be expressed as either a SOP with six product terms or a POS with two sum terms. Reading this as a POS, we get $F(A,B,C) = (A + \overline{B} + C) \bullet (\overline{A} + \overline{B} + C)$, which simplifies to $F(A,B,C) = (\overline{B} + C)$.

We now convert back to the original notation. Recalling that B = (y == 0) and C = (z == 0), we note that B' = (y != 0) and the condition for calling the function fzero becomes ((y != 0) || (z == 0)). So the equivalent (and much simpler) expression is

```
if ((y != 0) || (z == 0) ) y = fzero()
```

Consider now the Boolean expression ((x == 0) || ((x != 0) && (y == 0))). In an attempt to simplify this expression we define two Boolean variables

A = (x == 0)
B = (y == 0)

Recall that (x != 0) = !(x == 0) = $\overline{A}$. In our terminology, the expression is,

$$F(A, B) = A + (\overline{A} \bullet B)$$

There are a number of ways to simplify this expression. The first, and least obvious, is to invoke the theorem of absorption, which states that the formula equals A + B.

To illustrate other options, we expand the above to canonical SOP and then examine it by means of both a truth table and a K-map. To expand the expression into canonical SOP, we need to have the first term contain a literal for the variable B.

$$A+\overline{A}\bullet B = A\bullet\left(\overline{B}+B\right)+\overline{A}+B = A\bullet\overline{B}+A\bullet B$$

The truth table for this expression is

A	B	F(A, B)
0	0	0
0	1	1
1	1	1
1	1	1

Representing this as a POS formula, we immediately get F(A, B) = (A + B), which translates to the C++ expression ((x == 0) || (y == 0)).

As a final example, consider the following Boolean expression in C++

((x == 0) || (y == 0) || (z == 0)) && ((x == 0) || (y == 0) || (z !=0)) && ((x == 0) || (y != 0) || (z == 0)) && ((x != 0) || (y == 0) || (z == 0))

Define A = (x == 0)

B = (y == 0)

C = (z == 0)

With these definitions our expression becomes

$$F(A,B,C)=(A+B+C)\bullet\left(A+B+\overline{C}\right)\bullet\left(A+\overline{B}+C\right)\bullet\left(\overline{A}+B+C\right)$$

This is known to simplify to

F(A, B, C) = (A + B)"(A + C)"(B + C)

So our Boolean expression in C++ simplifies to

((x == 0) || (y == 0)) && ((x == 0) || (z == 0)) && (y == 0) || (z == 0))

Inspection of the above shows that we want at least two of (x == 0), (y == 0), and (z == 0) to be true. Compare this with the original derivation of the function

F(A, B, C) = (A + B)"(A + C)"(B + C)

used for the carry-out of a Full-Adder, which is 1 if two or three of the inputs are 1.

POS SIMPLIFICATION

K-Maps for Product of Sums simplification are constructed similarly to those for Sum of Products simplification, except that the POS copy rule must be enforced: 1 for a negated variable and 0 for a non-negated (plain) variable. As our first example we consider F(A, B, C) = (3, 5) = (A + B' + C')"(A' + B + C'). Recall that the term (A + B' + C') corresponds to 011 and that (A' + B + C') to 101.

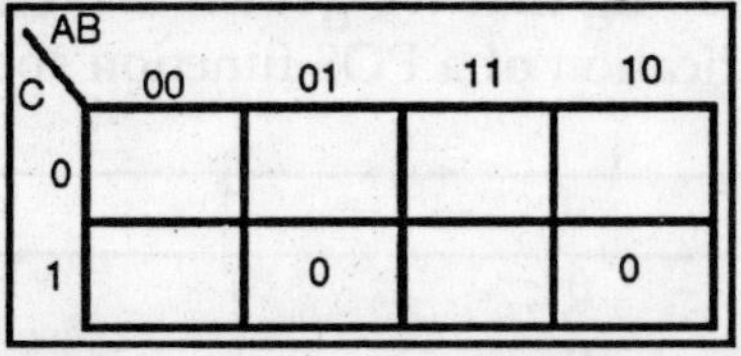

This is really somewhat of a trick question used only to illustrate placing of the terms for POS. Place a 0 at each location, rather than the 1 placed for SOP. Note that the two 0's placed are not adjacent, so we cannot simplify the expression. For the next example consider F2 = (A + B + C)•(A + B + C')•(A + B' + C)•(A' + B + C). Using the POS copy rule, we translate this to 000, 001, 010, and 100. Before we attempt to simplify F2, we note that it is a very good candidate for simplification. Compare the first term 000 to each of the following three terms. The term 000 differs from the term 001 in exactly one position. The same applies for comparison to the other two terms. Any two terms that differ in exactly one position can be combined in a simplification.

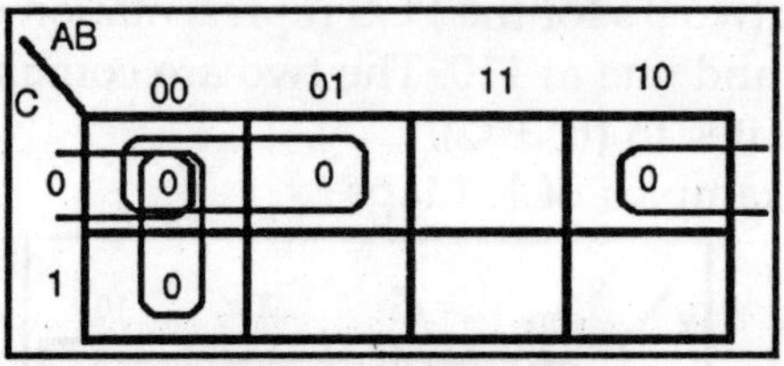

We begin the K-Map for POS simplification by placing a 0 in each of the four positions 000, 001, 010, 100. Noting that 000 is adjacent to 001, just below it, we combine to get 00- or (A + B). The term 000 is adjacent to 010 to its right to get 0-0 or (A + C). The term 000 is adjacent to 100 to its"left" to get -

00 or (B + C). As a result, we get the simplified form. F2 = (A + B)•(A + C)•(B + C). Just for fun, we simplify this expression algebraically, using the derived Boolean identity

X•X•X = X for any Boolean expression X.

F2 = (A + B + C)•(A + B + C')•(A + B' + C)•(A' + B + C)

= (A + B + C)•(A + B + C')•(A + B + C)•(A + B' + C)•(A + B + C)•(A' + B + C)

= (A + B)•(A + C)•(B + C)

It is encouraging that we get the same answer. We now consider simplification of a POS function specified by a truth table.

A	B	C	F
0	0	0	1
0	0	1	1
0	1	0	0
0	1	1	1
1	0	0	1
1	0	1	1
1	1	0	0
1	1	1	1

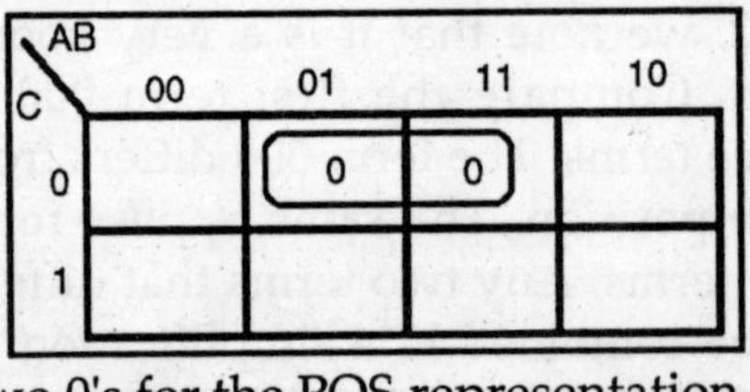

We plot two 0's for the POS representation of the function - one at 010 and one at 110. The two are combined to get -10, which translates to (B' + C).

More Examples of K-Maps

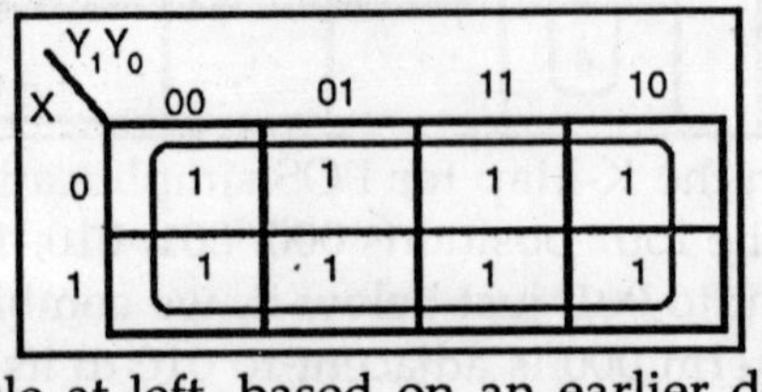

The sample at left, based on an earlier design shows a particularly simple problem. We find that all the entries in

the K-Map are covered with a single grouping, thus removing all three variables. Since the entire K-Map is covered, the simplification is F = 1.

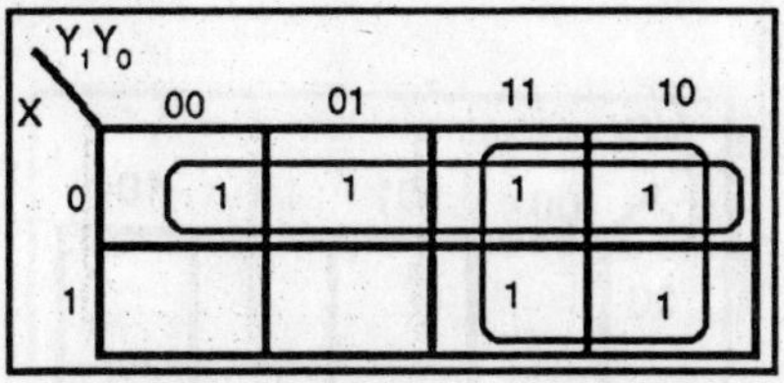

The K-Map at right shows an example with overlap of two groupings of 1's. All 1's in the map must be covered and some should be covered twice. The top row corresponds to X'. We then form the 2-by-2 grouping at the right to obtain the term Y1. Thus F = X' + Y1.

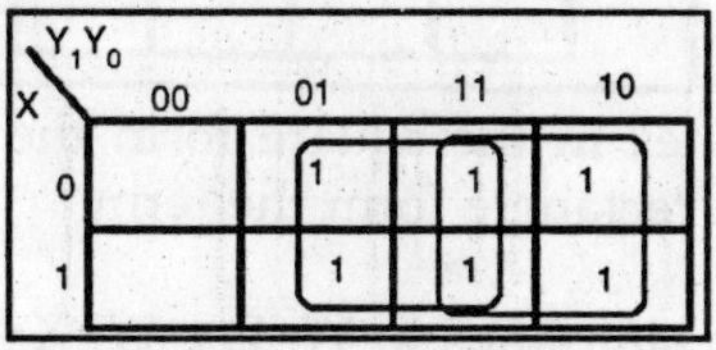

There is another simplification that should be considered. This corresponds to two 2-by-2 groupings. The 2-by-2 grouping at the right still corresponds to Y1. The new 2-by-2 grouping in the middle gives rise to Y0, so we get another simplification F = Y0 + Y1.

Just One More K-Map: Overlapping Circles: We close the discussion of K-Maps with a technique that applies to both SOP and POS simplifications. We shall apply it to SOP simplification.

Consider the following K-Map.

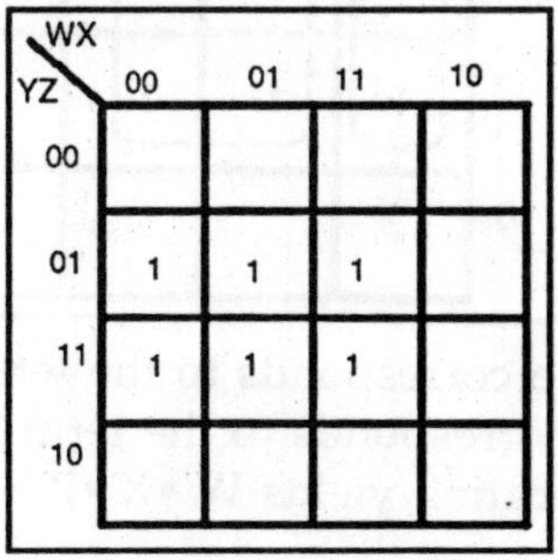

The six ones can be grouped in a number of ways. Consider the following.

This grouping of four and two covers the six one's in the K-Map.

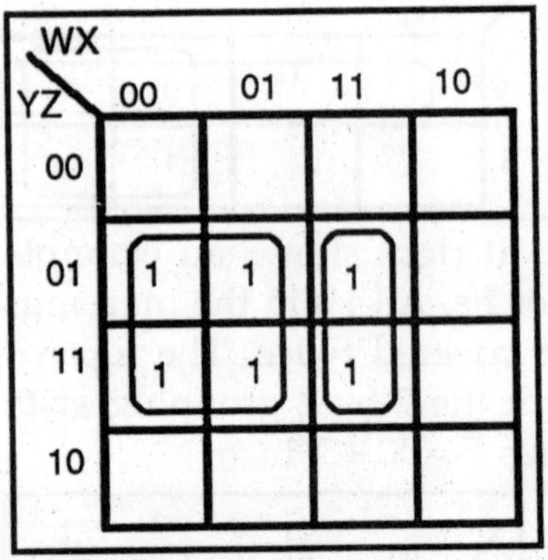

The four ones in the square form the term W'•Z. The two ones in the rectangle form the term
W•X•Z.

The K-Map simplifies to W•Z + W•X•Z.

Another way to consider the simplification of the K-Map is to group the rectangle and the square as in the figure at right.

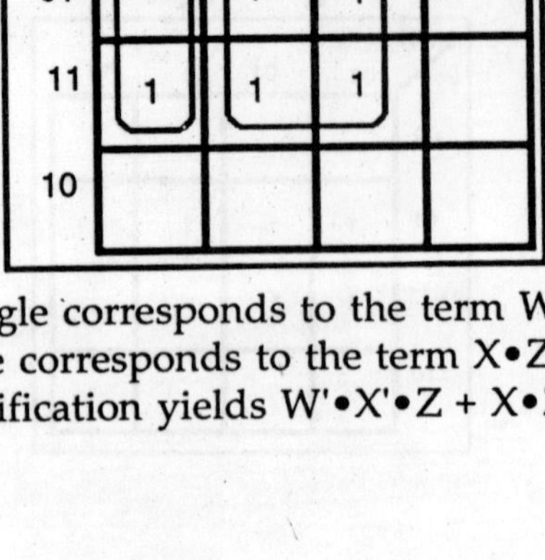

The rectangle corresponds to the term W'•X'•Z.
The square corresponds to the term X•Z.
This simplification yields W'•X'•Z + X•Z.

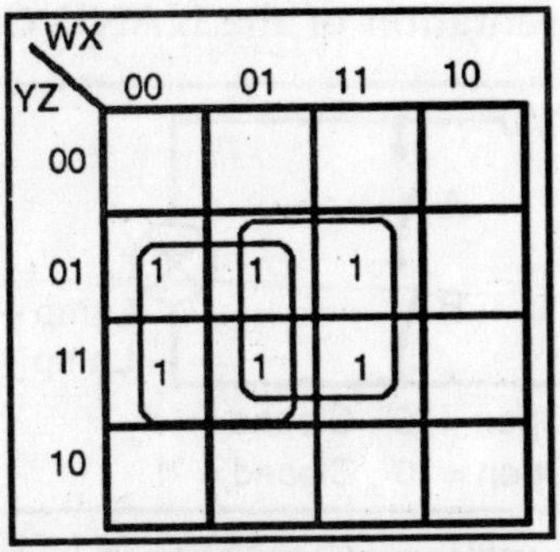

It is important to note that the groupings can overlap if this yields a simpler reduction.

Here we show two overlapping squares.

The square at left corresponds to the term W'•Z.

The square at right corresponds to the term X•Z.

This simplification yields W'•Z + X•Z, which is simpler than either of the other two forms validly produced by the K-Map method.

Try 1: W'•Z + W•X•Z

Try 2: W'•X'•Z + X•Z

Try 3: W'•Z + X•Z. This seems better.

Consider the POS formula (A + B)•(A + C)•(A + B + C). Again, the first term (A + B) is included in the third term (A + B + C), as is the second term.

NAND AND NOR GATE

THE NAND

The NAND or Not AND function is a combination of two separate functions, the AND function and theNOT function connected together in series, and can be expressed by the Boolean expression of, A.B

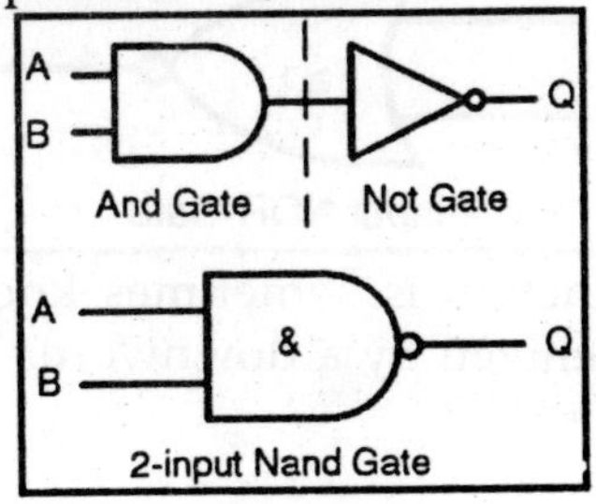

Switch Representation of the NAND Gate

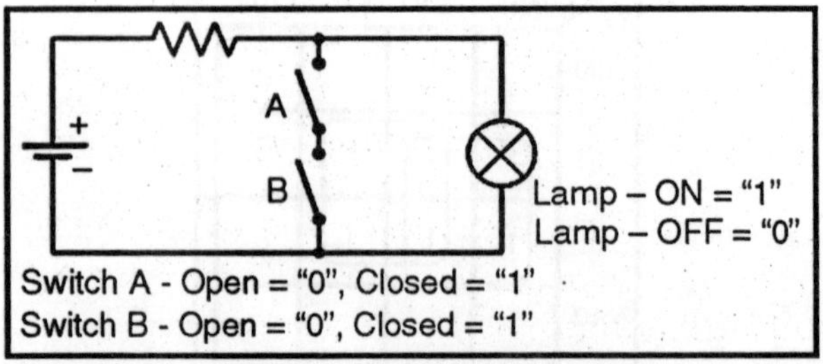

The NAND Function is sometimes known as the Sheffer Stroke Function and is denoted by a vertical bar or upwards arrow operator, for example, A NAND B = A|B or A?B.

NAND Gates are used as the basic"building blocks" to construct other logic gate functions and are available in standard i.c. packages such as the very common TTL 74LS00 Quadruple 2-input NANDGates, the TTL 74LS10 Triple 3-input NAND Gates or the 74LS20 Dual 4-input NAND Gates. There is even a single chip 74LS30 8-input NAND Gate.

THE NOR

Like the NAND Gate above, the NOR or Not OR Gate is also a combination of two separate functions, theOR function and the NOT function connected together in series and is expressed by the Boolean expression as, A + B

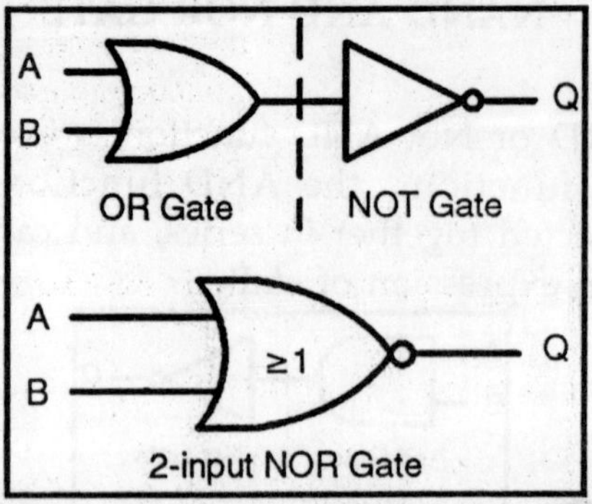

The NOR Function is sometimes known as the Pierce Function and is denoted by a downwards arrow operator as shown, A NOR B = A↓B.

NOR Gates are available as standard i.c. packages such as the TTL 74LS02 Quadruple 2-input NORGate, the TTL 74LS27 Triple 3-input NOR Gate or the 74LS260 Dual 5-input NOR Gate.

NAND and NOR Gates

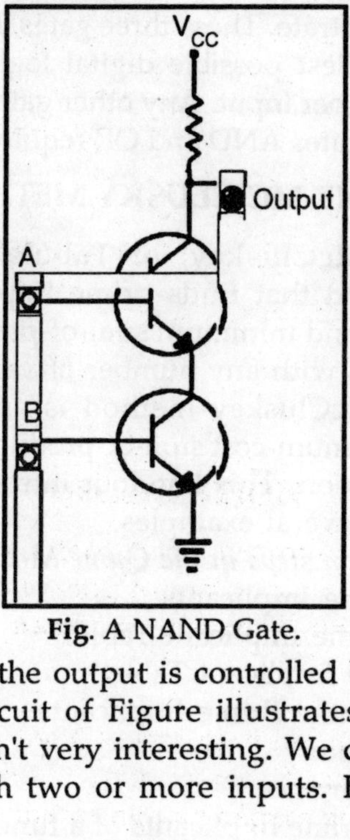

Fig. A NAND Gate.

The value of the output is controlled by the two inputs A and B. The circuit of Figure illustrates some important concepts, but it isn't very interesting. We can do more if we build circuits with two or more inputs. Figure 4. shows a NAND gate.

The name NAND is a contraction of not-and. Current can flow, and produce a voltage drop across the resistor, only if both transistors are conducting. Having either transistor switched off is enough to block current flow and hold the output high.

The NAND gate has its transistors connected in series. Recall from the Electric Circuits Web Lecture that switches can be connected in series or parallel. If we connect transistors in parallel as shown in Figure above, applying a signal to the base of eithertransistor is sufficient to allow current to flow through the resistor and pull the output voltage to near zero.

This is the NOR gate. The name NOR is a contraction of not-or. Although the gates shown here are simplified by comparison to the actual construction of integrated circuits, you could go to an electrical engineering lab and build the circuits of Figures. If you did, they would function just as the animations demonstrate. These three gates, NOT, NAND, and NOR are the simplest possible digital logic gates. Each has only one transistor per input. Any other gate, and in particular the non-inverting gates AND and OR require more transistors.

QUINE MC-CLUSKY METHOD

The Quine-McCluskey, or Tabular, method is an algorithmic method that finds prime implicants, necessary prime implicants, and minimum sum-of-products expressions for digital systems with any number of variables.

The Quine-McCluskey method is an exact algorithm which finds a minimum-cost sum-of-products implementation of a Boolean function. This handout introduces the method and applies it to several examples.

There are 4 main steps in the Quine-McCluskey algorithm:

Generate Prime Implicants

Construct Prime Implicant Table

Reduce Prime Implicant Table

Remove Essential Prime Implicants

Row Dominance

Column Dominance

Step #1, the prime implicants of a function are generated using an iterative procedure. In Step #2, a prime implicant table is constructed. The columns of the table are the prime implicants of the function. The rows are minterms of where the function is 1, called *ON-set minterms*. The goal of the method is to cover all the rows using a minimum-cost *cover* of prime implicants.

The reduction step (Step #3) is used to reduce the size of the table. This step has three sub-steps which are iterated until no further table reduction is possible! At this point, the reduced table is either (i) empty or (ii) non-empty. If the reduced table is empty, the removed essential prime implicants form a minimum-cost solution. However, if the reduced table is *not* empty, the table must be "solved" (Step #4). The table can be solved using either "Petrick's method" or the "branching method".

This handout focuses on Petrick's method. The branching method is discussed in the books by McCluskey, Roth, etc., but you will not be responsible for the branching method. The remainder of this handout illustrates the details of the Quine-McCluskey method.

RULES OF TABULAR METHOD

Consider a function of three variables f(A, B, C): $\overline{A}BC$ is represented by 011 ¬ Binary notation, where A = 0, B = 1 and c = 1

$A\overline{B}\overline{C}$ is represented by 100

$A\overline{C}$ is represented by 1-0

BC is represented by –11

Consider the function:

$$f(A,B,C,D) = \Sigma(1110,1111) = ABC\overline{D} + ABCD = ABC$$

Listing the two minterms shows they can be combined

```
A B C D
1 1 1 0 ←┐
         ├─ Can combine (Differs in one digit position)
1 1 1 1 ←┘
-------
1 1 1 –
```

Now consider the following:

$$f(A,B,C,D) = \Sigma(1101,1110) = AB\overline{C}D + ABC\overline{D}$$

Note that these variables cannot be combined

```
A B C D
1 1 0 1 ←┐
         ├─ Cannot Combine (Differs in more than one
1 1 1 0 ←┘   Digit Position)
-------
   ?
```

This is because the FIRST RULE of the Tabular method for two terms to combine, and thus eliminate one variable, is that they must differ in only one digit position. Bear in mind that when two terms are combined, one of the combined terms has one digit more at logic 1 than the other combined term. This indicates that the number of 1's in a term is significant and is referred to as its index.

For example: f(A, B, C, D)
0000..................Index 0
0010, 1000.............Index 1
1010, 0011, 1001.......Index 2
1110, 1011.............Index 3
1111..................Index 4

The necessary condition for combining two terms is that the indices of the two terms must differ by one logic variable which must also be the same.

COMBINATIONAL CIRCUITS

Combinational logic is probably the easiest circuitry to design. The outputs from a combinational logic circuit depend only on the current inputs. The circuit has no remembrance of what it did at any time in the past.

Much of logic design involves connecting simple, easily understood circuits to construct a larger circuit that performs a much more complicated function. Several simple, often-used combinational logic circuits are the following: Logic circuits for digital systems may be combinational or sequential.

A combinational circuit consists of logic gates whose outputs at any time are determined by combining the values of the applied inputs using logic operations. A combinational circuit performs an operation that can be specified logically by a set of Boolean expression. In addition to using logic gates, sequential circuits employ elements that store bit values. Sequential circuit outputs are a function of inputs and the bit value in storage elements. These values, in turn, are a function of previously applied inputs and stored values.

As a consequence, the outputs of a sequential circuit depend not only on the presently applied values of the inputs, but also on pas inputs, and the behaviour of the circuit must be specified by a sequence in time of inputs and internal stored bit values. A combinational circuit consists of input variables, output variables, logic gates and interconnections. The interconnected logic gates accept signals from the inputs and generate signals at the output. The n input variables come from the environment of the circuit, and the m output variables are available for use by the environment. Each input and output variable exists physically as a binary signal that represents logic 1 or logic 0. For n input variables, there are 2^n possible binary input combinations. For each binary combination of the input variables, there is one possible binary value on each output. Thus, a combinational circuit can be specified by a truth table that lists the output values for each combination of the input variables. A combinational circuit can also be described by m Boolean function, one for each output variable. Each such function is expressed as function of the n input variables. A combinational circuit performs an operation that can be specified logically by a set of Boolean expression. In addition to using logic gates, sequential circuits employ elements that store bit values.

Sequential circuit outputs are a function of inputs and the bit value in storage elements. These values, in turn, are a function of previously applied inputs and stored values. As a consequence, the outputs of a sequential circuit depend not only on the presently applied values of the inputs, but also on pas inputs, and the behaviour of the circuit must be specified by a sequence in time of inputs and internal stored bit values. A combinational circuit consists of input variables, output variables, logic gates and interconnections. The interconnected logic gates accept signals from the inputs and generate signals at the output. The n input variables come from the environment of the circuit, and the m output variables are available for use by the environment. Each input and output variable exists physically as a binary signal that represents logic 1 or logic 0.

ANALYSIS PROCEDURE

The bulk of the Combinational Analysis module is accessed through a single window of that name allowing you to view truth tables and Boolean expressions. This window can be opened in two ways.

VIA THE WINDOW MENU

Select Combinational Analysis, and the current Combinational Analysis window will appear. If you haven't viewed the window before, the opened window will represent no circuit at all. Only one Combinational Analysis window exists within Logisim, no matter how many projects are open. There is no way to have two different analysis windows open at once.

VIA THE PROJECT MENU

From a window for editing circuits, you can also request that Logisim Analyse the current circuit by selecting the Analyse Circuit option from the Project menu. Before Logisim opens the window, it will compute Boolean expressions and a truth table corresponding to the circuit and place them there for you to view.

For the analysis to be successful, each input must be attached to an input pin, and each output must be attached to an output pin. Logisim will only Analyse circuits with at most eight of each type, and all should be single-bit pins. Otherwise, you will see an error message and the window will not open.

In constructing Boolean expressions corresponding to a circuit, Logisim will first attempt to construct a Boolean expressions corresponding exactly to the gates in the circuit. But if the circuit uses some non-gate components (such as a multiplexer), or if the circuit is more than 100 levels deep (unlikely), then it will pop up a dialog box telling you that deriving Boolean expressions was impossible, and Logisim will instead derive the expressions based on the truth table, which will be derived by quietly trying each combination of inputs and reading the resulting outputs.

After analysing a circuit, there is no continuing relationship between the circuit and the Combinational Analysis window. That is, changes to the circuit will not be reflected in the window, nor will changes to the Boolean expressions and/or truth table in the window be reflected in the circuit. Of course, you are always free to Analyse a circuit again; and, as we will see later, you can replace the circuit with a circuit corresponding to what appears in the Combinational Analysis window.

LIMITATIONS

Logisim will not attempt to detect sequential circuits: If you tell it to Analyse a sequential circuit, it will still create a truth table and corresponding Boolean expressions, although these will not accurately summarize the circuit behaviour. (In fact, detecting sequential circuits is provably impossible, as it would amount to solving the Halting Problem. Of course, you might hope that Logisim would make at least some attempt - perhaps look for flip-flops or cycles in the wires - but it does not.) As a result, the Combinational Analysis system should not be used indiscriminately: Only use it when you are indeed sure that the circuit you are analysing is indeed combinational! Logisim will make a change to the original circuit that is perhaps unexpected: The Combinational Analysis system requires that each input and output have a unique name that conforming to the rules for Java identifiers. (Roughly, each character must either a letter or a digit, and the first character must be a letter. No spaces allowed!) It attempts to use the pins' existing labels, and to use a list of defaults if no label exists. If an existing label doesn't follow the Java-identifier rule, then Logisim will attempt to extract a valid name from the label if at all possible. Incidentally, the ordering of the inputs in the truth table will match their top-down ordering in the original circuit, with ties being broken in left-right order.

DESIGN PROCEDURE

Logic circuits for digital systems may be combinational or sequential. A combinational circuit consists of logic gates whose outputs at any time are determined by combining the values of the applied inputs using logic operations. A combinational circuit performs an operation that can be specified logically by a set of Boolean expression. In addition to using logic gates, sequential circuits employ elements that store bit values. Sequential circuit outputs are a function of inputs and the bit value in storage elements. These values, in turn, are a function of previously applied inputs and stored values. As a consequence, the outputs of a sequential circuit depend not only on the presently applied values of the inputs, but also on pas inputs, and the behaviour of the circuit must be specified by a sequence in time of inputs and internal stored bit values. A combinational circuit consists of input variables, output variables, logic gates and interconnections. The interconnected logic gates accept signals from the inputs and generate signals at the output. The n input variables come from the environment of the circuit, and the m output variables are available for use by the environment.

Each input and output variable exists physically as a binary signal that represents logic 1 or logic 0. For n input variables, there are 2^n possible binary input combinations. For each binary combination of the input variables, there is one possible binary value on each output. Thus, a combinational circuit can be specified by a truth table that lists the output values for each combination of the input variables. A combinational circuit can also be described by m Boolean function, one for each output variable. Each such function is expressed as function of the n input variables.

BINARY ADDER-SUBTRACTOR

HALF ADDER/SUBTRACTOR

This figure shows the configuration for a Half Adder/ Subtractor. The first logic gate which is a XOR allows the circuit to do the complement of the binary bit when we want to do a subtraction. In the case that is needed to implement a addition the XOR keep the number the same.

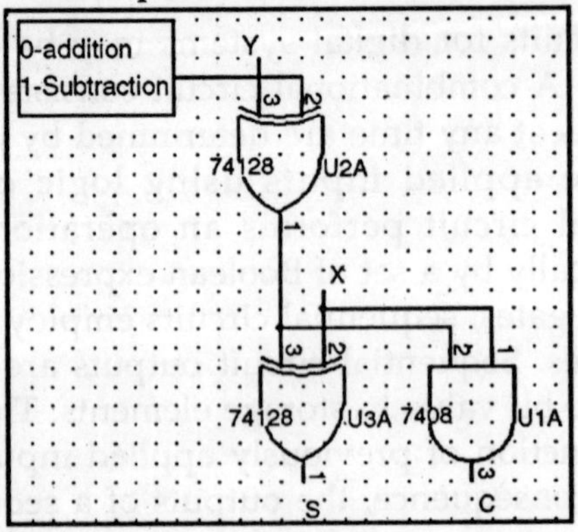

FULL ADDER/SUBTRACTOR

Full Adder Circuit

This circuit adds two binary one bit numbers. Also, it manages a carry that could come from another circuit.

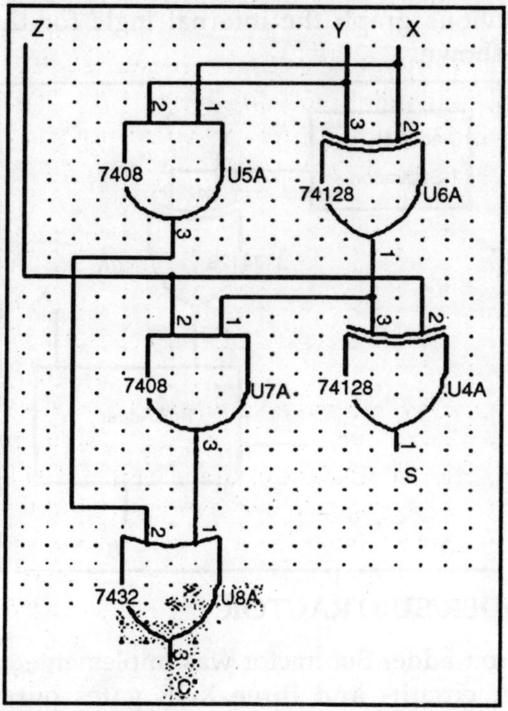

[(AA)'*(BB)']' = A+B

X	Y	Z	C	S
0	0	0	0	0
0	0	1	0	1
0	1	0	0	1
0	1	1	1	0
1	0	0	0	1
1	0	1	1	0
1	1	0	1	0
1	1	1	1	1

This figure shows the configuration for a Full Adder/ Subtractor. The box with the name of"Full Adder" has all the logic to do the addition and subtraction depending of the inputs that it receives. The XOR gate that is outside the box allows the circuit to do the complement of the binary bit when we want to do a subtraction. In the case that is needed to implement an addition the XOR keep the number the same. In the previous graph the internal logic for the box"Full Adder" is shown.

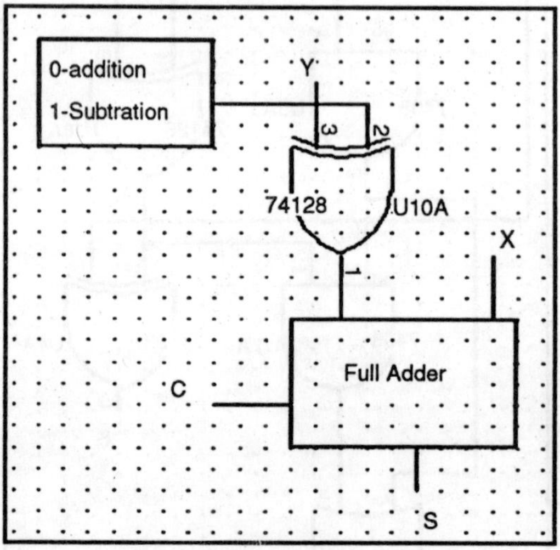

3-BIT ADDER/SUBTRACTOR

The 3-bit adder/Subtractor was implemented with three Full adder circuits and three XOR gates outside which implemented the operation (addition/subtraction) selected by the user. In this circuit, we have three inputs for the first three bits binary number and three inputs for the second three bits binary number.

When the addition is selected the XOR gates keep the binary numbers the same and add them together. On the other hand, when a subtraction is selected the XOR gates complement the second number which is represented with a"Y" and after that, the Full Adder circuit adds both numbers together. The 3-bit Adder/Subtractor circuit has four outputs. The first three outputs represent the three bits that were the result of the subtraction or addition.

BINARY MULTIPLIER

Binary multiplication uses the same technique as decimal multiplication. In fact, binary multiplication is much easier because each digit we multiply by is either zero or one. Consider the simple problem of multiplying 1102 by 102. We can use this problem to review some terminology and illustrate the rules for binary multiplication.

- First, we note that 1102 is our multiplicand and 102 is our multiplier.

$$\begin{array}{r} 110 \\ \times\ 10 \\ \hline \end{array}$$

- We begin by multiplying 1102 by the rightmost digit of our multiplier which is 0. Any number times zero is zero, so we just write zeros below. 110

$$\begin{array}{r} 110 \\ \times\ 10 \\ \hline 000 \end{array}$$

- Now we multiply the multiplicand by the next digit of our multiplier which is 1. To perform this multiplication, we just need to copy the multiplicand and shift it one column to the left as we do in decimal multiplication.

$$\begin{array}{r} 110 \\ \times\ 10 \\ \hline 000 \\ 110 \end{array}$$

- Now we add our results together. The product of our multiplication is 11002. 110

$$\begin{array}{r} 110 \\ \times\ 10 \\ \hline 000 \\ 110 \\ \hline 1100 \end{array}$$

When performing binary multiplication, remember the following rules:

- Copy the multiplicand when the multiplier digit is

1. Otherwise, write a row of zeros.

- Shift your results one column to the left as you move to a new multiplier digit.
- Add the results together using binary addition to find the product.

MAGNITUDE COMPARATOR

74L85 4-BIT MAGNITUDE COMPARATOR

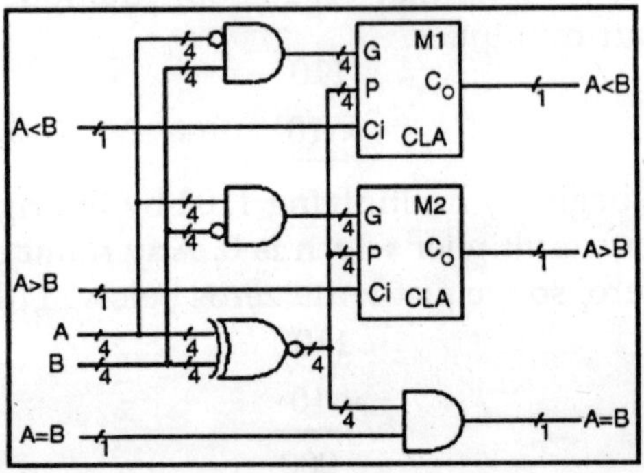

STATISTICS

11 inputs; 3 outputs; 33 gates;

FUNCTION

The 74L85 magnitude comparator can be functionally modeled as above. This is a simplification of implementing a magnitude comparator by a carry function with an inverted input bus as shown.

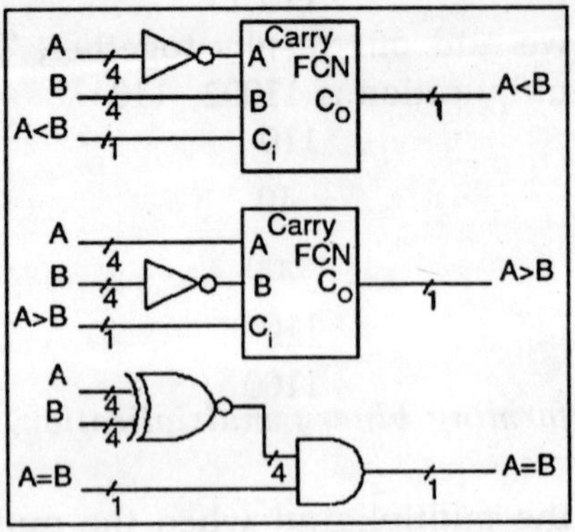

Using this concept, common elements of the three comparator functions A < B, A > B, and A = B are combined to construct the model shown above, which maps directly onto the gate-level realisation of the 74L85.

DECODERS

INTRODUCTION

In both the multiplexer and the demultiplexer, part of the circuits decode the address inputs, *i.e.* it translates a binary number of n digits to 2n outputs, one of which (the one that corresponds to the value of the binary number) is 1 and the others of which are 0. It is sometimes advantageous to separate this function from the rest of the circuit, since it is useful in many other applications. Thus, we obtain a new combinatorial circuit that we call the decoder.

a2	a1	a0	d7	d6	d5	d4	d3	d2	d1	d0
0	0	0	0	0	0	0	0	0	0	1
0	0	1	0	0	0	0	0	0	1	0
0	1	0	0	0	0	0	0	1	0	0
0	1	1	0	0	0	0	1	0	0	0
1	0	0	0	0	0	1	0	0	0	0
1	0	1	0	0	1	0	0	0	0	0
1	1	0	0	1	0	0	0	0	0	0
1	1	1	1	0	0	0	0	0	0	0

DECODER GENERATION

X86's decoder is generated using an ISA description like all the other ISAs, although how it does that is a bit different. Most of the instructions for most of the other ISAs are defined by passing chunks of code that perform the instruction into an instruction format. The format is basically a template which puts wraps that bit of code in the structure needed to support it and you have your instruction object. Because almost all of the instructions in x86 are microcoded and many can be encoded in multiple ways and hence appear in the decoder more than once, and because the same non-trivial decoding rules apply to many different instructions, X86 uses the decoder as a layer of indirection and defines the majority of its instructions elsewhere. X86 almost exclusively uses only two different instruction formats, Inst and MultiInst. MultiInst is just a compact way of describing multiple related Insts. An Inst essentially selects an instruction like XOR and provides a specification for its operands. Inside the instruction format, the instruction name and operand specification are passed to a python function called"specializeInst" which figures out what to do with it. If the operand specification describes more than one version of the instruction, for instance one that uses memory and one that uses registers, the instruction's information is passed into another funciton,"do Split Decode", which separates out those versions and passes each individually back through the same system. This goes on until the instructions have been fully split out and code has been generated to figure out what version to use. As a nice bonus, the MultiInst format doesn't add much complexity to this model since it can simply jump right into do Split Decode and continue as normal.

3 TO 8 DECODER

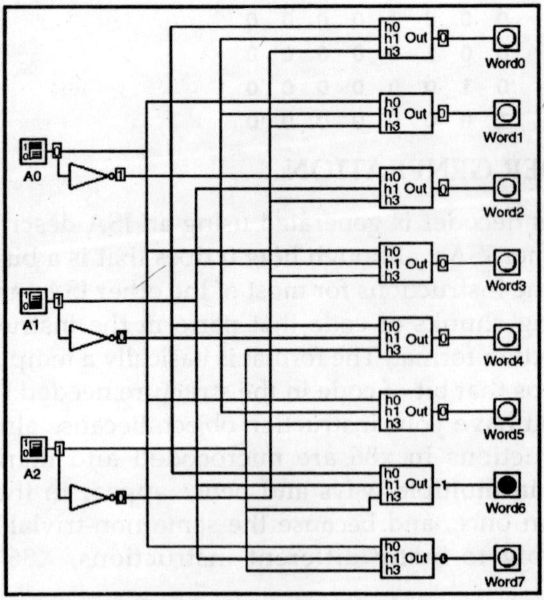

The 3 to 8 decoder unit takes 3 address lines as input and outputs 8 address enable lines. Which of the 8 output is enabled is dependant upon the configuration of the 3 address line. If A0, A1, and A2 are all 0, then address 0 is enabled. If A0=0, A1=1, A2=0, then address 3 is enables. With 3 address lines, the number of words that can be addressed is 8 (2^3=8).

ENCODERS

An encoder is a circuit that changes a set of signals into a code. Lets begin making a 2-to-1 line encoder truth table by reversing the 1-to-2 decoder truth table.

D_1	D_0	A
0	1	0
1	0	1

This truth table is a little short. A complete truth table would be,

D_1	D_0	A
0	0	
0	1	0
1	0	1
1	1	

One question we need to answer is what to do with those other inputs? Do we ignore them? Do we have them generate an additional error output? In many circuits this problem is solved by adding sequential logic in order to know not just what input is active but also which order the inputs became active. A more useful application of combinational encoder design is a binary to 7-segment encoder. The seven segments are given according,

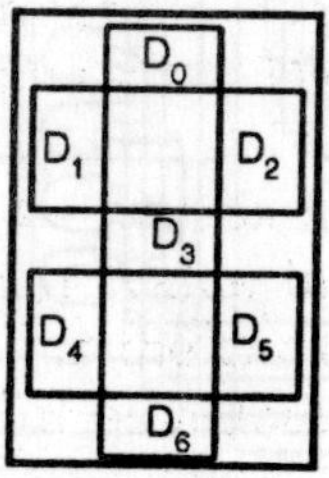

Our truth table is:

I_3	I_2	I_1	I_0	D_6	D_5	D_4	D_3	D_2	D_1	D_0
0	0	0	0	1	1	1	0	1	1	1
0	0	0	1	0	0	1	0	0	1	0
0	0	1	0	1	0	1	1	1	0	1
0	0	1	1	1	0	1	1	0	1	1
0	1	0	0	0	1	1	1	0	1	0
0	1	0	1	1	1	0	1	0	1	1
0	1	1	0	1	1	0	1	1	1	1
0	1	1	1	1	0	1	0	0	1	0
1	0	0	0	1	1	1	1	1	1	1
1	0	0	1	1	1	1	1	0	1	1

Deciding what to do with the remaining six entries of the truth table is easier with this circuit. This circuit should not be expected to encode an undefined combination of inputs, so we can leave them as"don't care" when we design the circuit. The boolean equations are

$$D_0 = l_3 + l_1 + \bar{l}_3\bar{l}_2\bar{l}_1\bar{l}_0 + \bar{l}_3\bar{l}_2\bar{l}_1\bar{l}_0$$

$$D_1 = l_3 + \bar{l}_2\bar{l}_1 + \bar{l}_2\bar{l}_1 + \bar{l}_2\bar{l}_0$$

$$D_2 = l_2 + \bar{l}_3\bar{l}_2\bar{l}_1\bar{l}_0 + \bar{l}_3\bar{l}_2\bar{l}_1\bar{l}_0$$

$$D_3 = l_3 + l_1\bar{l}_0 + l_2\bar{l}_1$$

$$D_4 = l_1\bar{l}_0 + \bar{l}_2\bar{l}_1\bar{l}_0$$

$$D_5 = l_3 + l_2 + l_0$$

$$D_6 = l_3 + l_1\bar{l}_0 + \bar{l}_3\bar{l}_2\bar{l}_1 + \bar{l}_3\bar{l}_2\bar{l}_1\bar{l}_0 + \bar{l}_3 l_2\bar{l}_1\bar{l}_0$$

and the circuit is

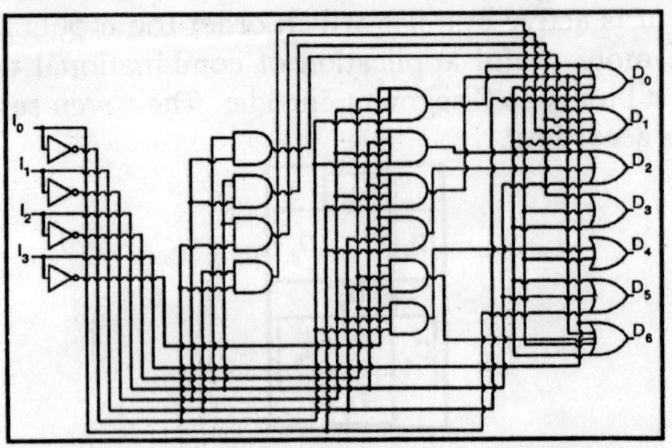

MULTIPLEXES

INTRODUCTION

A multiplexer is a combinatorial circuit that is given a certain number (usually a power of two) data inputs, let us say 2n, and n address inputs used as a binary number to select one of the data inputs. The multiplexer has a single output, which has the same value as the selected data input.

In other words, the multiplexer works like the input selector of a home music system. Only one input is selected at a time, and the selected input is transmitted to the single output. While on the music system, the selection of the input is made manually, the multiplexer chooses its input based on a binary number, the address input.

The truth table for a multiplexer is huge for all but the smallest values of n. We therefore use an abbreviated version of the truth table in which some inputs are replaced by `-' to indicate that the input value does not matter.

Here is such an abbreviated truth table for n = 3. The full truth table would have 2(3 + 23) = 2048rows.

a_2	a_1	a_0	d_7	d_6	d_5	d_4	d_3	d_2	d_1	d_0	|	x
-	-	-	-	-	-	-	-	-	-	-	---	-
0	0	0	-	-	-	-	-	-	-	0	|	0
0	0	0	-	-	-	-	-	-	-	1	|	1
0	0	1	-	-	-	-	-	-	0	-	|	0
0	0	1	-	-	-	-	-	-	1	-	|	1
0	1	0	-	-	-	-	-	0	-	-	|	0
0	1	0	-	-	-	-	-	1	-	-	|	1
0	1	1	-	-	-	-	0	-	-	-	|	0
0	1	1	-	-	-	-	1	-	-	-	|	1
1	0	0	-	-	-	0	-	-	-	-	|	0
1	0	0	-	-	-	1	-	-	-	-	|	1
1	0	1	-	-	0	-	-	-	-	-	|	0
1	0	1	-	-	1	-	-	-	-	-	|	1
1	1	0	-	0	-	-	-	-	-	-	|	0
1	1	0	-	1	-	-	-	-	-	-	|	1
1	1	1	0	-	-	-	-	-	-	-	|	0
1	1	1	1	-	-	-	-	-	-	-	|	1

We can abbreviate this table even more by using a letter to indicate the value of the selected input, like this:

a_2	a_1	a_0	d_7	d_6	d_5	d_4	d_3	d_2	d_1	d_0	x
-	-	-	-	-	-	-	-	-	-	-	-
0	0	0	-	-	-	-	-	-	-	c	c
0	0	1	-	-	-	-	-	-	c	-	c
0	1	0	-	-	-	-	-	c	-	-	c
0	1	1	-	-	-	-	c	-	-	-	c
1	0	0	-	-	-	c	-	-	-	-	c
1	0	1	-	-	c	-	-	-	-	-	c
1	1	0	-	c	-	-	-	-	-	-	c
1	1	1	c	-	-	-	-	-	-	-	c

The same way we can simplify the truth table for the multiplexer, we can also simplify the corresponding circuit. Indeed, our simple design method would yield a very large circuit. The simplified circuit looks like this:

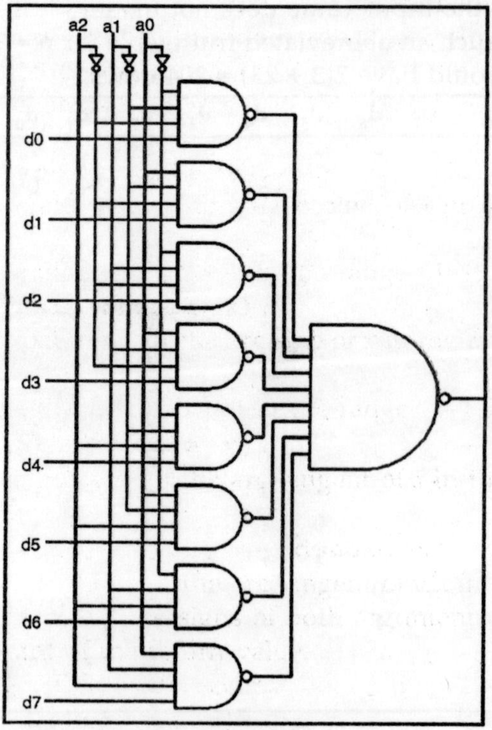

A multiplexer performs the function of selecting the input on any one of'n' input lines and feeding this input to one output line. Multiplexers are used as one method of reducing the number of integrated circuit packages required by a particular circuit design. This in turn reduces the cost of the system. Assume that we have four lines, C0, C1, C2 and C3, which are to be multiplexed on a single line, Output (f). The four input lines are also known as the Data Inputs. Since there are four inputs, we will need two additional inputs to the multiplexer, known as the Select Inputs, to select which of the C inputs is to appear at the output. Call these select lines A and B. The gate implementation of a 4-line to 1-line multiplexer is shown below:

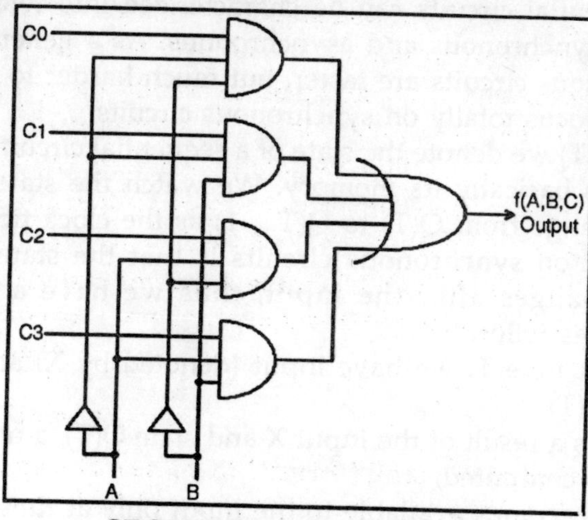

SEQUENTIAL CIRCUITS

Digital electronics is classified into combinational logic and sequential logic. Combinational logic output depends on the inputs levels, whereas sequential logic output depends on stored levels and also the input levels.

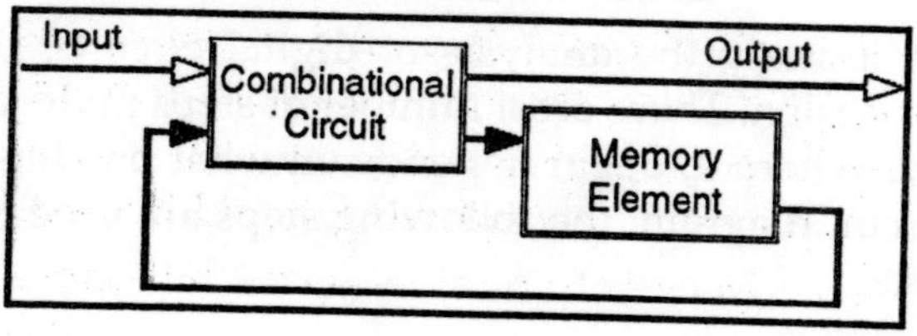

The following figure shows a way to consider sequential circuits.

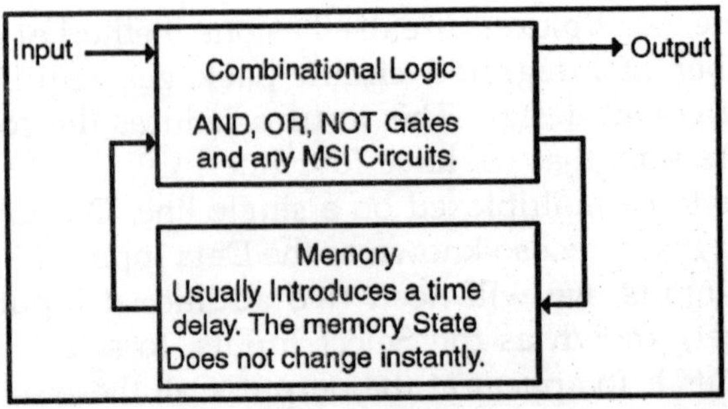

Fig. Sequential Logic

Sequential circuits can be characterized into two broad classes - synchronous and asynchronous. As a general rule, asynchronous circuits are faster, but much harder to design. We shall focus totally on synchronous circuits.

By Q(T) we denote the state of a sequential circuit at time T - this is basically its memory. We watch the state of the circuit change from Q(T) to Q(T + 1) as the clock ticks. The constraint on synchronous circuits is that the state of the circuit changes after the input, thus we have a typical sequence as follows:

- At time T, we have input (denoted by X) and state Q(T).
- As a result of the input X and state Q(T), a new state is computed,

This becomes available to the input only at time (T + 1) and so is called Q(T + 1). The fact that the new state, computed as a result of X and Q(T), is not available to the input of the sequential circuit until the next time step greatly facilitates the design and analysis of the specific circuit.

CIRCUIT ANALYSIS

We first study the analysis of digital circuits, then we study their design. There are a number of steps in the analysis of a circuit. Where to begin depends on what one has. When given a circuit diagram, the following steps are used to begin the analysis.

- Determine the inputs and outputs of the circuit. Assign variables to represent these.
- Determine the inputs and outputs of the flip-flops.
- Construct the Next State and Output Tables.
- Construct the State Diagram.
- If possible, identify the circuit. There are no good rules for this step.

Consider the following circuit. We want to discover what it does.

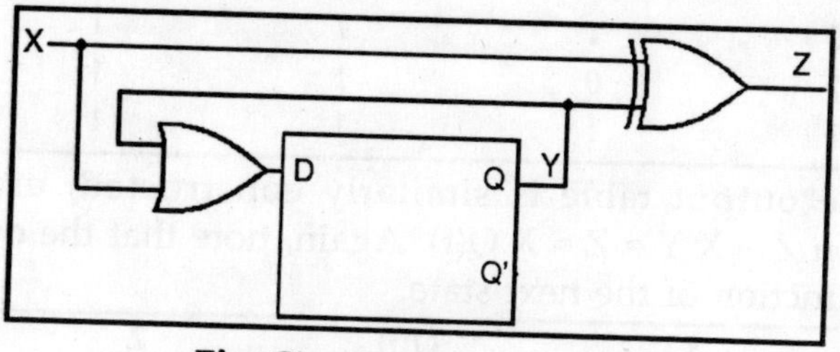

Fig. Circuit to Be Analysed

Step 1: Identify and Label the Inputs, Outputs, and Internal States. We use the following variables in the analysis of this circuit with a single flip-flop.

X denotes the input, Y denotes the output of the flip-flop (Y' also), and Z the output of the circuit. If we had more than one flip-flop, we would label the flip-flop with a number beginning at 0 and use that as a subscript, so flip-flop 0 would have output Y0, etc.

Step 2: Determine the Inputs and Outputs of the Flip-flops

The next step is to determine the equations for Z, the output, and D, the input to the flip-flop. By inspection, we determine the following for the equations:

$$Z = X \oplus Y$$

$$D = X + Y$$

Step 3: Construct the Next State and Output Tables.

We begin this state by recalling the characteristic table of each flip-flop that is used in the design. Here we have only one flip-flip, a D with a very simple characteristic table that is better represented as an equation: Q(t+1) = D - the next state is what you put in now. Noting that Q(t) = Y (the state of a flip-flop is also its output) we construct the following

Next-State diagram for the flip-flop, based on the characteristic table of a D flip-flop and the equation we derived for the D input: D = X + Y. One simple caution here is that the input to a flip-flop is a function of the present state only, having nothing to do with the next state (as we have no crystal balls). Thus Y = Q(t). Here is the present state (PS)/ next state (NS) diagram for the circuit.

X	Q(t) = Y	D = X + Y	Q(t+1)
0	0	0	0
0	1	1	1
1	0	1	1
1	1	1	1

The output table is similarly constructed, using the equation Z = X Y = Z = X Q(t). Again, note that the output is not a function of the next state.

X	Q(t)	Z
0	0	0
0	1	1
1	0	1
1	1	0

These two tables are combined to form the transition/ output table.

X	Q(t) = Y	D = X + Y	Q(t+1)/Z
0	0	0	0/0
0	1	1	1/1
1	0	1	1/1
1	1	1	1/0

At this point, we should produce a state table in the standard format. This involves assigning labels to each of the two states, currently identified only as Q(t) = 0 and Q(t) = 1. For lack of anything more imaginative, we label the states 0 and 1.

Present State	Next State/Output	
	X = 0	X = 1
0	0/0	1/1
1	1/1	1/0

Figure: State Table for Circuit to be Analysed

Step 4: Construct the State Diagram

The final step in the process may be the creation of the state diagram.

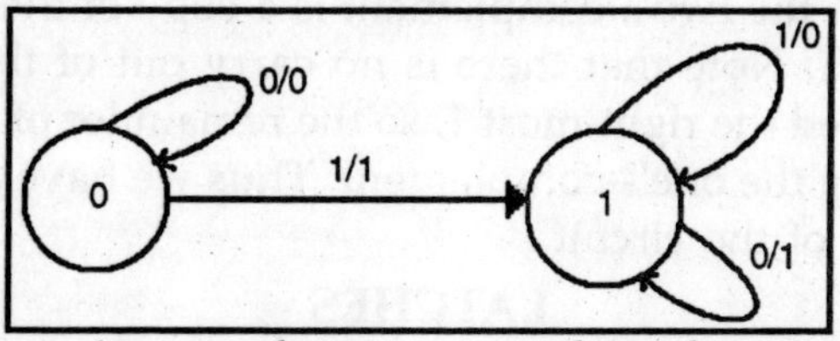

At this point, we have a complete description of the circuit. It may be possible to proceed from this diagram to obtain an understanding of what the circuit does.

Step 5: If possible, identify the circuit.

This circuit is a 2-state device, with memory represented by one bit. The circuit stays in state 0 from the start until a 1 is input at which time it transitions to state 1 and remains there. Note the relation of the output to the input, depending on the state of the machine.

Input	Q(t)	Output	
0	0	0	For Q(t) = 0, the output is X
1	0	1	
0	1	1	For Q(t) = 1, the output is X'.
1	1	0	

A verbal description of the circuit is then that it copies its input to the output until the first 1 is encountered in the input stream. After that event, all input is output as complemented.

What this circuit does is take the two's-complement of a binary integer, presented to the circuit least-significant bit first. It is easy to prove that such a strategy produces the two's complement of a number. First, consider a number ending in 1, say X_nX_n–1.... X_2X_{11}.

The one's complement of this number is Xn'Xn-1' .... X_2'X_1'0. Adding 1 to this produces the number Xn'X_{n-1}' .... X_2'X_1'1, in which the least significant 1 is copied and the remaining bits are complemented. The proof is completed by supposing that the number terminates in a one or more zeroes;

i.e., its least significant bits are 10 .... 0, where the count of zeroes is not important. The one's-complement of this number will end with 01 .... 1, where each zero in the original has turned to a 1. But 01 .... 1 + 1 = 10 .... 0, and up to the least significant 1 the two's-complement is a copy of the bits in the integer itself. Note that there is no carry out of the addition that produced the right-most 1, so the remainder of the integer is formed by the one's-complement. Thus we have a complete description of the circuit.

LATCHES

When showing either latches or flip-flops as circuit elements, it is undesirable to show the"internals" of the device. Here are the symbols for SR and D latches.

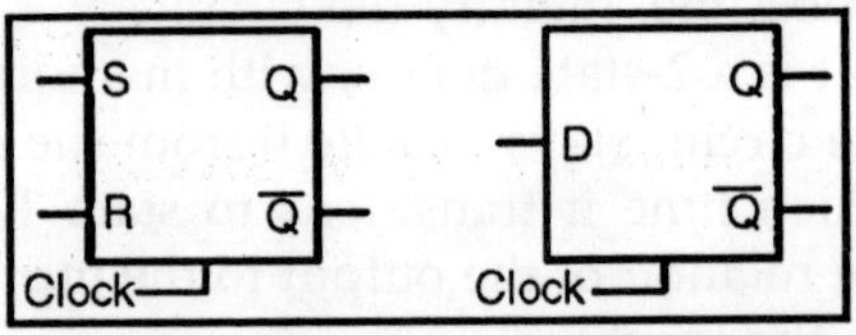

FLIP FLOPS

A flip-flop is a"bit box"; it stores a single binary bit. By Q(t), we denote the state of the flip-flop at the present time, or present tick of the clock; either Q(t) = 0 or Q(t) = 1. The student will note that throughout this textbook we make the assumption that all circuit elements function correctly, so that any binary device is assumed to have only two states. A flip-flop must have an output; this is called either Q or Q(t).

This output indicates the current state of the flip-flop, and as such is either a binary 0 or a binary 1. We shall see that, as a result of the way in which they are constructed, all flip-flops also output $\overline{Q(t)}$, the complement of the current state.

Each flip-flop also has, as input, signals that specify how the next state, Q(t + 1), is to relate to the present state, Q(t). Every flip-flop also has an input derived from the system clock, which allows it to function as a synchronous circuit. It also has connections to power and ground. Here are the symbols for SR and D flip-flops, which we have not yet defined. Note the small triangles on the clock input; this says"edge triggered".

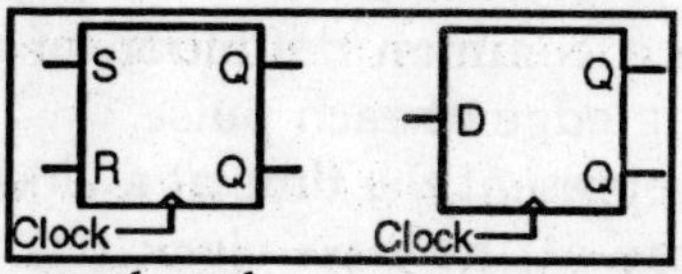

One should note that the more common symbols for flip-flops show the clock input coming in"from the side" as shown in the next figure.

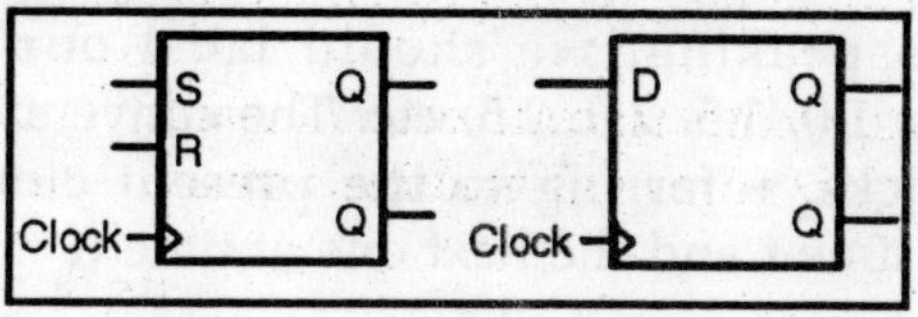

THE CLOCK

The most fundamental characteristic of synchronous sequential circuits is a system clock. This is an electronic circuit that produces a repetitive train of logic 1 and logic 0 at a regular rate, called the clock frequency.

Most computer systems have a number of clocks, usually operating at related frequencies; for example - 2 GHz, 1GHz, 500MHz, and 125MHz. The inverse of the clock frequency is the clock cycle time. As an example, we consider a clock with a frequency of 2 GHz (2"109 Hertz). The cycle time is 1.0/ (2"109) seconds, or 0.5"10-9 seconds = 0.500 nanoseconds = 500 picoseconds. Synchronous sequential circuits are sequential circuits that use a clock input to order events.

Asynchronous sequential circuits do not use a common clock and, as hinted at above, are much harder to design and test. As we shall focus only on synchronous circuits, we immediately launch a discussion of the clock. The following figure illustrates some of the terms commonly used for a clock.

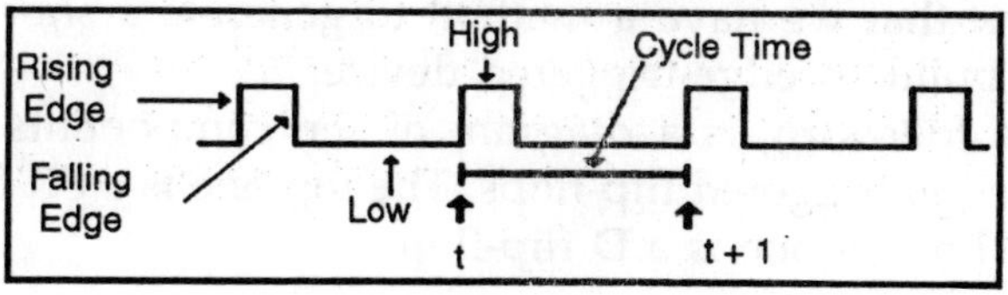

The clock input is very important to the concept of a sequential circuit. At each"tick" of the clock the output of a sequential circuit is determined by its input and by its state. We now provide a common definition of a"clock tick" - it occurs at the rising edge of each pulse.

We use t to represent the time at a clock tick and (t + 1) to denote the time at the next clock tick - the difference between the two is the clock cycle time. Suppose a 2 GHz clock, which corresponds to a clock cycle time of 0.5 nanosecond.

Strictly speaking, we should label our timings in nanoseconds: 1.0, 1.5. 2.0. 2.5, etc. The convention is just to count the ticks, referring to the present clock pulse as occurring at time t and the next one at time (t + 1).

DESCRIPTION

By definition, a flip-flop is an edge-triggered latch. We must now show how achieve edge triggering. In essence, what we shall do is take a level triggered latch and give it a clock pulse with a very short positive (logical 1) phase.

The key component of an edge-triggered flip-flop is a pulse generator that we studied in a previous chapter. This could be based on the gate delay of a NOT gate. More modern devices likely use a different circuit so as to generate a shorter pulse.

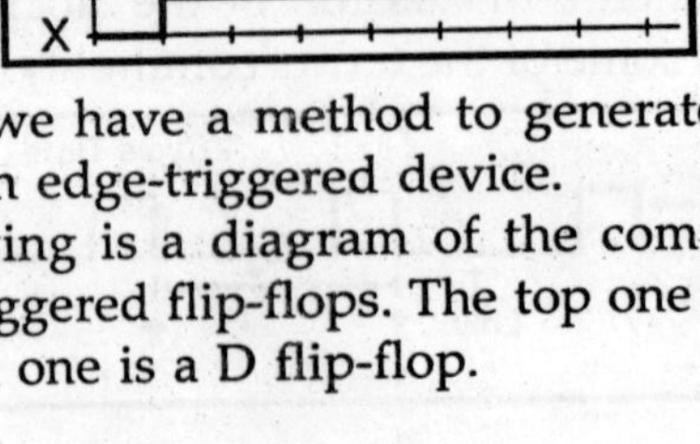

Now that we have a method to generate a short pulse, we can build an edge-triggered device.

The following is a diagram of the components of two typical edge-triggered flip-flops. The top one is a SR flip-flop and the bottom one is a D flip-flop.

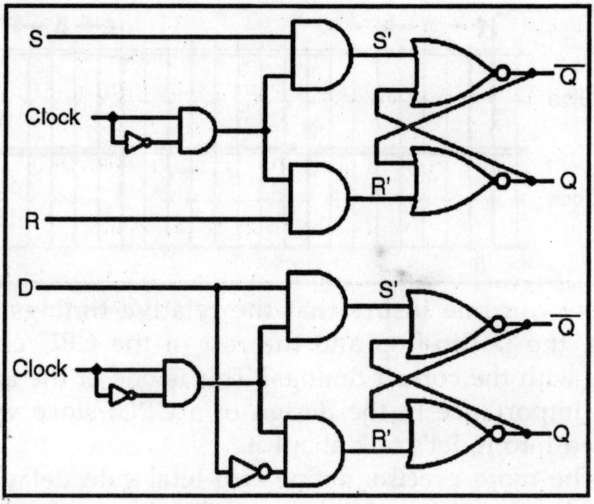

TYPES OF FLIP-FLOPS

In order to avoid the simple example, we shall examine the general case. Here is the circuit for consideration. We postulate a total of gate delays (including that of the D flip-flop) to be the time interval signified by Δ. Thus at time Δ after the D latch is first sensitive to its input, the circuitry has output a new value to become D. But the flip-flop is activated by a short pulse, of time length δ.

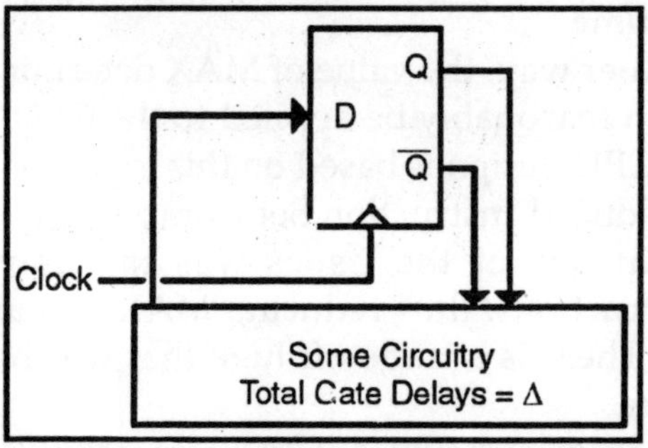

The timing diagram below shows the interruption of the uncontrolled feedback loop. By the time that the output of the circuitry has changed, the D flip-flop is no longer sensitive to input. The input will not become effective until the beginning of the next clock cycle.

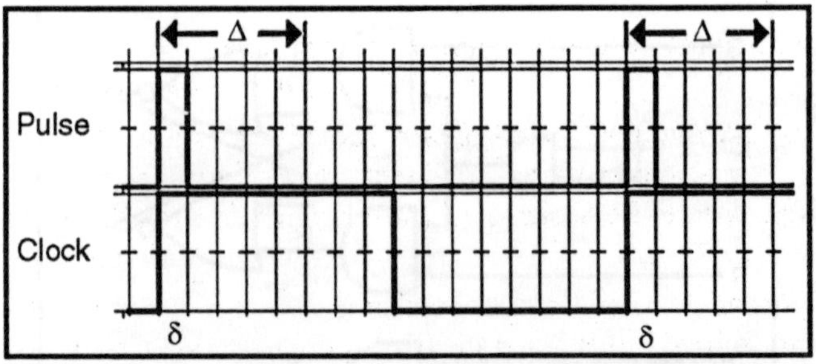

How can one insure that the relative timings of two circuits, the D flip-flop and the rest of the CPU circuitry, operate with the correct timings? This is one of the issues of central importance in the design of a CPU; since we have stumbled into it, let's talk about it.

To be more precise, define two total gate delays: Δ_{MIN} and Δ_{MAX}. Δ_{MIN} is the total time delay for the fastest CPU operation and Δ_{MAX}. the delay for the slowest. We must haveΔ_{MIN} >, or the circuit would occasionally display uncontrolled feedback. Conservatively, we might say Δ_{MIN} 1.5•. The next criterion is a bit more difficult to state precisely, but it might be stated something like T 1.5•δ Δ_{MAX}, where T denotes the clock period. What we say here is that the clock period must be long enough for the CPU output to"settle". Note, however, that a value of T much larger than MAX is just wasted time.

Put another way, the value of MAX determines the fastest clock that can reasonably be applied to the CPU. A good part of the art of CPU design is based on this issue. When we study the RISC (Reduced Instruction Set Computer) movement, we shall see that one of the issues was to remove the more complex instructions, thus reducing MAX and allowing for a faster clock. There is a trade-off here that we shall explore in later chapters.

To be honest, the sum of CPU gate delays is not always the limiting factor in the clock speed. Some recent CPUs have been designed with a"hot clock" that is hot in both ways. It is very fast, being of the order of 4 to 5 GHz. It is also hot in the literal sense, in that the CPU, operating at that clock rate, emits so much heat that it overheats itself. The art of CPU design is always bumping up against those messy laws of physics.

The SR Flip-Flop

We have completely defined the SR flip-flop, based on the idea of an SR latch. While we could just leave the topic and proceed, it is appropriate at this time to review the subject and state, in one place, what the student is expected to know. We begin with a depiction of the SR flip-flop that will be used in all future discussions.

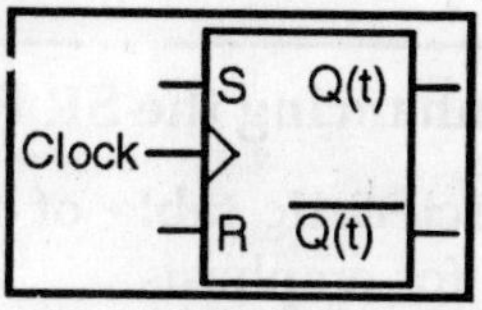

At this point we are no longer interested in the internal construction of the flip-flop, but on its operational characteristics. These are given in the characteristic table.

S	R	Q(t + 1)
0	0	Q(t)
0	1	0
1	0	1
1	1	ERROR

We next address an issue that commonly arises in the use of flip-flops in circuit design. We have a number of scenarios. For each, we know Q(t) and what Q(t + 1) should be. The question is how to achieve that change. For example, if Q(t) = 0 and we want Q(t + 1) = 0, we have two choices: either S = 0 and R = 0, or S = 0 and R = 1.

The first option, keeps the state unchanged at 0; the second forces it to 0. As S = 0 is sufficient to do this without regard to the value of R, we say that the input is S = 0 and R = d; the d standing for"don't care". On the other hand, if Q(t) = 0 and Q(t + 1) = 1, only S = 1 and R = 0 will do. This is the only combination that will give a next state of 1 when the present state is 0. If we have Q(t) = 1 and want Q(t + 1) = 0, then our choice is simple: S = 0 and R = 1.

If we have Q(t) = 1 and want Q(t + 1) = 1, then we can choose either S = 0 and R = 0, or

S = 1 and R = 0. This is denoted as S = d and R = 0.

The above discussions lead to the excitation table for the SR flip-flop.

Q(t)	Q(t + 1)	S	R
0	0	0	d
0	1	1	0
1	0	0	1
1	1	d	0

The JK Flip-Flop: Enhancing the SR Flip-Flop

Recall the characteristic table of the SR flip-flop. We repeat the table here for emphasis.

S	R	Q(t + 1)
0	0	Q(t)
0	1	0
1	0	1
1	1	ERROR

The theoretician examining this table would note two facts immediately.

- The input S = 1 and R = 1 is disallowed; we would like to do something with it.
- The values for Q(t + 1) are three of the possible four Boolean functions of 1 variable.

Considering Q as a Boolean variable, we now show that there are exactly four Boolean functions of this Boolean variable. These are f(Q) = 0, f(Q) = 1, f(Q) = Q, and f(Q) = $\overline{Q}$. We do this by showing the truth table for each of these functions and noting that there are only four different ways to put 0's and 1's into the two row entries for a function..

Table. The Four Boolean Functions of Boolean Variable Q

Q	0	Q	$\overline{Q}$	1
0	0	0	1	1
1	0	1	0	1

Given this, our enhanced SR flip-flop would have Q(t + 1) = $\overline{Q}$ (t) as one possible output. For maximal compatibility with the existing SR, we would want to leave the existing valid inputs alone and just make good use of the invalid one. What we get is a JK flip-flop.

Recalling that an SR flip-flop is so called because it is a Set-Reset device, we may ask for the meaning of JK. One is tempted to make up some story related to names in German, but the basic answer is that"I don't know".

In any case, we present the characteristic table for the JK flip-flop and then ask how one might modify an SR flip to achieve that goal.

Here is the desired characteristic table.

J	K	Q(t + 1)
0	0	Q(t)
0	1	0
1	0	1
1	1	$\overline{Q}$ (t)

Viewing this as a modification of the SR flip-flop, we ask how to generate each of S and R from the inputs J and K under the following constraints;

- Except when J = 1 and K = 1, we want to have S = J and R = K.
  Under these circumstances, the behaviour is identical.
- When J = 1, K = 1, and Q = 0, we want S = 1 and R = 0. This makes Q(t + 1) = 1.
- When J = 1, K = 1, and Q = 1, we want S = 0 and R = 1. This makes Q(t + 1) = 0.

When in doubt about how to create a circuit, we make a truth table. The inputs to the truth table are J, K, and Q (the present state). The outputs are S and R.

Row	Q	J	K	S	R
0	0	0	0	0	0
1	0	0	1	0	1
2	0	1	0	1	0
3	0	1	1	1	0
4	1	0	0	0	0

5	1	0	1	0	1
6	1	1	0	1	0
7	1	1	1	0	1

We have two patterns that almost work: $S = J \bullet \overline{Q}$ and R = K"Q. Let's examine each case. $S = J \bullet \overline{Q}$ produces the expected result for all rows except row 6. In that row we have Q = 1, J = 1, and K = 0. We want Q(t + 1) to be 1. But S = 0 and R = 0 will cause. Q(t + 1) = Q(t) = 1, exactly what we want. So this simple formula causes no trouble.

R = K•Q produces the expected result for all rows except row 1. In that row we have Q = 0, J = 0, and K = 1. We want Q(t + 1) to be 0. But S = 0 and R = 0 will cause Q(t + 1) = Q(t) = 0, exactly what we want. So again we have no trouble.

Here is the basic detailed circuit for the JK flip-flop.

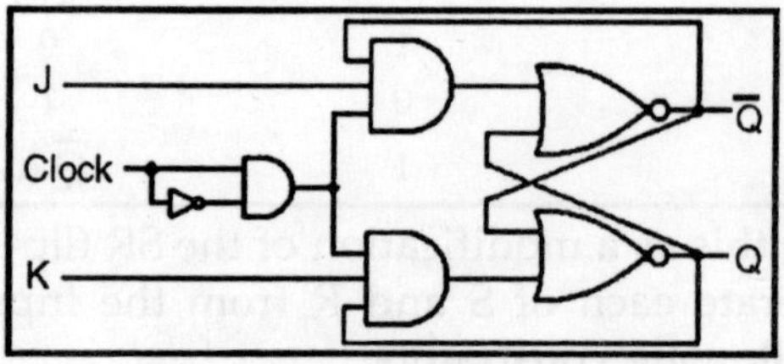

We now give the standard representation of the JK flip-flop as will be used in future discussions. Again, note the triangle symbol on the clock input, indicating edge triggering.

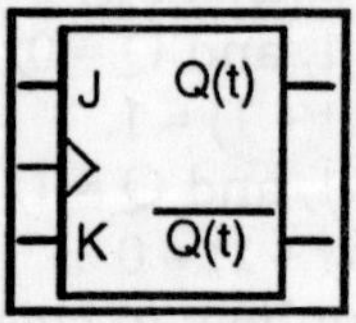

We have already presented the characteristic table for the JK flip-flop. Here it is again.

J	K	Q(t + 1)
0	0	Q(t)
0	1	0
1	0	1
1	1	$\overline{Q}$ (t)

We now create the excitation table for the JK.

If Q(t) = 0 and Q(t + 1) is to be 0, we can use either J = 0 and K = 0, or J = 0 and K = 1. If Q(t) = 0 and Q(t + 1) is to be 1, we can use either J = 1 and K = 0, or J = 1 and K = 1. Note that this is a new option, not available for an SR flip-flop. If Q(t) = 1 and Q(t + 1) is to be 0, we can use either J = 0 and K = 1, or J = 1 and K = 1.

Note that this also is a new option, not available for an SR flip-flop. If Q(t) = 1 and Q(t + 1) is to be 1, we can use either J = 0 and K = 0, or J = 1 and K = 0.

This gives the excitation table for the JK flip-flop.

Q(t)	Q(t + 1)	J	K
0	0	0	d
0	1	1	d
1	0	d	1
1	1	d	0

The D Flip-Flop

We have already examined the D latch. The input is labeled"D" for"Data". The D flip-flop has a characteristic table identical to that of a D latch.

D	Q(t + 1)
0	0
1	1

The device is so simple that it does not require an excitation equation. We just use an excitation equation, which simply states"Give it what you want".

D = Q(t + 1)

The T Flip-Flop

This is the fourth and last of the major types of flip-flops. The input to this flip-flop is labeled"T" for toggle. When T = 0, the state remains the same. When T = 1, the flip-flop changes state. This gives rise to the following characteristic table.

T	Q(t + 1)
0	Q(t)
1	$\overline{Q}$ (t)

The excitation table for this flip-flop is almost obvious.

Q(t)	Q(t + 1)	T
0	0	0
0	1	1
1	0	1
1	1	0

This gives rise to an excitation equation.

$T = Q(t) \oplus Q(t+1)$

JK as a General Flip-Flop

We now take notice that the JK can be configured to function as any of the other 3 flip-flop types. In this, it is the most general type of flip-flop.

JK as a D Flip-Flop

To convert a JK to a D flip-flop, connect the inputs as follows.

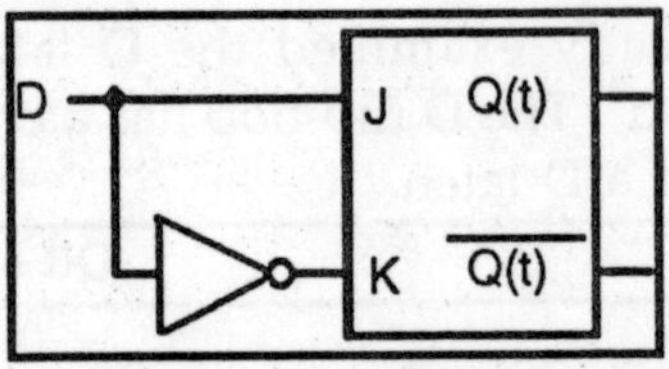

If D = 0, then J = 0, K = 1, and Q(t + 1) = 0, If D = 1, then J = 1, K = 0, and Q(t + 1) = 1.

The JK As A T Flip-Flop. To convert a JK to a T flip-flop, connect the inputs as follows.

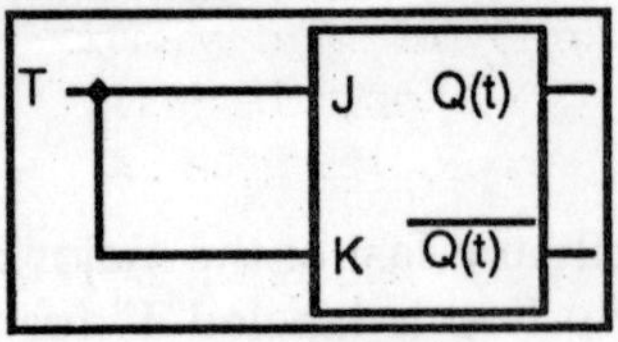

If T = 0, then J = 0, K = 0, and Q(t + 1) = Q(t). If T = 1, then J = 1, K = 1, and Q(t + 1) = $\overline{Q}$ (t)

CLOCKED SEQUENTIAL CIRCUITS

Analysis consists of obtaining a state-table or a state-diagram from a given sequential circuit implementation. In other words analysis closes the loop by forming state-table from a given circuit-implementation. We will show the analysis procedure by deriving the state table of the example circuit we considered in synthesis.

The circuit is shown in Figure.

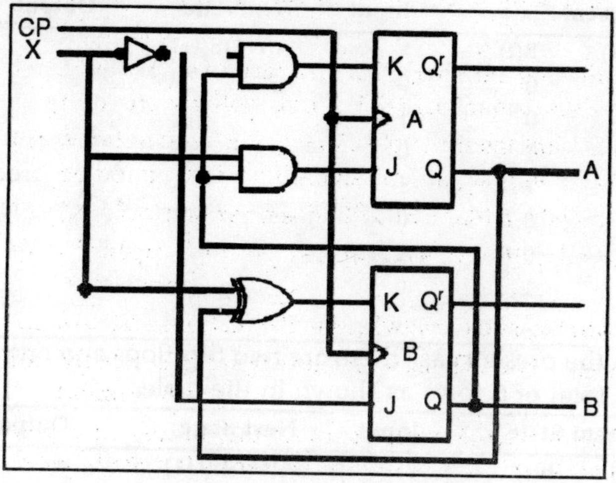

Fig.A Clocked Sequential Circuit

The circuit has:

- Clock input, CP.
- One input x
- One output y
- One clocked JK flip-flop
- One clocked D flip-flop (the machine can be in maximum of 4 states)

A State table is representation of sequence of inputs, outputs, and flip-flop states in a tabular form. Two forms of state tables are shown.

Present State		**Next State**	**Output**
x = 0	**x = 1**	**x = 0**	**x = 1**
A	B	AB	yy
0	0		
0	1		
1	0		
1	1		

Analysis is the generation of state table from the given sequential circuit. The number of rows in the state table is equal to 2 (number of flip-flops+ number of inputs). For the circuit under consideration, number of rows = $2^{(2+1)} = 2^{(3)} = 8$

Table -Form 2

Present State		**Input**	**NextState**	**Output**
A(t)	B(t)	x	A(t+1)B(t+1)	y
0	0	0		
0	0	1		
0	1	0		
0	1	1		
1	0	0		
1	0	1		
1	1	0		
1	1	1		

In the present case there are two flip-flops and one input, thus a total of 8 rows as shown in the table.

Present State		**Input**	**Next State**		**Output**
A(t)	B(t)	x	A(t+1)B(t+1)		y
0	0	0	0	0	0
0	0	1	0	1	0
0	1	0	1	0	0
0	1	1	0	1	0
1	0	0	0	0	0
1	0	1	0	0	0
1	1	1	1	1	0
1	1	1	0	1	1

The analysis can start from any arbitrary state. Let us start deriving the state table from the initial state 00. As a first step, the input equations to the flip-flops and to the combinational circuit must be obtained from the given logic diagram.

These equations are:

$J_A = BX'$

$K_A = BX + B'X'$

$D_B = X$

$y = ABX$

The first row of the state-table is obtained as follows:

When input X = 0; and present states A = 0 and B = 0 (as in the first row); then, using the above equations we get:

$$y = 0, J_A = 0, K_A = 1, \text{ and } D_B = 0.$$

The resulting state table is exactly same from which we started our design example. Thus analysis is opposite to design and combined they act as a closed loop.

STATE REDUCTION

The problem of state reduction is to find ways of reducing the number of states in a sequential circuit without altering the input-output relationships. In other words, to reduce the number of states, redundant states should be eliminated. A redundant state Si is a state which is equivalent to another state Sj. Two states are said to be equivalent if, for each member of the set of inputs, they give exactly the same output and send the circuit either to the same state or to an equivalent state. Since'm' flip-flops can describe a state machine of up to 2m states, reducing the number of states may (or may not) result in a reduction in the number of flip-flops. For example, if the number of states are reduced from 8 to 5, we still need 3 flip-flops. However, state reduction will result in more don't care states. The increased number of don't care states can help obtain a simplified circuit for the state machine.

Consider the shown state diagram.

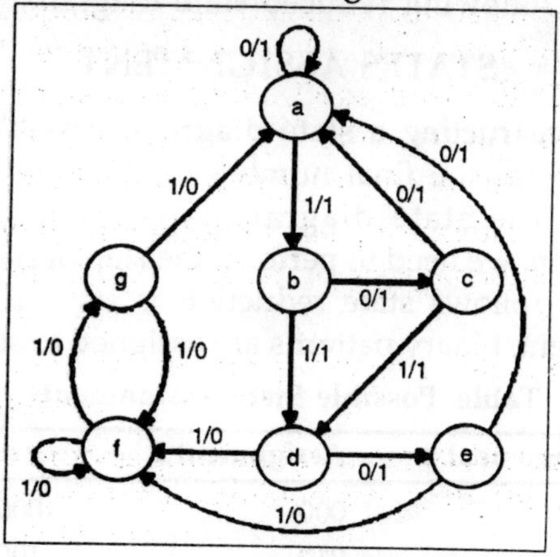

Fig. State Diagram

The state reduction proceeds by first tabulating the information of the state diagram into its equivalent state-table form (as shown in the table) The problem of state reduction requires identifying equivalent states. Each N states is replaced by 1 state.

Consider the following state table.

Present State	Next State		Output	
	x = 0	x = 1	x = 0	x = 1
a	a	b	1	1
b	c	d	1	1
c	a	d	1	1
d	e	~~f~~d	1	0
e	a	~~f~~d	1	0
~~f~~	~~g~~e	f	1	0
~~g~~	a	f	1	0

States'g' and'e' produce the same outputs, *i.e.*'1' and'0', and take the state machine to same next-states,'a' and'f', on inputs'0' and'1' respectively. Thus, states'g' and'e' are equivalent states. We can now remove state'g' and replace it with'e' as shown. We next note that the above change has caused the states'd' and'f' to be equivalent. Thus in the next step, we remove state'f' and replace it with'd'. There are no more equivalent states remaining. The reduced state table results in the following reduced state diagram.

STATES ASSIGNMENT

When constructing a state diagram, variable names are used for states as the final number of states is not known a priori. Once the state diagram is constructed, prior to implementation, we need to perform the step of'state reduction'. The step that follows state reduction is state assignment. In state assignment, binary patterns are assigned to state variables.

Table: Possible State Assignments

State	Assignment 1	Assignment 2	Assignment 3
a	001	000	000
b	010	010	100

c	011	011	010
d	100	101	101
e	101	111	011

For a given machine, there are several state assignments possible. Different state assignments may result in different combinational circuits of varying complexities. State assignment procedures try to assign binary values to states such that the cost (complexity) of the combinational circuit is reduced. There are several heuristics that attempt to choose good state assignments (also known as state encoding) that try to reduce the required combinational logic complexity, and hence cost.

As mentioned earlier, for the reduced state machine obtained in the previous example, there can be a number of possible assignments. As an example, three different state assignments are shown in the table for the same machine.

DESIGN PROCEDURE

DESIGN WITH UNUSED STATES

There are occasions when a sequential circuit, implemented using m flip-flops, may not utilize all the possible 2m states

Table: Reduced Table with binary Assignment

Present State	Next State		Output	
	x = 0	x = 1	x = 0	x = 1
a	a	b	1	1
b	c	d	1	1
c	a	d	1	1
d	e	d	1	0
e	a	d	1	0

In the previous example of machine with 5 states, we need three flip-flops. Let us choose assignment 1, which is binary assignment for our sequential machine example (shown in the table). The unspecified states can be used as don't-cares and will therefore help in simplifying the logic. The excitation table of previous example is shown. There are three states, 000, 110, and 111 that are not listed in the table under present state and input.

Exciation Table

Present State			Input	Next state			Flip-flop inputs						output
A	B	C	X	A	B	C	SA	RA	SB	RB	SC	RC	Y
0	0	1	0	0	0	1	0	X	0	X	X	0	1
0	0	1	1	0	0	1	0	X	1	0	0	1	1
0	1	0	0	0	1	0	0	X	X	0	1	0	1
0	1	0	1	0	1	0	1	0	0	1	0	X	1
0	1	1	0	0	1	1	0	X	0	1	X	1	1
0	1	1	1	0	1	1	1	0	0	1	0	0	1
1	0	0	0	0	0	0	1	0	0	1	0	1	1
1	0	0	0	1	0	0	x	0	0	X	1	0	1
1	0	1	0	1	0	1	0	1	0	X	X	0	1
1	0	1	1	1	0	1	X	0	0	X	0	1	0

With the inclusion of input 1 or 0, we obtain six don't-care minterms: 0, 1, 12, 13, 14, and 15.

The K-maps of SA and RA is shown in the figure. Other K-Maps can be obtained similarly and the equations derived are shown in the figure. The logic diagram thus obtained is shown in the figure.

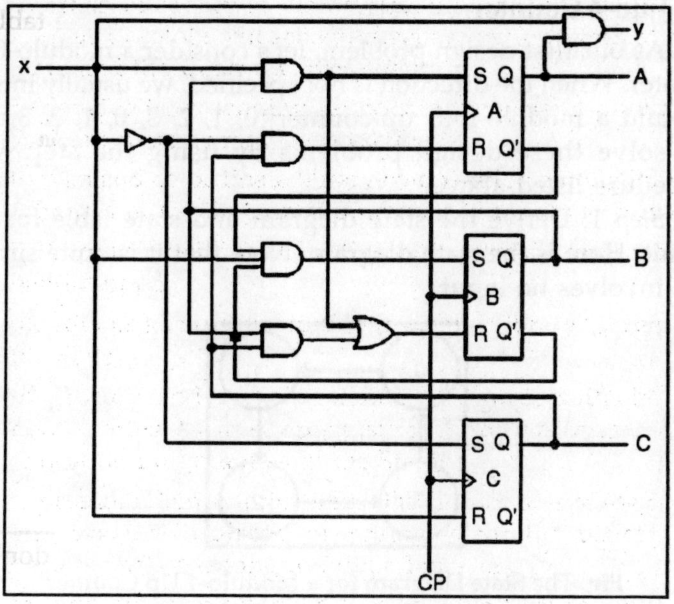

Fig. Logic Diagram

SA = BX

RA = Cx′

SB = A′B′X

RB = BC +Bx

SC = x′

RC = x

y = A′ + x′ = (Ax)′

Note that the design of the sequential circuit is dependent on binary codes for states. A different binary state codes set may have resulted in some different combinational circuit.

DESIGN OF SEQUENTIAL CIRCUITS

Having seen how to Analyse digital circuits, we now investigate how to design digital circuits. We assume that we are given a complete and unambiguous description of the circuit to be designed as a starting point.

At this level, most design problems focus on one of two topics: modulo-N counters and sequence detectors.

Modulo-4 Counter

As our first design problem, let's consider a modulo-four counter. When the direction is not specified, we usually intend to build a modulo-four up-counter: 0, 1, 2, 3, 0, 1, 2, 3, etc. We solve these design problems by using the step-wise procedure listed above.

Step 1: Derive the state diagram and state table for the circuit. Here is the state diagram. Note that it is quite simple and involves no input.

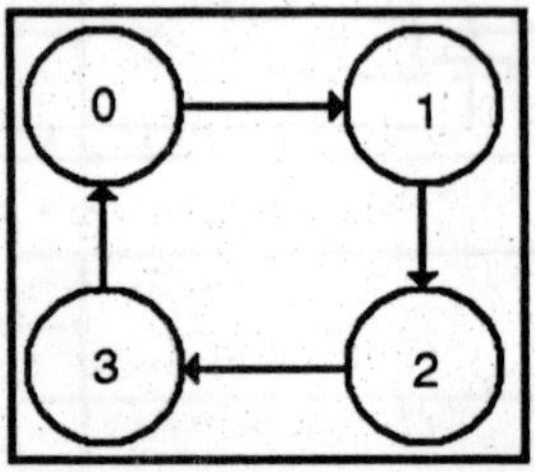

Fig. The State Diagram for a Modulo-4 Up Counter

The state table is simply a rearrangement of the state diagram into a tabular form.

Present State	Next State
0	1
1	2
2	3
3	0

Step 2: Count the number of states in the state diagram (call it N) and calculate the number of flip-flops needed (call it P) by solving the equation $2^{P-1} < N \leq 2^P$.

The number of states on a modulo-N counter is simply N; these are labeled 0 through (N - 1). Specifically, a modulo-4 counter has four states: labeled 0, 1, 2, and 3.

We solve the equation $2^{P-1} < 4 \leq 2^P$ by noting that $2^1 = 2$ and $2^2 = 4$, so we have determined that $2^1 < 4 \leq 22$, hence P = 2. We shall see later that there are valid solutions with more than two flip-flops, but there are none with fewer.

Step 3 Assign a unique P-bit binary number (state vector) to each state.

Often, the first state = 0, the next state = 1, etc. Some sequential circuits suggest an innovative numbering system, but modulo-N counters never do. We go with the obvious labeling, generated by assigning each decimal number its two-bit binary equivalent as an unsigned integer in the range from 0 to 3.

State	2-bit Vector
0	00
1	01
2	10
3	11

Step 4 Derive the state transition table and the output table.

There is no output table for any modulo-N counter, as the output associated with this type of table is the output on a transition, as is seen in a sequence detector. The transition table is a direct translation of the state table, using the assignments from the previous step.

Present State		Next State
0	00	01
1	01	10
2	10	11
3	11	00

Step 5 Separate the state transition table into P tables, one for each flip-flop.

Here we separate the state transition table into 2 tables, one for each flip-flop. Note that the flip-flops will be numbered 0 and 1, with flip-flop 0 storing the least significant bit of the state information. Thus, we shall refer to the state information as Y1Y0.

Flip-Flop 1		Flip-Flop 0	
Present State	**Next State**	**Present State**	**Next State**
Y_1 Y_0	$Y_1(T+1)$	Y_1 Y_0	$Y_0(T+1)$
0 0	0	0 0	1
0 1	1	0 1	0
1 0	1	1 0	1
1 1	0	1 1	0

Step 6 Decide on the types of flip-flops to use. When in doubt, use all JK's. Up to this point, we have made no assumptions about the type of flip-flop to use.

In order to proceed any farther with the design, we must now commit to a specific type. In line with this author's preferences, he chooses to use two JK flip-flops.

Q(t)	Q(t+1)	J	K
0	0	0	d
0	1	1	d
1	0	d	1
1	1	d	0

The excitation table for a JK flip-flop is shown at right. Recall that the"d" stands for"Don't Care". For example, if we have Q(t) = 0 and want Q(t+1) = 0, we can use either J = 0, K = 0 or J = 0, K = 1. Similarly either J = 1 and K = 0 or J = 1 and K = 1 will take Q(t) = 0 to Q(t + 1) = 1.

Step 7 Derive the input table for each flip-flop using the excitation tables for the type.

First look at flip-flop 1, representing the high-order bit. Note that we compare the present state of Y1 to its next state in order to determine J1 and K1.

PS	NS	Input	
Y1 Y0	Y1	J1	K1
0 0	0	0	d
0 1	1	1	d
1 0	1	d	0
1 1	0	d	1

Note that in deciding on the input, we must match only the 0's and 1's. We ignore the don't-cares. Note that the"d" for"don't-care" is not a variable to be assigned a value. It is a value that does not need to be matched. At the moment, Y0 is included in the table for future use only. It plays no part in determining the values of J1 and K1.

Here is the table for Y0

PS	NS	Input	
Y1 Y0	Y0	J0	K0
0 0	1	1	d

0 1	0	d	1
1 0	1	1	d
1 1	0	d	1

Again, Y1 is included in the table for future use only. It plays no part in determining the values of J0 and K0.

Step 8 Derive the input equations for each flip-flop based as functions of the input and current state of all flip-flops.

At this point, we try to derive an expression that matches each column. Formal methods can be used, but generally are more trouble than they are worth. Here is this author's set of rules to match an expression to a given column.

- If a column does not have a 0 in it, match it to the constant value 1.
  If a column does not have a 1 in it, match it to the constant value 0.
- If the column has both 0's and 1's in it, try to match it to a single variable, which must be part of the present state. Only the 0's and 1's in a column must match the suggested function.
- If every 0 and 1 in the column is a mismatch, match to the complement of a function.
- If all the above fails, try for simple combinations of the present state.

Let's look at the input table for Y1.

PS	NS	Input
Y_1 Y_0	Y_1	J_1 K_1
0 0	0	0 d
0 1	1	1 d
1 0	1	d 0
1 1	0	d 1

Note that the column for J1 has a 0 and a 1 in it as does the column for K1. Each column has two"don't cares" in it, but we ignore these. Because each column has both a 0 and a 1 in it, neither is a match for a constant function. We now try to match J1. J1 does not match Y1, because Y1 is 0 in the same row (0 1) as J1 is 1. J1 matches Y0. In row 0 0, both Y0 and J1 are 1. In row 0 1, both Y0 and J1 are 1.

In rows 1 0 and 1 1, J1 is a"don't care", so we do not need to match it. Similar logic shows that K1 matches Y0 also.

So now we have the following matches for J1 and K1.

PS	NS	Input	
$Y_1\ Y_0$	Y_1	J_1	K_1
0 0	0	0	d
0 1	1	1	d
1 0	1	d	0
1 1	0	d	1

$J_1 = Y_0 \quad K_1 = Y_0$

We now examine Y_0

PS	NS	Input	
$Y_1\ Y_0$	Y_0	J_0	K_0
0 0	1	1	d
0 1	0	d	1
1 0	1	1	d
1 1	0	d	1

Note that there are no 0's in either the J0 or K0 column. The simplest (and best) match is J0 = 1 and K0 = 1.

Step 9 Summarize the equations by writing them in one place. Here they are.

J1 = Y0 K1 = Y0

J0 = 1 K0 = 1

This is a counter, so there is no Z output.

Step 10 Draw the circuit diagram.

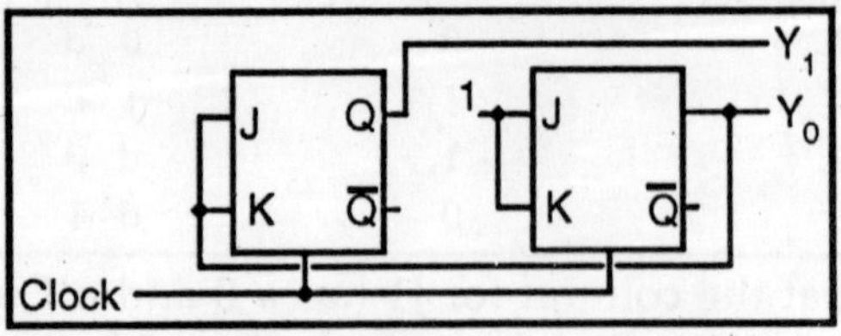

But wait - there is another solution hidden here. Recall that a JK flip-flop can be used to emulate a T flip-flop by setting the J input equal to the K input. Note that the design has the following interesting property.

J1 = K1 = Y0

J0 = K0 = 1

Given this, we can replace each JK flip-flop with a T flip-flop, arriving at this design.

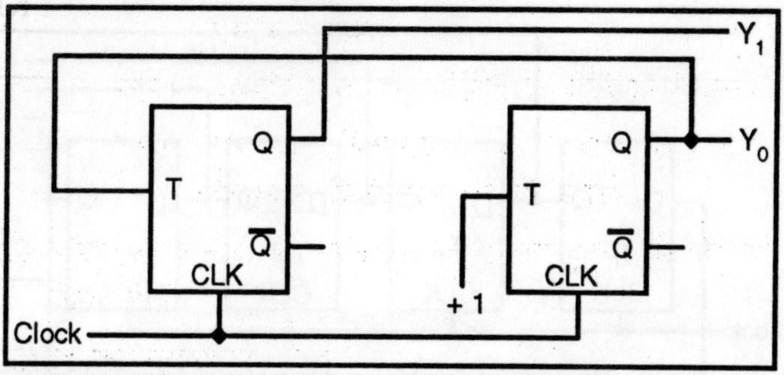

The modulo-4 counter just designed outputs binary codes for the time pulses. Specifically, we assume that it is initialized to Y1Y0 = 00 and then outputs 01, 10, 11, 00, 01, 10, 11, etc.

A more realistic circuit would output discrete pulses corresponding to the decoded output, so that first T0 = 1 and all others are 0, then T1 = 1 and all others are 0, etc. In order to produce the discrete signals T0, T1, T2, and T3, we need to add a decoding phase to the counter.

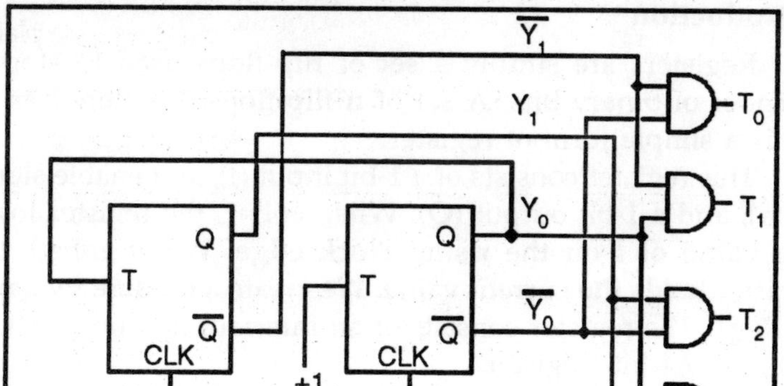

Note that the above design is simplified by the fact that the outputs Y1' and Y0' are available directly from the flip-flops and do not need to be synthesized using NOT gates. One can achieve a simpler design at the cost of additional flip-flops. The following design is called a one-hot design, in that it uses a shift register in which exactly one flip-flop at a time is storing a 1. This design also works as a modulo-4 counter and skips the decoder delays.

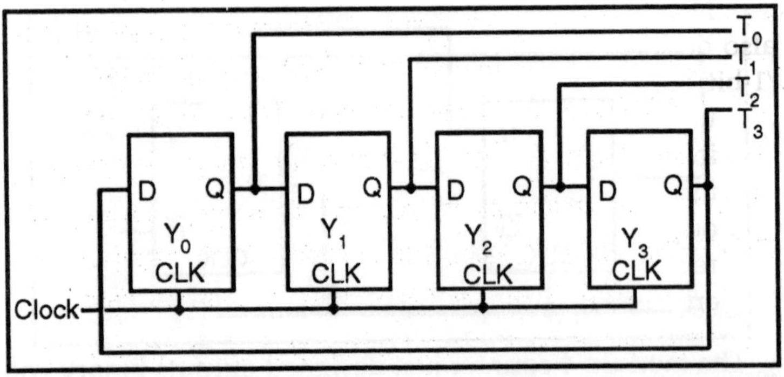

When the counter is initialized, we set Y0 = 1, and Y1 = Y2 = Y3 = 0. As the clock ticks, the single 1 is shifted by the shift register, so that the discrete signals become high in sequence.

REGISTERS AND COUNTERS

REGISTERS

Introduction

Registers are simply a set of flip-flops used to store a number of binary bits. A set of n flip-flops can store bits. 1-bit is a simple form of register.

This register consists of a 1-bit input (I), and enable signal (enb), and a 1-bit output (Q). When enb=1, the register loads the value of I on the rising clock edge. When enb=0, the register holds the current value. We create a module by name of Reg1. The register consists of an interface of 4 ports, clk, I, enb, Q. //1-bit Register

module Reg1(clk, I enb, Q);
endmodule

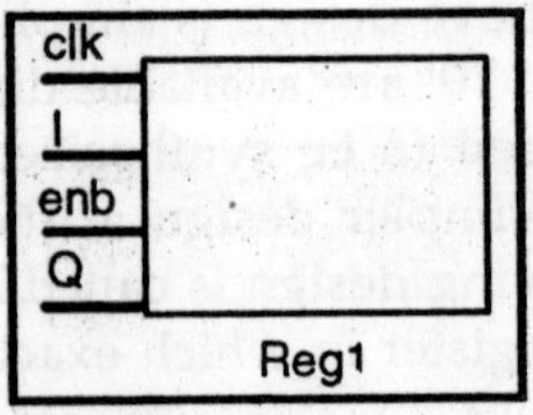

We next specify what type the ports are. In this example, clk, I, and enb are input ports. Port Q is an output port.

Notice in addition to declaring Q as an output, we must also declare Q as a register so we can assign values to Q. /
/1-bit Register

```
module Reg1(clk, I enb, Q);
input clk;
input I, enb;
output Q;
reg Q;
endmodule
```

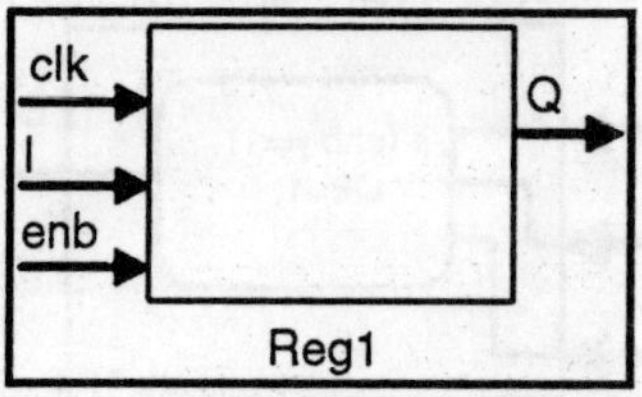

We then create a sensitivity list, which executes the code between the"begin" and"end" statements onv every rising edge of the clk.//1-bit Register

```
module Reg1(clk, I enb, Q);
input clk;
input I, enb;
output Q;
reg Q;
always @ (posedge clk)
begin
end
endmodule
```

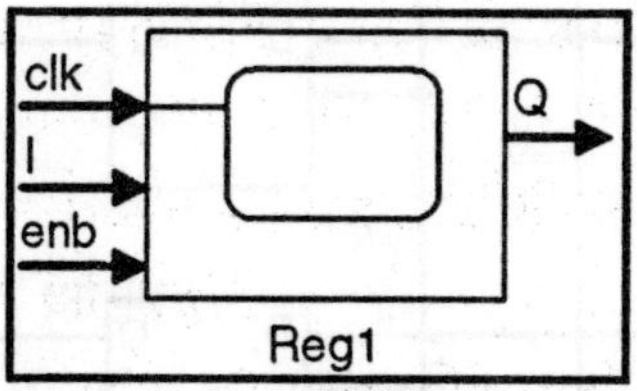

If enb=1 on the rising edge of the clk, then we store the value of input I. //1-bit Register

```
module Reg1(clk, I enb, Q);
input clk;
input I, enb;
output Q;
reg Q;
always @ (posedge clk)
begin
if(enb == 1 )
Q <= I;
end
endmodule
```

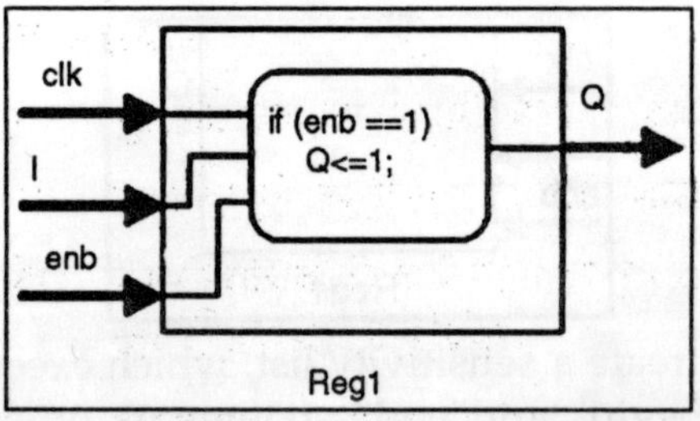

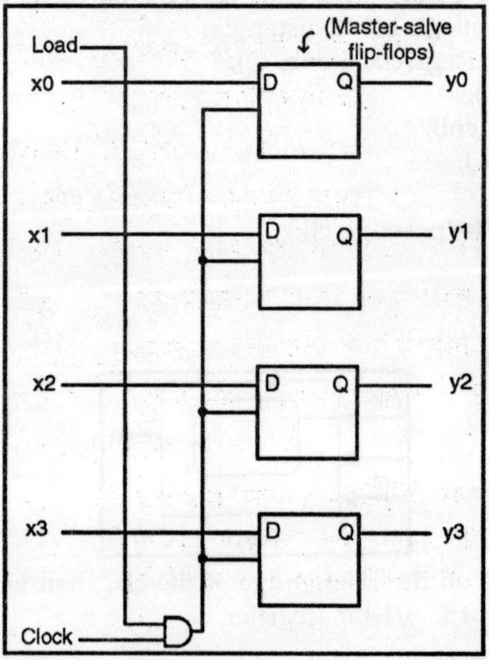

Description

A CPU contains very fast memory called registers. For example, a MIPS ISA stores 32 32-bit registers.

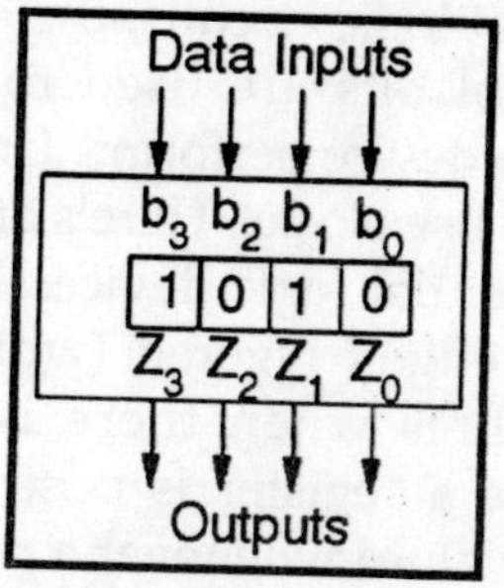

In some sense, this is not really a black box, because we have some idea of what's in it. However, let's not worry about that. The black box shown above has four inputs. The register can do one of two things: it can parallel load the inputs, that is, it can read in all four inputs and store the four bits into the array.

Each element of the array can store a single bit. It can also choose to ignore the inputs, and the values of the arrays remain unchanged. In this case, we say the array is"holding" its values.

The array's values is continuously being sent as output. Thus, if we could measure the output of the register (say, with a voltmeter), the four bits being output would correspond to the four bits currently being stored in the array. This output is sent to the outside world where other devices can read the values, if they want to.

A register can have more than 4 bits stored in it. In fact, modern CPUs either store 32 or 64 bits in registers. In reality, one bit of a register is really a flip flop, which is a device that can store one bit. We will discuss flip flops at some later point.

Parallel Load Register

This register has a name. It's called a parallel load register. It supports two operations. The operation is controlled by a single control bit, called c.

c	Operation
0	Hold
1	Parallel Load

Like combinational logic circuits, the c refers to a control bit. Recall that control bits are used to determine which operation or function a device performs. Unlike combinational logic circuits, registers use clocks. Here's an important feature of registers (and sequential logic devices in general).

A device that is edge-triggered (which this register is) can only change values when there is a clock edge. In particular, we assume a register is positive-edge triggered, so it can only change values whenever a positive edge occurs. Specifically, when the clock reaches a positive edge, the register detects this event.

It then reads in the value of c, the control bit, and based on the value, either parallel loads (*i.e.*, sets $z_3z_2z_1z_0 = x_3x_2x_1x_0$) or it holds. If a clock is not at a positive edge, then the value of the registers is held, and does not change.

COUNTERS

Counters can be classified into two broad categories according to the way they are clocked:

- Asynchronous (Ripple) Counters - the first flip-flop is clocked by the external clock pulse, and then each successive flip-flop is clocked by the Q or Q' output of the previous flip-flop.
- Synchronous Counters - all memory elements are simultaneously triggered by the same clock.

Asynchronous (Ripple) Counters

A two-bit asynchronous counter is shown on the left. The external clock is connected to the clock input of the first flip-flop (FF0) only. So, FF0 changes state at the falling edge of each clock pulse, but FF1 changes only when triggered by the falling edge of the Q output of FF0.

Because of the inherent propagation delay through a flip-flop, the transition of the input clock pulse and a transition of the Q output of FF0 can never occur at exactly the same time. Therefore, the flip-flops cannot be triggered simultaneously, producing an asynchronous operation.

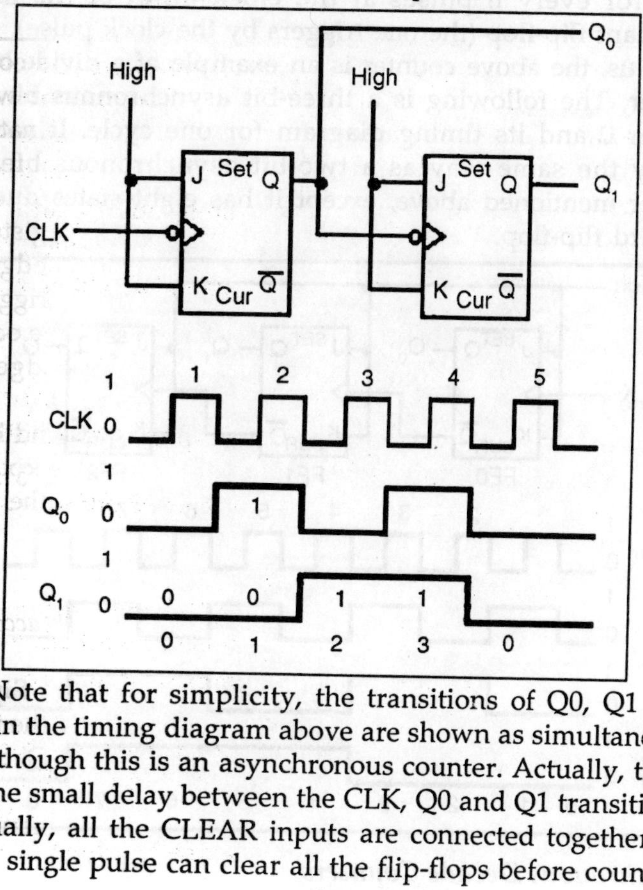

Note that for simplicity, the transitions of Q0, Q1 and CLK in the timing diagram above are shown as simultaneous even though this is an asynchronous counter. Actually, there is some small delay between the CLK, Q0 and Q1 transitions. 0 Usually, all the CLEAR inputs are connected together, so that a single pulse can clear all the flip-flops before counting starts.

The clock pulse fed into FF0 is rippled through the other counters after propagation delays, like a ripple on water, hence the name Ripple Counter. The 2-bit ripple counter circuit above has four different states, each one corresponding to a count value.

Similarly, a counter with n flip-flops can have 2 to the power n states. The number of states in a counter is known as its mod (modulo) number. Thus a 2-bit counter is amod-4 counter. A mod-n counter may also described as a divide-by-n counter. This is because the most significant flip-flop (the furthest flip-flop from the original clock pulse) produces one pulse for every n pulses at the clock input of the least significant flip-flop (the one triggers by the clock pulse).

Thus, the above counter is an example of a divide-by-4 counter. The following is a three-bit asynchronous binary counter 0 and its timing diagram for one cycle. It works exactly the same way as a two-bit asynchronous binary counter mentioned above, except it has eight states due to the third flip-flop.

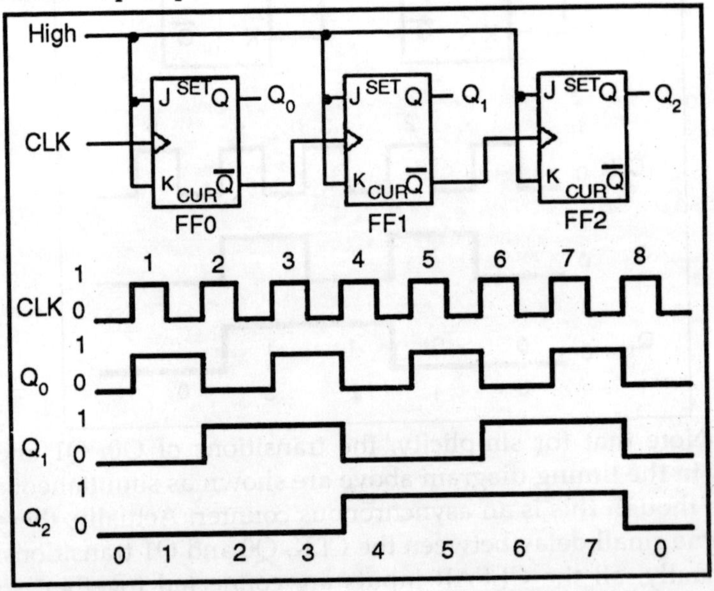

Asynchronous Decade Counters

The binary counters previously introduced have two to the power n states. But counters with states less than this number are also possible. They are designed to have the number of states in their sequences, which are called truncated sequences.

These sequences are achieved by forcing the counter to recycle before going through all of its normal states. A common modulus for counters with truncated sequences is ten. A counter with ten states in its sequence is called a decade counter. The circuit below is an implementation of a decade counter.

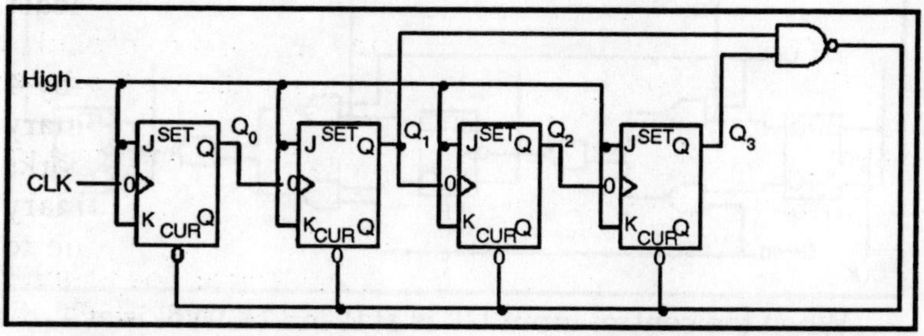

Once the counter counts to ten (1010), all the flip-flops are being cleared. Notice that only Q1 and Q3 are used to decode the count of ten. This is called partial decoding, as none of the other states (zero to nine) have both Q1 and Q3 HIGH at the same time.

The sequence of the decade counter is shown in the table below:

Clock Pulse	Q3	Q2	Q1	Q0
0	0	0	0	0
1	0	0	0	1
2	0	0	1	0
3	0	0	1	1
4	0	1	0	0
5	0	1	0	1
6	0	1	1	0
7	0	1	1	1
8	1	0	0	0
9	1	0	0	1

Asynchronous Up-Down Counters

In certain applications a counter must be able to count both up and down. The circuit below is a 3-bit up-down counter. It counts up or down depending on the status of the control signals UP and DOWN.

When the UP input is at 1 and the DOWN input is at 0, the NAND network between FF0 and FF1 will gate the non-inverted output (Q) of FF0 into the clock input of FF1. Similarly, Q of FF1 will be gated through the other NAND network into the clock input of FF2. Thus the counter will count up.

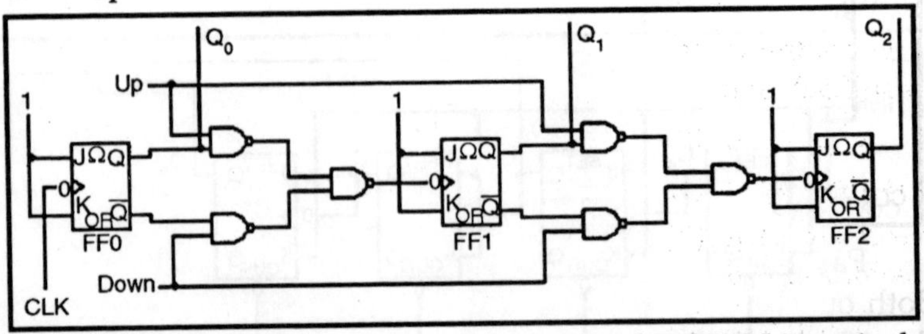

When the control input UP is at 0 and DOWN is at 1, the inverted outputs of FF0 and FF1 are gated into the clock inputs of FF1 and FF2 respectively. If the flip-flops are initially reset to 0's, then the counter will go through the following sequence as input pulses are applied.

FF2	FF1	FF0
0	0	0
1	1	1
1	1	0
1	0	1
1	0	0
0	1	1
0	1	0
0	0	1

Notice that an asynchronous up-down counter is slower than an up counter or a down counter because of the additional propagation delay introduced by the NAND networks.

Synchronous Counters

In synchronous counters, the clock inputs of all the flip-flops are connected together and are triggered by the input pulses. Thus, all the flip-flops change state simultaneously (in parallel). The circuit below is a 3-bit synchronous counter. The J and K inputs of FF0 are connected to HIGH. FF1 has its J and K inputs connected to the output of FF0, and the J and K inputs of FF2 are connected to the output of an AND gate that is fed by the outputs of FF0 and FF1.

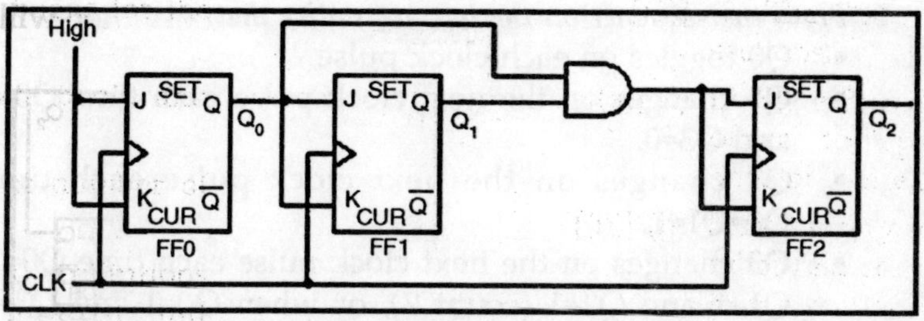

Pay attention to what happens after the 3rd clock pulse. Both outputs of FF0 and FF1 are HIGH. The positive edge of the 4th clock pulse will cause FF2 to change its state due to the AND gate.

Synchronous Decade Counters

Similar to an asynchronous decade counter, a synchronous decade counter counts from 0 to 9 and then recycles to 0 again.

This is done by forcing the 1010 state back to the 0000 state. This so called truncated sequence can be constructed by the following circuit.

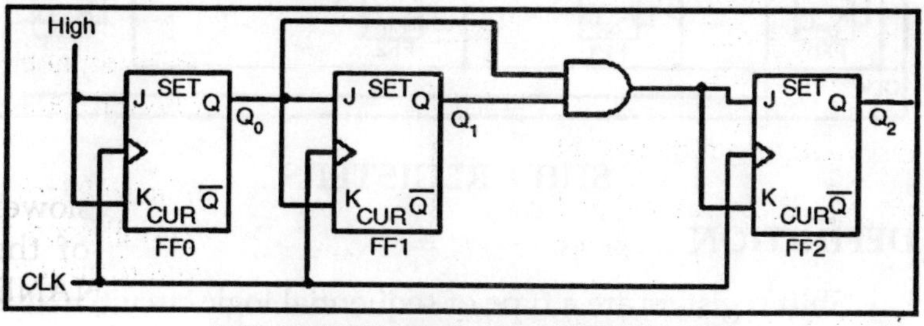

Clock Pulse	Q3	Q2	Q1	Q0
0	0	0	0	0
1	0	0	0	1
2	0	0	1	0
3	0	0	1	1
4	0	1	0	0
5	0	1	0	1
6	0	1	1	0
7	0	1	1	1
8	1	0	0	0
9	1	0	0	1

From the sequence on the left, we notice that:

- Q0 toggles on each clock pulse.
- Q1 changes on the next clock pulse each time Q0=1 and Q3=0.
- Q2 changes on the next clock pulse each time Q0=Q1=1.
- Q3 changes on the next clock pulse each time Q0=1, Q1=1 and Q2=1 (count 7), or when Q0=1 and Q3=1 (count 9).

Synchronous Up-Down Counters

A circuit of a 3-bit synchronous up-down counter and a table of its sequence are shown below. Similar to an asynchronous up-down counter, a synchronous up-down counter also has an up-down control input. It is used to control the direction of the counter through a certain sequence.

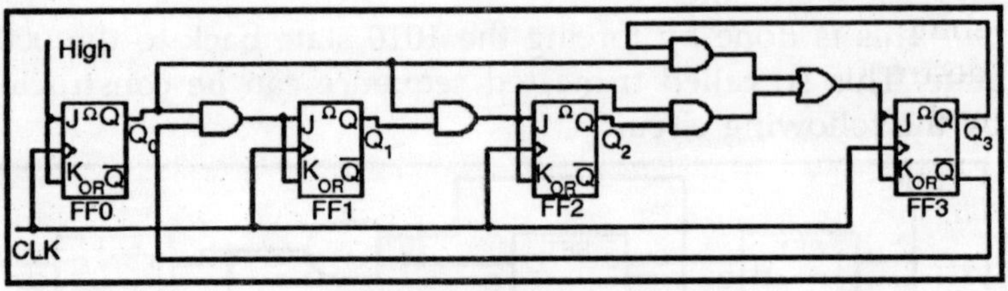

SHIFT REGISTERS

DEFINITION

Shift registers are a type of sequential logic circuit, mainly for storage of digital data. They are a group of flip-flops connected in a chain so that the output from one flip-flop becomes the input of the next flip-flop. Most of the registers possess no characteristic internal sequence of states. All the flip-flops are driven by a common clock, and all are set or reset simultaneously.

SERIAL IN - SERIAL OUT SHIFT REGISTERS

A basic four-bit shift register can be constructed using four D flip-flops, as shown below. The operation of the circuit is as follows. The register is first cleared, forcing all four outputs to zero. The input data is then applied sequentially to the D input of the first flip-flop on the left (FF0).

During each clock pulse, one bit is transmitted from left to right. Assume a data word to be 1001. The least significant bit of the data has to be shifted through the register from FF0 to FF3.

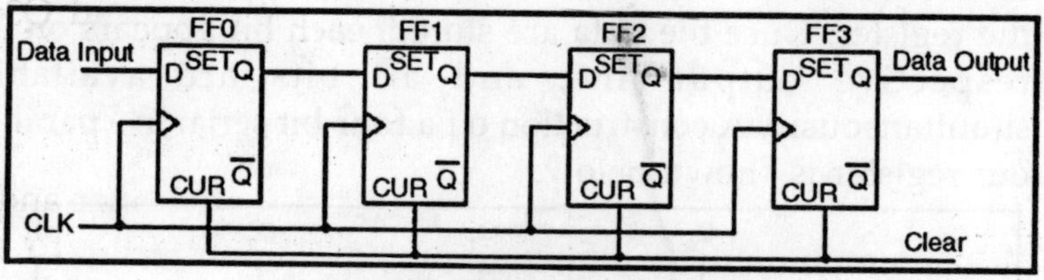

	FF0	FF1	FF2	FF3
Clear	0	0	0	0

In order to get the data out of the register, they must be shifted out serially. This can be done destructively or non-destructively. For destructive readout, the original data is lost and at the end of the read cycle, all flip-flops are reset to zero.

	FF0	FF1	FF2	FF3	
0000	1	0	0	1	0000

To avoid the loss of data, an arrangement for a non-destructive reading can be done by adding two AND gates, an OR gate and an inverter to the system. The construction of this circuit is shown below.

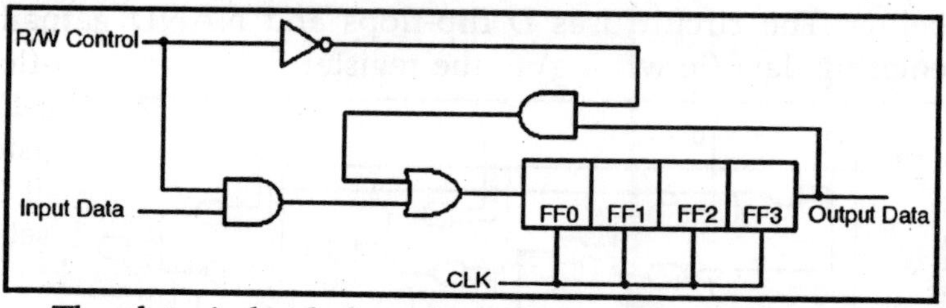

The data is loaded to the register when the control line is HIGH (ie WRITE). The data can be shifted out of the register when the control line is LOW (ie READ). This is shown in the animation below.

Write	FF0	FF1	FF2	FF3
1001	0	0	0	0

SERIAL IN - PARALLEL OUT SHIFT REGISTERS

For this kind of register, data bits are entered serially in the same manner as discussed in the last section. The difference is the way in which the data bits are taken out of the register. Once the data are stored, each bit appears on its respective output line, and all bits are available simultaneously. A construction o f a four-bit serial in - parallel out register is shown below.

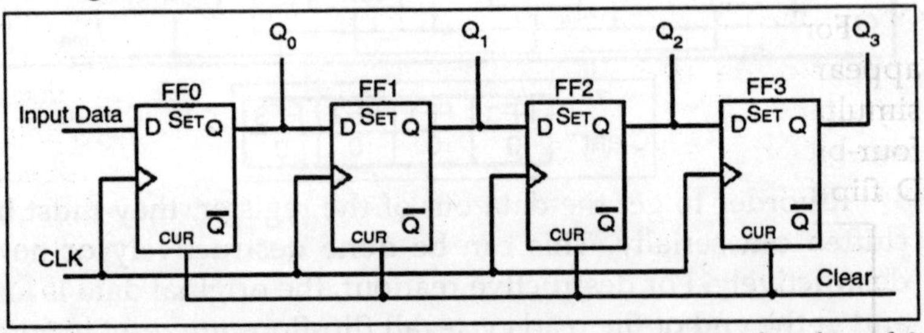

In the animation below, we can see how the four-bit binary number 1001 is shifted to the Q outputs of the register.

Clear	Q0	Q1	Q2	Q3
1001	0	0	0	0

PARALLEL IN - SERIAL OUT SHIFT REGISTERS

A four-bit parallel in - serial out shift register is shown below. The circuit uses D flip-flops and NAND gates for entering data (ie writing) to the register.

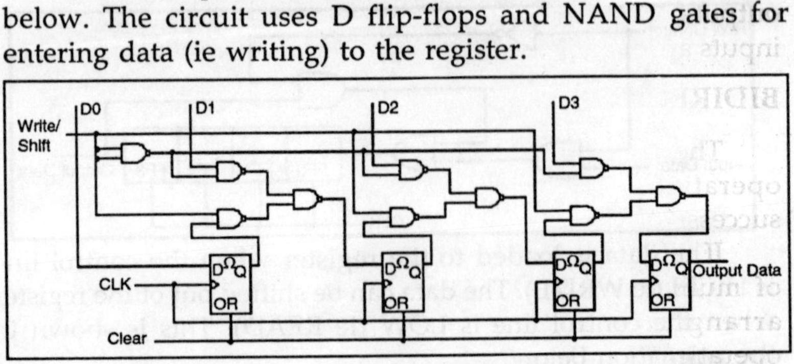

D0, D1, D2 and D3 are the parallel inputs, where D0 is the most significant bit and D3 is the least significant bit. To write data in, the mode control line is taken to LOW and the data is clocked in. The data can be shifted when the mode control line is HIGH as SHIFT is active high. The register performs right shift operation on the application of a clock pulse, as shown in the animation below.

	Q0	Q1	Q2	Q3
Clear	0	0	0	0

PARALLEL IN - PARALLEL OUT SHIFT REGISTERS

For parallel in - parallel out shift registers, all data bits appear on the parallel outputs immediately following the simultaneous entry of the data bits. The following circuit is a four-bit parallel in - parallel out shift register constructed by D flip-flops.

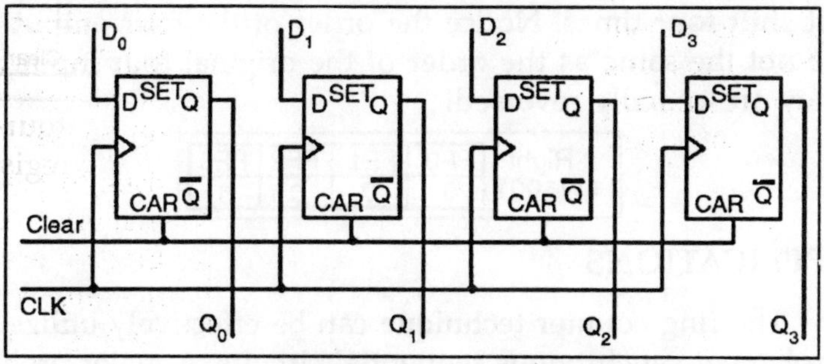

The D's are the parallel inputs and the Q's are the parallel outputs. Once the register is clocked, all the data at the D inputs appear at the corresponding Q outputs simultaneously.

BIDIRECTIONAL SHIFT REGISTERS

The registers discussed so far involved only right shift operations. Each right shift operation has the effect of successively dividing the binary number by two.

If the operation is reversed (left shift), this has the effect of multiplying the number by two. With suitable gating arrangement a serial shift register can perform both operations.

A bidirectional, or reversible, shift register is one in which the data can be shift either left or right. A four-bit bidirectional shift register using D flip-flops is shown below.

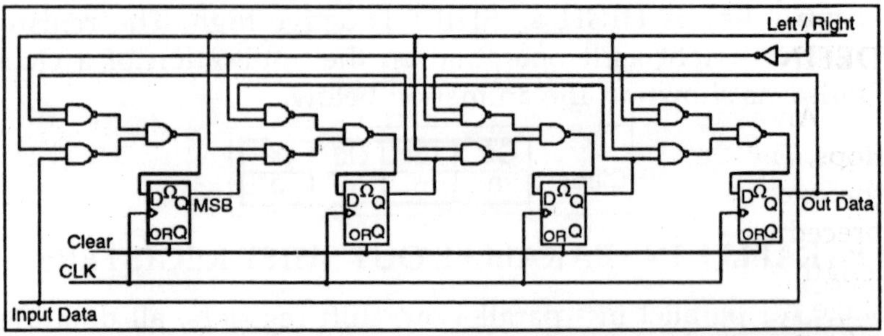

Here a set of NAND gates are configured as OR gates to select data inputs from the right or left adjacent bistables, as selected by the LEFT/RIGHT control line.

The animation below performs right shift four times, then left shift four times. Notice the order of the four output bits are not the same as the order of the original four input bits. They are actually reversed!

Right	FF0	FF1	FF2	FF3
11111001	0	0	0	0

APPLICATIONS

The ring counter technique can be effectively utilized to implement synchronous sequential circuits. A major problem in the realisation of sequential circuits is the assignment of binary codes to the internal states of the circuit in order to reduce the complexity of circuits required. By assigning one flip-flop to one internal state, it is possible to simplify the combinational logic required to Realise the complete sequential circuit.

When the circuit is in a particular state, the flip-flop corresponding to that state is set to HIGH and all other flip-flops remain LOW. A computer or microprocessor-based system commonly requires incoming data to be in parallel format. But frequently, these systems must communicate with external devices that send or receive serial data. So, serial-to-parallel conversion is required. As shown in the previous sections, a serial in - parallel out register can achieve this.

RIPPLE COUNTER

DEFINITION

An n-stage counter that is formed from n cascaded flip-flops. The clock input to each of the individual flip-flops, with the exception of the first, is taken from the output of the preceding one. The count thus ripples along the counter's length due to the propagation delay associated with each stage of counting. A ripple counter contains a chain of flip-flops with the output of each one feeding the input of the next. A flip-flop output changes state every time the input changes from high to low (on the falling-edge). This simple arrangement works well, but there is a slight delay as the effect of the clock'ripples' through the chain of flip-flops.

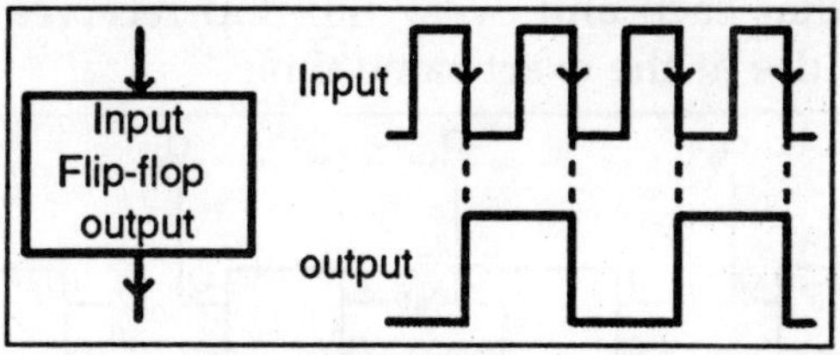

In most circuits the ripple delay is not a problem because it is far too short to be seen on a display. However, a logic system connected to ripple counter outputs will briefly see false counts which may produce'glitches' in the logic system and may disrupt its operation. For example a ripple counter changing from 0111 (7) to 1000 (8) will very briefly show 0110, 0100 and 0000 before 1000!

LINKING RIPPLE COUNTERS

The diagram below shows how to link standard ripple counters. Notice how the highest output QD of each counter drives the clock (CK) input of the next counter. This works because ripple counters have clock inputs that are'active-low' which means-that the count advances as the clock input becomes low, on the falling-edge. Remember that with all ripple counters there will be a slight delay before the later outputs respond to the clock signal, especially with a long counter chain. This is not a problem in simple circuits driving displays, but it may cause glitches in logic systems connected to the counter outputs.

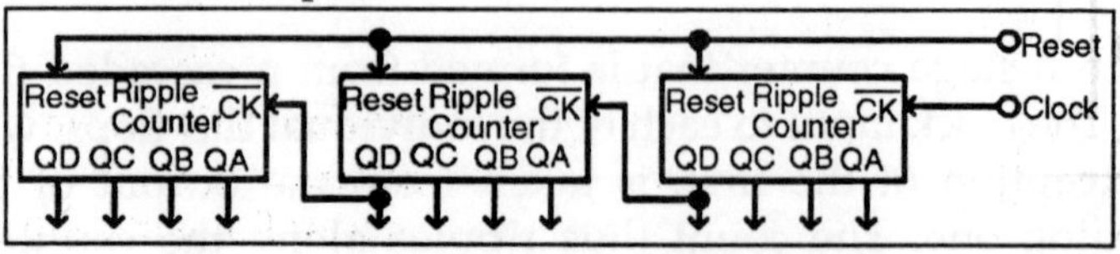

SYNCHRONOUS COUNTER

DESCRIPTION

A synchronous counter, in contrast to an asynchronous counter, is one whose output bits change state simultaneously, with no ripple. The only way we can build such a counter circuit from J-K flip-flops is to connect all the clock inputs together, so that each and every flip-flop receives the exact same clock pulse at the exact same time:

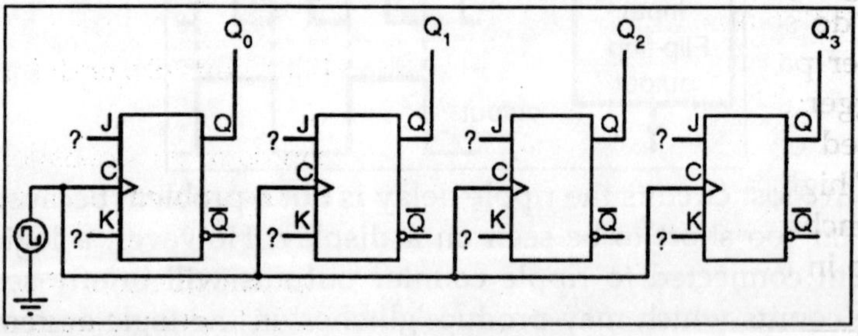

OPERATION

Now, the question is, what do we do with the J and K inputs? We know that we still have to maintain the same divide-by-two frequency pattern in order to count in a binary sequence, and that this pattern is best achieved utilizing the"toggle" mode of the flip-flop, so the fact that the J and K inputs must both be (at times)"high" is clear. However, if we simply connect all the J and K inputs to the positive rail of the power supply as we did in the asynchronous circuit, this would clearly not work because all the flip-flops would toggle at the same time: with each and every clock pulse!

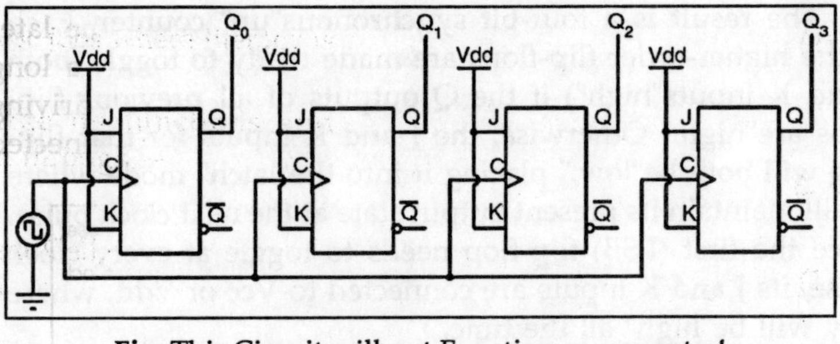

Fig. This Circuit will not Function as a counter!

EXAMPLE

Let's examine the four-bit binary counting sequence again, and see if there are any other patterns that predict the toggling of a bit. Asynchronous counter circuit design is based on the fact that each bit toggle happens at the same time that the preceding bit toggles from a"high" to a"low" (from 1 to 0). Since we cannot clock the toggling of a bit based on the toggling of a previous bit in a synchronous counter circuit (to do so would create a ripple effect) we must find some other pattern in the counting sequence that can be used to trigger a bit toggle: If we enable each J-K flip-flop to toggle based on whether or not all preceding flip-flop outputs (Q) are"high," we can obtain the same counting sequence as the asynchronous circuit without the ripple effect, since each flip-flop in this circuit will be clocked at exactly the same time:

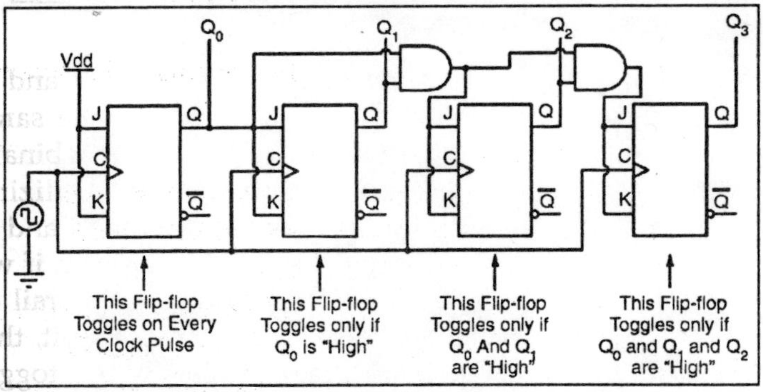

Fig. A Four-bit Synchronous "up" Counter

The result is a four-bit synchronous"up" counter. Each of the higher-order flip-flops are made ready to toggle (both J and K inputs"high") if the Q outputs of all previous flip-flops are"high." Otherwise, the J and K inputs for that flip-flop will both be"low," placing it into the"latch" mode where it will maintain its present output state at the next clock pulse. Since the first (LSB) flip-flop needs to toggle at every clock pulse, its J and K inputs are connected to Vcc or Vdd, where they will be"high" all the time.

The next flip-flop need only"recognize" that the first flip-flop's Q output is high to be made ready to toggle, so no AND gate is needed. However, the remaining flip-flops should be made ready to toggle only when all lower-order output bits are"high," thus the need for AND gates.

3

Computer Organisation and Architecture

REPRESENTING NUMBERS

Humans use base 10, commonly assumed to be due to us having ten fingers. Digital computers use the base 2 or *binary* number representation, each digit of which is known as a *bit* (*b*inary dig*it*). The number of bytes for the exponent and mantissa components of floating point numbers varies. Here, each bit is represented as a voltage that is either "high" or "low," thereby representing "1" or "0," respectively. To represent signed values, we tack on a special bit—the *sign bit*—to express the sign.

The computer's memory consists of an ordered sequence of *bytes*, a collection of eight bits. A byte can therefore represent an unsigned number ranging from 0 to255. If we take one of the bits and make it the sign bit, we can make the same byte to represent numbers ranging from "128to 127. But a computer cannot represent *all* possible real numbers. The fault is not with the binary number system; rather having only a finite number of bytes is the problem. While a gigabyte of memory may seem to be a lot, it takes an infinite number of bits to represent ð.

Since we want to store many numbers in a computer's memory, we are restricted to those. that have a *finite* binary representation. Large integers can be represented by an ordered sequence of bytes. Common lengths, usually expressed in terms of the number of bits, are 16, 32, and 64.

Thus, an unsigned 32-bit number can represent integers ranging between 0 and2^{32}–1 (4,294,967,295), a number almost big enough to enumerate every human in the world.

FIXED-POINT NUMBERS

DESCRIPTION

Fixed-point numbers and their data types are characterized by their word size in bits, binary point, and whether they are signed or unsigned. The Simulink Fixed Point software supports integers, fixed-point numbers. The main difference among these data types is their binary point.

SIGNED FIXED-POINT NUMBERS

Computer hardware typically represents the negation of a binary fixed-point number in three different ways: sign/ magnitude, one's complement, and two's complement. Two's complement is the preferred representation of signed fixed-point numbers and supported by the Simulink Fixed Point software.

Negation using two's complement consists of a bit inversion (translation into one's complement) followed by the addition of a one. For example, the two's complement of 000101 is 111011.

Whether a fixed-point value is signed or unsigned is usually not encoded explicitly within the binary word; that is, there is no sign bit. Instead, the sign information is implicitly defined within the computer architecture.

BINARY POINT INTERPRETATION

The binary point is the means by which fixed-point numbers are scaled. It is usually the software that determines the binary point. When performing basic math functions such as addition or subtraction, the hardware uses the same logic circuits regardless of the value of the scale factor. In essence, the logic circuits have no knowledge of a scale factor. They are performing signed or unsigned fixed-point binary algebra as if the binary point is to the right of b_0.

SCALING

The dynamic range of fixed-point numbers is much less than floating-point numbers with equivalent word sizes. To avoid overflow conditions and minimize quantization errors, fixed-point numbers must be scaled.

With the Simulink Fixed Point, you can select a fixed-point data type whose scaling is defined by its binary point, or you can select an arbitrary linear scaling that suits your needs. This section presents the scaling choices available for fixed-point data types. You can represent a fixed-point number by a general slope and bias encoding scheme.

$$V = \tilde{V} = SQ + B$$

where,

- V is an arbitrarily precise real-world value
- $\tilde{V}$ is the approximate real-world value
- Q, the stored value, is an integer that encodes V
- $S = F\,2^E$ is the slope
- B is the bias

The slope is partitioned into two components:

- 2^E specifies the binary point. E is the fixed power-of-two exponent.
- F is the slope adjustment factor. It is normalized such that $1 \leq F < 2$

Note: S and B are constants and do not show up in the computer hardware directly. Only the quantization value Q is stored in computer memory.

Binary-Point-Only Scaling

Binary-point-only or power-of-two scaling involves moving the binary point within the fixed-point word. The advantage of this scaling mode is to minimize the number of processor arithmetic operations.

With binary-point-only scaling, the components of the general slope and bias formula have the following values:

- $F = 1$
- $S = F2^E = 2^E$
- $B = 0$

The scaling of a quantized real-world number is defined by the slope *S*, which is restricted to a power of two. The negative of the power-of-two exponent is called the fraction length. The fraction length is the number of bits to the right of the binary point.

For Binary-Point-Only scaling, specify fixed-point data types as:

- *Signed types*: Fixdt(1, word length, fraction length)
- *Unsigned types*: Fixdt(0, word length, fraction length)

Integers are a special case of fixed-point data types. Integers have a trivial scaling with slope 1 and bias 0, or equivalently with fraction length 0. Specify integers as

- *Signed integer*: Fixdt(1, word length, 0)
- *Unsigned integer:* Fixdt(0, Word length, 0)

Slope and Bias Scaling

When you scale by slope and bias, the slope *S* and bias *B* of the quantized real-world number can take on any value.

The slope must be a positive number. Using slope and bias, specify fixed-point data types as

- Fixdt(signed, word length, slope, bias)

Unspecified Scaling

Specify fixed-point data types with an unspecified scaling as:

- Fixdt(signed, word length)

Simulink signals, parameters, and states must never have unspecified scaling. When scaling is unspecified, you must use some other mechanism such as automatic best precision scaling to determine the scaling used.

QUANTIZATION

The quantization *Q* of a real-world value *V* is represented by a weighted sum of bits. Within the context of the general slope and bias encoding scheme, the value of an unsigned fixed-point quantity is given by

$$\tilde{V} = S \cdot \left[\sum_{i=0}^{ws-1} b_i 2^i \right] + B$$

while the value of a signed fixed-point quantity is given by:

$$\tilde{V} = S\cdot\left[-b_{WS-1}2^{WS-1} + \sum_{i=0}^{ws-1} b_i 2^i\right] + B$$

where,

- b_i are binary digits, with $b_i = 1, 0$.
- The word size in bits is given by *ws*, with *ws* = 1, 2, 3,..., 128.
- *S* is given by $F\,2^E$, where the scaling is unrestricted because the binary point does not have to be contiguous with the word.
- b_i are called *bit multipliers* and 2^i are called the *weights*.

EXAMPLE: FIXED-POINT FORMAT

Formats for 8-bit signed and unsigned fixed-point values are shown in the following:

0	0	1	1	0	1	0	1	Unsigned Data Type
1	0	1	1	0	1	0	1	Signed Data Type

Note that you cannot discern whether these numbers are signed or unsigned data types merely by inspection since this information is not explicitly encoded within the word. The binary number 0011.0101 yields the same value for the unsigned and two's complement representation because the MSB = 0.

Setting *B* = 0 and using the appropriate weights, bit multipliers, and scaling, the value is

$$\tilde{V} = \left(F2^E\right)\cdot Q = 2^E\left[\sum_{i=0}^{ws-1} b_i 2^i\right]$$

$$= 2^{-4}\cdot\left(0.2^7 + 0\cdot 2^6 + 1\cdot 2^5 + 1\cdot 2^4 + 0\cdot 2^3 + 1\cdot 2^2 + 0\cdot 2^1 + 1\cdot 2^0\right)$$

$$= 3.3125$$

Conversely, the binary number 1011.0101 yields different values for the unsigned and two's complement representation since the MSB = 1.

Setting $B = 0$ and using the appropriate weights, bit multipliers, and scaling, the unsigned value is

$$\tilde{V} = \left(F2^{E}\right)\cdot Q = 2^{E}\left[\sum_{i=0}^{ws-1} b_i 2^i\right]$$

$$= 2^{-4}\cdot\left(0.2^7 + 0\cdot 2^6 + 1\cdot 2^5 + 1\cdot 2^4 + 0\cdot 2^3 + 1\cdot 2^2 + 0\cdot 2^1 + 1\cdot 2^0\right)$$

$$= 11.3125$$

While the two's complement value is

$$\tilde{V} = \left(F2^{E}\right)\cdot Q = 2^{E}\left[-B_{WS-1}2^{WS-1}\sum_{i=0}^{ws-1} b_i 2^i\right]$$

$$= 2^{-4}\cdot\left(0.2^7 + 0\cdot 2^6 + 1\cdot 2^5 + 1\cdot 2^4 + 0\cdot 2^3 + 1\cdot 2^2 + 0\cdot 2^1 + 1\cdot 2^0\right)$$

$$= -4.6875$$

RANGE AND PRECISION

The *range* of a number gives the limits of the representation, while the *precision* gives the distance between successive numbers in the representation. The range and precision of a fixed-point number depends on the length of the word and the scaling.

Range

The range of representable numbers for an unsigned and two's complement fixed-point number of size *ws*, scaling *S*, and bias *B* is illustrated in the following:

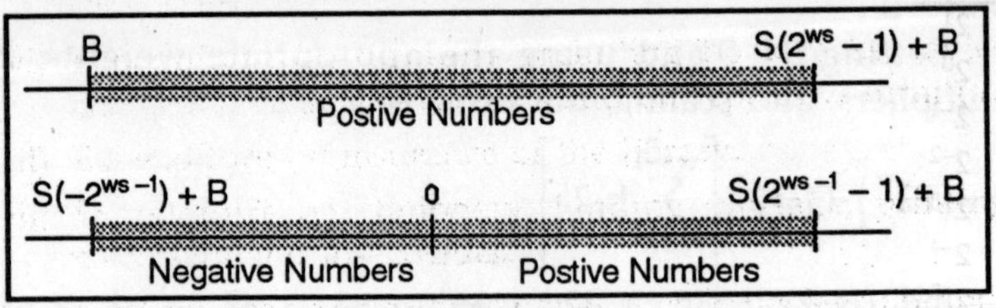

For both the signed and unsigned fixed-point numbers of any data type, the number of different bit patterns is 2^{ws}. For example, if the fixed-point data type is an integer with scaling defined as $S = 1$ and $B = 0$, then the maximum unsigned value is $2^{ws} - 1$, because zero must be represented. In two's complement, negative numbers must be represented as well as zero, so the maximum value is $2^{ws-1} - 1$. Additionally, since there is only one representation for zero, there must be an unequal number of positive and negative numbers. This means there is a representation for -2^{ws-1} but not for 2^{ws-1}.

Precision

The precision of a data type is given by the slope. In this usage, precision means the difference between neighbouring representable values.

FIXED-POINT DATA TYPE PARAMETERS

The low limit, high limit, and default binary-point-only scaling for the supported fixed-point data types discussed in Binary Point Interpretation are given in the following table.

Range of Binary-Point-Only Scaling

The precisions, range of signed values, and range of unsigned values for an 8-bit generalized fixed-point data type with binary-point-only scaling are listed in the follow table. Note that the first scaling value (2^1) represents a binary point that is not contiguous with the word.

Scaling	Precision	Range of signed values (low, high) (low, high)	Range of unsigned values
2^1	2.0	–256, 254	0, 510
2^0	1.0	–128, 127	0, 255
2^{-1}	0.5	–64, 63.5	0, 127.5
2^{-2}	0.25	–32, 31.75	0, 63.75
2^{-3}	0.125	–16, 15.875	0, 31.875
2^{-4}	0.0625	–8, 7.9375	0, 15.9375
2^{-5}	0.03125	–4, 3.96875	0, 7.96875
2^{-6}	0.015625	–2, 1.984375	0, 3.984375
2^{-7}	0.0078125	–1, 0.9921875	0, 1.9921875
2^{-8}	0.00390625	–0.5, 0.49609375	0, 0.99609375

FLOATING POINT NUMBER

There are several ways to represent real numbers on computers. Fixed point places a radix point somewhere in the middle of the digits, and is equivalent to using integers that represent portions of some unit. For example, one might represent 1/100ths of a unit; if you have four decimal digits, you could represent 10.82, or 00.01. Another approach is to use rationals, and represent every number as the ratio of two integers. Floating-point representation - the most common solution - basically represents reals in scientific notation. Scientific notation represents numbers as a base number and an exponent. For example, 123.456 could be represented as 1.23456×10^2. In hexadecimal, the number 123.abc might be represented as $1.23abc \times 16^2$. Floating-point solves a number of representation problems.

Fixed-point has a fixed window of representation, which limits it from representing very large or very small numbers. Also, fixed-point is prone to a loss of precision when two large numbers are divided. Floating-point, on the other hand, employs a sort of "sliding window" of precision appropriate to the scale of the number. This allows it to represent numbers from 1,000,000,000,000 to 0.0000000000000001 with ease.

STORAGE LAYOUT

IEEE floating point numbers have three basic components: the sign, the exponent, and the mantissa. The mantissa is composed of the *fraction*and an implicit leading digit (explained below). The exponent base (2) is implicit and need not be stored.

THE SIGN BIT

The sign bit is as simple as it gets. 0 denotes a positive number; 1 denotes a negative number. Flipping the value of this bit flips the sign of the number.

THE EXPONENT

The exponent field needs to represent both positive and negative exponents. To do this, a *bias* is added to the actual exponent in order to get the stored exponent. For IEEE single-precision floats, this value is 127. Thus, an exponent of zero means that 127 is stored in the exponent field. A stored value of 200 indicates an exponent of (200-127), or 73. For reasons discussed later, exponents of -127 (all 0s) and +128 (all 1s) are reserved for special numbers. For double precision, the exponent field is 11 bits, and has a bias of 1023.

THE MANTISSA

The *mantissa,* also known as the *significant,* represents the precision bits of the number. It is composed of an implicit leading bit and the fraction bits. To find out the value of the implicit leading bit, consider that any number can be expressed in scientific notation in many different ways.

For example, the number five can be represented as any of these:

5.00×10^0

0.05×10^2

5000×10^{-3}

In order to maximize the quantity of representable numbers, floating-point numbers are typically stored in *normalized* form. This basically puts the radix point after the first non-zero digit. In normalized form, five is represented as 5.0×10^0.

A nice little optimization is available to us in base two, since the only possible non-zero digit is 1. Thus, we can just assume a leading digit of 1, and don't need to represent it explicitly. As a result, the mantissa has effectively 24 bits of resolution, by way of 23 fraction bits.

PUTTING IT TOGETHER

So, to sum up:

- The sign bit is 0 for positive, 1 for negative.
- The exponent's base is two.
- The exponent field contains 127 plus the true exponent for single-precision, or 1023 plus the true exponent for double precision.
- The first bit of the mantissa is typically assumed to be 1.*f*, where *f* is the field of fraction bits.

RANGES OF FLOATING-POINT NUMBERS

Let's consider single-precision floats for a second. Note that we're taking essentially a 32-bit number and re-jiggering the fields to cover a much broader range. Something has to give, and it's precision.

For example, regular 32-bit integers, with all precision centered around zero, can precisely store integers with 32-bits of resolution. Single-precision floating-point, on the other hand, is unable to match this resolution with its 24 bits. It does, however, approximate this value by effectively truncating from the lower end. For example:

```
  11110000 11001100 10101010 00001111//32-
bit integer
  = +1.1110000 11001100 10101010 x 2^31    //
Single- Precision Float
  = 11110000 11001100 10101010 00000000    //
Corresponding Value
```

This approximates the 32-bit value, but doesn't yield an exact representation. On the other hand, besides the ability to represent fractional components (which integers lack completely), the floating-point value can represent numbers around 2^{127}, compared to 32-bit integers maximum value around 2^{32}.

FIXED VS FLOATING POINT

Digital Signal Processing can be divided into two categories, fixed point and floating point. These refer to the format used to store and manipulate numbers within the devices. Fixed point DSPs usually represent each number with a minimum of 16 bits, although a different length can be used. For instance, Motorola manufactures a family of fixed point DSPs that use 24 bits.

There are four common ways that these 2^{16} = 65536 possible bit patterns can represent a number. In unsigned integer, the stored number can take on any integer value from 0 to 65,535. Similarly, signed integer uses two's complement to make the range include negative numbers, from –32,768 to 32,767. With unsigned fraction notation, the 65,536 levels are spread uniformly between 0 and 1. Lastly, the signed fraction format allows negative numbers, equally spaced between –1 and 1. In comparison, floating point DSPs typically use a minimum of 32 bits to store each value. This results in many more bit patterns than for fixed point, $2^{32} = 4,294,967,296$ to be exact. A key feature of floating point notation is that the represented numbers are *not* uniformly spaced. In the most common format (ANSI/IEEE Std. 754 -1985), the largest and smallest numbers are $\pm 3.4 \times 10^{38}$ and 1.2×10^{-38}, respectively.

The represented values are unequally spaced between these two extremes, such that the gap between any two numbers is about ten-million times smaller than the value of the numbers. This is important because it places large gaps between large numbers, but small gaps between small numbers.

All floating point DSPs can also handle fixed point numbers, a necessity to implement counters, loops, and signals coming from the ADC and going to the DAC. However, this doesn't mean that fixed point math will be carried out as quickly as the floating point operations; it depends on the internal architecture.

For instance, the SHARC DSPs are optimized for both floating point and fixed point operations, and executes them with equal efficiency. For this reason, the SHARC devices are often referred to as "32-bit DSPs," rather than just "Floating Point." On the other hand, fixed point DSPs have traditionally been cheaper than floating point devices.

Nothing changes more rapidly than the price of electronics; anything you find in a book will be out-of-date before it is printed. Nevertheless, cost is a key factor in understanding how DSPs are evolving, and we need to give you a general idea. If you want to find out what the prices are *today,* you need to look *today.*

Now let's turn our attention to *performance;* what can a 32-bit floating point system do that a 16-bit fixed point can't? The answer to this question is signal-to-noise ratio. Suppose we store a number in a 32 bit floating point format. As previously mentioned, the gap between this number and its adjacent neighbour is about one ten-millionth of the value of the number. To store the number, it must be round up or down by a maximum of one-half the gap size. In other words, each time we store a number in floating point notation, we add *noise* to the signal. The same thing happens when a number is stored as a 16-bit fixed point value, except that the added noise is much worse.

This is because the gaps between adjacent numbers are much larger. For instance, suppose we store the number 10,000 as a signed integer (running from –32,768 to 32,767). The gap between numbers is one ten-thousandth of the value of the number we are storing. If we want to store the number 1000, the gap between numbers is only one one-thousandth of the value.

Noise in signals is usually represented by its *standard deviation*. For here, the important fact is that the standard deviation of this quantization noise is about one-third of the gap size. This means that the signal-to-noise ratio for storing a floating point number is about 30 million to one, while for a fixed point number it is only about ten-thousand to one. In other words, floating point has roughly 30,000 times less quantization noise than fixed point.

This brings up an important way that DSPs are different from traditional microprocessors. Suppose we implement an FIR filter in fixed point. To do this, we loop through each coefficient, multiply it by the appropriate sample from the input signal, and add the product to an accumulator. Here's the problem.

In traditional microprocessors, this accumulator is just another 16 bit fixed point variable. To avoid overflow, we need to scale the values being added, and will correspondingly add quantization noise on each step. In the worst case, this quantization noise will simply add, greatly lowering the signal-to-noise ratio of the system. For instance, in a 500 coefficient FIR filter, the noise on each output sample may be 500 times the noise on each input sample. The signal-to-noise ratio of *ten-thousand to one* has dropped to a ghastly *twenty to one.* Although this is an extreme case, it illustrates the main point: when many operations are carried out on each sample, it's bad, really bad. DSPs handle this problem by using an extended precision accumulator.

This is a special register that has 2-3 times as many bits as the other memory locations. For example, in a 16 bit DSP it may have 32 to 40 bits, while in the SHARC DSPs it contains 80 bits for fixed point use. This extended range virtually eliminates round-off noise while the accumulation is in progress.

The only round-off error suffered is when the accumulator is scaled and stored in the 16 bit memory. This strategy works very well, although it does limit how some algorithms must be carried out. In comparison, floating point has such low quantization noise that these techniques are usually not necessary. In addition to having lower quantization noise, floating point systems are also easier to develop algorithms for. Most DSP techniques are based on repeated multiplications and additions.

In fixed point, the possibility of an overflow or underflow needs to be considered after each operation. The programmer needs to continually understand the amplitude of the numbers, how the quantization errors are accumulating, and what scaling needs to take place. In comparison, these issues do not arise in floating point; the numbers take care of themselves (except in rare cases).

To give you a better understanding of this issue, Fig. below shows a table from the SHARC user manual. This describes the ways that multiplication can be carried out for both fixed and floating point formats. First, look at how floating point numbers can be multiplied; there is only one way!

Fixed point		**Floating point**
$\left\lvert\begin{matrix}\text{Rn}\\\text{MRF}\\\text{MRB}\end{matrix}\right\rvert^{=\text{Rx*Ry}}$	$\left(\left\lvert\begin{matrix}\text{S}\\\text{U}\end{matrix}\right\rvert\left\lvert\begin{matrix}\text{S}\\\text{U}\end{matrix}\right\rvert\left\lvert\begin{matrix}\text{F}\\\text{I}\\\text{FR}\end{matrix}\right\rvert\right)$	Fn = Fx* Fy

$$\left|\begin{array}{l} Rn = MRF \\ MRF = MRB \\ MRF = MRF \\ MRB = MRB \end{array}\right|^{\pm Rx*Ry} \qquad \left(\left|\begin{array}{c} S \\ U \end{array}\right|\left|\begin{array}{c} S \\ U \end{array}\right|\left|\begin{array}{c} F \\ I \\ FR \end{array}\right|\right)$$

$$\left|\begin{array}{l} Rn = MRF \\ Rn = MRB \\ MRF = MRF \\ MRB = MRB \end{array}\right|^{\pm Rx*Ry} \qquad \left(\left|\begin{array}{c} S \\ U \end{array}\right|\left|\begin{array}{c} S \\ U \end{array}\right|\left|\begin{array}{c} F \\ I \\ FR \end{array}\right|\right)$$

$$\left|\begin{array}{l} Rn = SATMRF \\ Rn = SATMRB \\ MRF = SATMRF \\ MRB = SATMRB \end{array}\right| \qquad \left|\begin{array}{c} (SI) \\ (UI) \\ (SF) \\ (UF) \end{array}\right|$$

$$\left|\begin{array}{l} Rn = RNDMRF \\ Rn = RNDMRB \\ MRF = RNDMRF \\ MRB = RNDMRB \end{array}\right| \qquad \left|\begin{array}{c} (SI) \\ (UF) \end{array}\right|$$

$$\left|\begin{array}{l} MRF \\ MRB \end{array}\right|^{=0}$$

$$\left|\begin{array}{l} MRxF \\ MRxB \end{array}\right|^{=Rn}$$

$$Rn = \left|\begin{array}{l} MRxF \\ MRxB \end{array}\right|$$

That is, Fn = Fx * Fy, where Fn, Fx, and Fy are any of the 16 data registers. It could not be any simpler. In comparison, look at all the possible commands for fixed point multiplication. These are the many options needed to efficiently handle the problems of round-off, scaling, and format.

In Fig. above shows, Rn, Rx, and Ry refer to any of the 16 data registers, and MRF and MRB are 80 bit accumulators. The vertical lines indicate *options*. For instance, the top-left entry in this table means that all the following are valid commands: Rn = Rx * Ry, MRF = Rx * Ry, and MRB = Rx * Ry. In other words, the value of any two registers can be multiplied and placed into another register, or into one of the extended precision accumulators. This table also shows that the numbers may be either signed or unsigned (S or U), and may be fractional or integer (F or I). The RND and SAT options are ways of controlling rounding and register overflow. There are other details and options in the table, but they are not important for our present discussion.

The important idea is that the fixed point programmer must understand *dozens* of ways to carry out the very basic task of multiplication. In contrast, the floating point programmer can spend his time concentrating on the algorithm. Given these tradeoffs between fixed and floating point, how do you choose which to use? Here are some things to consider.

First, look at how many bits are used in the ADC and DAC. In many applications, 12-14 bits per sample is the crossover for using fixed versus floating point. For instance, television and other video signals typically use 8 bit ADC and DAC, and the precision of fixed point is acceptable. In comparison, professional audio applications can sample with as high as 20 or 24 bits, and almost certainly need floating point to capture the large dynamic range.

The next thing to look at is the complexity of the algorithm that will be run. If it is relatively simple, think fixed point; if it is more complicated, think floating point. For example, FIR filtering and other operations in the time domain only require a few dozen lines of code, making them suitable for fixed point. In contrast, frequency domain algorithms, such as spectral analysis and FFT convolution, are very detailed and can be much more difficult to programme. While they can be written in fixed point, the development time will be greatly reduced if floating point is used.

Lastly, think about the money: how important is the cost of the product, and how important is the cost of the development? When fixed point is chosen, the cost of the product will be reduced, but the development cost will probably be higher due to the more difficult algorithms. In the reverse manner, floating point will generally result in a quicker and cheaper development cycle, but a more expensive final product.

IEEE STANDARDS

IEEE reserves exponent field values of all 0s and all 1s to denote special values in the floating-point scheme.

ZERO

As mentioned above, zero is not directly representable in the straight format, due to the assumption of a leading 1 (we'd need to specify a true zero mantissa to yield a value of zero). Zero is a special value denoted with an exponent field of zero and a fraction field of zero. Note that –0 and +0 are distinct values, though they both compare as equal.

DENORMALIZED

If the exponent is all 0s, but the fraction is non-zero (else it would be interpreted as zero), then the value is a *denormalized* number, which does *not* have an assumed leading 1 before the binary point. Thus, this represents a number $(-1)^s \times 0.f \times 2^{-126}$, where s is the sign bit and f is the fraction. For double precision, denormalized numbers are of the form $(-1)^s \times 0.f \times 2^{-1022}$. From this you can interpret zero as a special type of denormalized number.

INFINITY

The values +infinity and -infinity are denoted with an exponent of all 1s and a fraction of all 0s. The sign bit distinguishes between negative infinity and positive infinity. Being able to denote infinity as a specific value is useful because it allows operations to continue past overflow situations. *Operations with infinite values are well defined in IEEE floating point.*

NOT A NUMBER

The value NaN (*Not a Number*) is used to represent a

value that does not represent a real number. NaN's are represented by a bit pattern with an exponent of all 1s and a non-zero fraction. There are two categories of NaN: QNaN (*Quiet NaN*) and SNaN (*Signalling NaN*).

A QNaN is a NaN with the most significant fraction bit set. QNaN's propagate freely through most arithmetic operations. These values pop out of an operation when the result is not mathematically defined.

An SNaN is a NaN with the most significant fraction bit clear. It is used to signal an exception when used in operations. SNaN's can be handy to assign to uninitialized variables to trap premature usage.

SPECIAL OPERATIONS

Operations on special numbers are well-defined by IEEE. In the simplest case, any operation with a NaN yields a NaN result.

Other operations are as follows:

Operation	Result
n ÷ ±Infinity	0
±Infinity × ±Infinity	±Infinity
±nonzero ÷ 0	±Infinity
Infinity + Infinity	Infinity
±0 ÷ ±0	NaN
Infinity - Infinity	NaN
±Infinity ÷ ±Infinity	NaN
±Infinity × 0	NaN

ERROR CODING

Error coding is a method of providing reliable digital data transmission and storage when the communication medium used has an unacceptable bit error rate (BER) and a low signal-to-noise ratio (SNR).

Error coding is used in many digital applications like computer memory, magnetic and optical data storage media, satellite and deep space communications, network communications, and cellular telephone networks. Rather than transmitting digital data in a raw bit for bit form, the data is encoded with extra bits at the source. The longer "code word" is then transmitted, and the receiver can decode it to retrieve the desired information. The extra bits transform the data into a valid code word in the coding scheme. The space of valid code words is smaller than the space of possible bit strings of that length, therefore the destination can recognize invalid code words.

If errors are introduced during transmission, they will likely be detected during the decoding process at the destination because the code word would be transformed into an invalid bit string. Given a data string to be transmitted that is k bits long, there are 2^k possible bit strings that the data can be. Error coding assumes the worst case scenario that the information to be encoded can be any of these bit strings. Therefore there will be 2^k valid code words. The code words will be n bits long, where $n > k$. So just having extra bits in the data transmission eliminates many of the possible 2^n bit strings as valid code words.

Perhaps the simplest example of error coding is adding a parity check bit. A bit string to be transmitted has a single bit concatenated to it to make a code word for transmission. The bit is a 1 or a 0 depending on the parity. If odd parity is being used, the parity bit will be added such that the sum of 1's in the code word is odd. If even parity is being used, the sum of 1's in the code word must be even.

The data can be four possible bit combinations, so the code word space is four out of the eight possible 3-bit strings. Here we are using odd parity. When data is transmitted using this coding scheme, any bit strings with even parity will be rejected because they are not valid code words. This simple coding scheme is limited because it can only detect an odd number of bit errors from the original data, and has no error correcting capabilities.

There are many other methods of error coding that provide better protection at the expense of increased bandwidth and complexity. The error detecting and correcting capabilities of a particular coding scheme is correlated with its code rate and complexity. The code rate is the ratio of data bits to total bits transmitted in the code words. A high code rate means information content is high and coding overhead is low. However, the fewer bits used for coding redundancy, the less error protection is provided. A tradeoff must be made between bandwidth availability and the amount of error protection required for the communication.

SHANNON'S THEOREM

Error coding techniques are based on information coding theory, an area developed from work. The theory states that a given code with a code rate R that is less than the communication channel capacity C, a code exists, for a block length of n bits, with code rate R that can be transmitted over the channel with an arbitrarily small probability of error.

Theoretically, we should be able to devise a coding scheme for a particular communication channel for any error rate, but no one has been able to develop a code that satisfies Shannon's theorem. This would indicate that there is still much work to be done improving error coding techniques. Cryptography, the method of encrypting data for security rather than reliability.

TRADEOFFS

When choosing a coding scheme for error protection, the types of errors that tend to occur on the communication channel must be considered. There are two types of errors that can occur on a communication channel: random bit errors and burst errors.

A channel that usually has random bit errors will tend to have isolated bit flips during data transmissions and the bit errors are independent of each other. A channel with burst errors will tend to have clumps of bit errors that occur during one transmission. Error codes have been developed to specifically protect against both random bit errors and burst errors.

Real-time systems must consider tradeoffs between coding delay and error protection. A coding scheme with high error-correcting capabilities will take longer to decode and will be non-deterministic. This could cause a missed deadline and failure if a piece of needed information is stuck being decoded. In embedded systems, error coding is especially important because the system may be used in critical applications and cannot tolerate errors. Coding schemes are becoming increasingly complex and probabilistic, making implementation of encoders and decoders in software attractive.

Since processing power is relatively fast and cheap, software coding is more feasible. However, software is much more prone to design defects and errors, making the coding algorithm less reliable. Pushing complexity into software introduces more errors in design and implementation.

TOOLS, TECHNIQUES, AND METRICS

There are two major types of coding schemes: linear block codes and convolutional codes. Linear block codes are characterized by segmenting a message into separate blocks of a fixed length, and encoding each block one at a time for transmission. Convolutional codes encode the entire data stream into one long code word and transmit it in pieces.

LINEAR BLOCK CODES

Linear block codes are so named because each code word in the set is a linear combination of a set of generator code words. If the messages are k bits long, and the code words are n bits long (where n > k), there are k linearly independent code words of length n that form a generator matrix. To encode any message of k bits, you simply multiply the message vector u by the generator matrix to produce a code word vector v that is n bits long.

Linear block codes are very easy to implement in hardware, and since they are algebraically determined, they can be decoded in constant time. They have very high code rates, usually above 0.95. They have low coding overhead, but they have limited error correction capabilities. They are very useful in situations where the BER of the channel is relatively low, bandwidth availability is limited in the transmission, and it is easy to retransmit data. One class of linear block codes used for high-speed computer memory are SEC/DED (single-error-correcting/double-error-detecting) codes. In high speed memory, bandwidth is limited because the cost per bit is relatively high compared to low-speed memory like disks.

The error rates are usually low and tend to occur by the byte so a SEC/DED coding scheme for each byte provides sufficient error protection. Error coding must be fast in this situation because high throughput is desired. SEC/DED codes are extremely simple and do not cause a high coding delay.

CRC CODES

Cyclic Redundancy Check (CRC) codes are a special subset of linear block codes that are very popular in digital communications. CRC codes have the cyclic shift property; when any code word is rotated left or right by any number of bit digits, the resulting string is still a word in the code space. This property makes encoding and decoding very easy and efficient to implement by using simple shift registers. The main drawback of using CRC codes is that they have only error detecting capabilities.

They cannot correct for any errors in the data once detected at the destination, and the data must be transmitted again to receive the message. For this reason, CRC codes are usually used in conjunction with another code that provides error correction. If CRC codes are the only ones used for an application, the raw BER of the channel is usually extremely low, and data is not time-critical. They are good for magnetic and optical storage, where a simple retransmit request to correct bit errors is feasible.

CONVOLUTIONAL CODES

Convolutional codes are generally more complicated than linear block codes, more difficult to implement, and have lower code rates (usually below 0.90), but have powerful error correcting capabilities. They are popular in satellite and deep space communications, where bandwidth is essentially unlimited, but the BER is much higher and retransmissions are infeasible. Convolutional codes are more difficult to decode because they are encoded using finite state machines that have branching paths for encoding each bit in the data sequence.

A well-known process for decoding convolutional codes quickly is the Viterbi Algorithm. The Viterbi algorithm is a maximum likelihood decoder, meaning that the output code word from decoding a transmission is always the one with the highest probability of being the correct word transmitted from the source.

ERROR DETECTION

The aim of an error detection technique is to enable the receiver of a message transmitted through a noisy (error-introducing) channel to determine whether the message has been corrupted. To do this, the transmitter constructs a value (called a checksum) that is a function of the message, and appends it to the message. The receiver can then use the same function to calculate the checksum of the received message and compare it with the appended checksum to see if the message was correctly received. For example, if we chose a checksum function which was simply the sum of the bytes in the message mod 256 (*i.e.* modulo 256), then it might go something as follows. All numbers are in decimal.

Message: 6 23 4

Message with checksum: 6 23 4 33

Message after transmission: 6 27 4 33

In the above, the second byte of the message was corrupted from 23 to 27 by the communications channel. However, the receiver can detect this by comparing the transmitted checksum (33) with the computer checksum of 37 (6 + 27 + 4). If the checksum itself is corrupted, a correctly transmitted message might be incorrectly identified as a corrupted one.

However, this is a safe-side failure. A dangerous-side failure occurs where the message and/or checksum is corrupted in a manner that results in a transmission that is internally consistent. Unfortunately, this possibility is completely unavoidable and the best that can be done is to minimize its probability by increasing the amount of information in the checksum (*e.g.* widening the checksum from one byte to two bytes).

Other error detection techniques exist that involve performing complex transformations on the message to inject it with redundant information. However, this document addresses only CRC algorithms, which fall into the class of error detection algorithms that leave the data intact and append a checksum on the end. *i.e.*:

NEED FOR COMPLEXITY

In the checksum example in the previous section, we saw how a corrupted message was detected using a checksum algorithm that simply sums the bytes in the message mod 256:

Message: 6 23 4

Message with checksum: 6 23 4 33

Message after transmission: 6 27 4 33

A problem with this algorithm is that it is too simple. If a number of random corruptions occur, there is a 1 in 256 chance that they will not be detected. For example:

Message: 6 23 4

Message with checksum: 6 23 4 33

Message after transmission: 8 20 5 33

To strengthen the checksum, we could change from an 8-bit register to a 16-bit register (*i.e.* sum the bytes mod 65536 instead of mod 256) so as to apparently reduce the probability of failure from 1/256 to 1/65536.

While basically a good idea, it fails in this case because the formula used is not sufficiently "random"; with a simple summing formula, each incoming byte affects roughly only one byte of the summing register no matter how wide it is. For example, in the second example above, the summing register could be a Megabyte wide, and the error would still go undetected. This problem can only be solved by replacing the simple summing formula with a more sophisticated formula that causes each incoming byte to have an effect on the entire checksum register. Thus, we see that at least two aspects are required to form a strong checksum function: *Width*: A register width wide enough to provide a low a-priori probability of failure (*e.g*. 32-bits gives a 1/2^32 chanceof failure). *Chaos*: A formula that gives each input byte the potential to change any number of bits in the register.

The term "checksum" was presumably used to describe early summing formulas, but has now taken on a more general meaning encompassing more sophisticated algorithms such as the CRC ones. The CRC algorithms to be described satisfy the second condition very well, and can be configured to operate with a variety of checksum widths.

BASIC ALGORITHMS

Where might we go in our search for a more complex function than summing? All sorts of schemes spring to mind. We could construct tables using the digits of pi, or hash each incoming byte with all the bytes in the register. We could even keep a large telephone book on-line, and use each incoming byte combined with the register bytes to index a new phone number which would be the next register value.

The possibilities are limitless.However, we do not need to go so far; the next arithmetic step suffices. While addition is clearly not strong enough to form an effective checksum, it turns out that division is, so long as the divisor is about as wide as the checksum register.

The basic idea of CRC algorithms is simply to treat the message as an enormous binary number, to divide it by another fixed binary number, and to make the remainder from this division the checksum. Upon receipt of the message, the receiver can perform the same division and compare the remainder with the "checksum" (transmitted remainder).

ERROR-CORRECTING CODES

INTRODUCTION

The theory of error detecting and correcting codes is that branch of engineering and mathematics which deals with the reliable transmission and storage of data. Information media are not 100% reliable in practice, in the sense that noise (any form of interference) frequently causes data to be distorted. To deal with this undesirable but inevitable situation, some form of redundancy is incorporated in the original data. With this redundancy, even if errors are introduced (up to some tolerance level), the original information can be recovered, or at least the presence of errors can be detected.

We saw in class how adding to the original message the parity bit or the arithmetic sum allows the detection of a (certain type of) error. However, that kind of redundancy doesn't allow for the correction of the error. Error-correcting codes do exactly this: they add redundancy to the original message in such a way that it is possible for the receiver to detect the error and correct it, recovering the original message. This is crucial for certain applications where the re-sending of the message is not possible (for example, for interplanetary communications and storage of data). The crucial problem to be resolved then is how to add this redundancy in order to detect and correct as many errors as possible in the most efficient way.

APPLICATIONS

The increasing reliance on digital communication and the emergence of the digital computer as an essential tool in a technological society have placed error-correcting codes in a most prominent position. We cite here a few specific applications, in an attempt to indicate their practicality and importance. Many computers now have error-correcting capabilities built into their random access memories; it is less expensive to compensate for errors through the use of error-correcting codes than to build integrated circuits that are 100% reliable.

The single error-correcting Hamming codes, and linear codes in general, are of use here. Disk storage is another area of computing where error-coding is employed. Storage capacity has been greatly increased through the use of disks of higher and higher density. With this increase in density, error probability also increases, and therefore information is now stored on many disks using error-correcting codes. In 1972, the *Mariner* space probe flew past Mars and transmitted pictures back to earth. The channel for such transmissions is space and the earth's atmosphere. Solar activity and atmospheric conditions can introduce errors into weak signals coming from the spacecraft.

In order that most of the pictures sent could be correctly recovered here on earth, the following coding scheme was used. The source alphabet consisted of 64 shades of gray. The source encoder encoded each of these into binary 6-tuples and the channel encoder produced binary 32-tuples. The source decoder could correct up to 7 errors in any 32-tuple. This was done with the Reed-Muller codes. The *Voyager* probes began transmitting colour pictures of Jupiter. For colour pictures the source alphabet needed to be much larger and was chosen to have 4096 colour shades.

The source encoder produced binary 12-tuples for each colour shade and the channel encoder produced 24-tuples (*i.e.* 24 dimensional vectors). This code would correct up to 3 errors in any 24-tuple, and is the Golay code. The increasing popularity of digital audio is due in part to the powerful error-correcting codes that the digitization process facilitates. Information is typically stored on a small aluminized disk as a series of microscopic pits and smooth areas, the pattern representing a sequence of 0's and 1's.

A laser beam is used as the playback mechanism to retrieve stored data. Because the data is digital, error correction schemes can be easily incorporated into such a system. Given an error-coded digital recording, a digital audio system can on playback, correct errors introduced by fingerprints, scratches, or even imperfections originally present in the storage medium. The compact disc system pioneered by Philips Corporation of the Netherlands in cooperation with Sony Corporation of Japan, allowing playback of pre-recorded digital audio disks, is an excellent example of the application of error-correcting codes to digital communication; *crossinterleaved Reed-Solomon* codes are used for error correction in this system. Digital audio tape (DAT) systems have also been developed, allowing digital recording as well as playback. Error-correcting codes are particularly suited when the transmission channel is noisy. This is the case of wireless communication. Nowadays, all digital wireless communications use error-correcting codes.

FUNDAMENTAL CONCEPTS

Let A be an alphabet of q symbols. For example, A = {a,b,c,...,z) is the standard lower case alphabet for the English language, and A = (0,1) is the binary alphabet.

Definition: A block code of length n containing M codewords over the alphabet A is a set of M n-tuples where each n-tuple takes its components from A. We refer to such a block code as an [n,M]-code over A.

In practice, we most frequently take A to be the binary alphabet. Given a code C of block length n over an alphabet A, those specific n-tuples over A which are in C are referred to as codeword's. Note that while the channel encoder transmits codeword's, the n-tuples received by the channel decoder may or may not be codeword's, due to the possible occurrence of errors during transmission.

ISSUES IN THE DESIGN OF ERROR-CORRECTING CODES

Designing a good code is a very hard problem. Also, lots of factors need to be taken in account. For instance, in practice the code should be designed appropriately depending on the expected rate of errors for the particular channel being employed.

If it is known that the probability that the channel will introduce 2 errors into any transmitted codeword is extremely small, then it is likely not necessary to construct a code that will correct all 2-bit error patterns. A single error correcting code will likely suffice. Conversely, if double errors are frequent and a single error correcting code is being used, then decoding errors will be frequent. From this brief introduction, a number of questions arise.

- Given n, M and d, can we determine if an [n Al] code with distance d exists?
- Assuming such a code does exist, how would one be constructed in practice?
- How should information k-tuples be associated with codeword n-tuples to facilitate efficient channel encoding?
- How should channel decoding be performed?

Lets examine the issue of channel decoding in greater detail. When a word is received and it's not a codeword, finding the closest codeword involves computing the distance from the received word to each codeword, requiring M comparisons. While this might be acceptable for small M, in practice we usually find M quite large.

Suppose a code C is used with M = 2^50 codeword's, which is not unrealistic. If we could carry out 1 million distance computations per second, it would take around 20 years to make a single correction. Clearly, this is not tolerable and more efficient techniques are required. Wishing to retain the nearest neighbour decoding strategy, we seek more efficient techniques for its implementation.

The theory of error-correcting code is concerned with constructing codes for various values of n, M and d, and the consideration of appropriate encoding and decoding techniques. Most of the best known codes are algebraic in nature like the linear codes. Linear codes are an important and general class of error-correcting codes.

For example, the*BCH codes* used for CDs are linear codes. They are heavily mathematical and an appropriate description here is not possible. The next session describes instead the last "discovery" in the theory of error correcting codes, the Turbo codes.

TURBO CODES

In this we introduced the Nearest Neighbour Decoding, we didn't mention the fact that what the decoding actually does is maximizing the probability P(r|c) that r is received, given that c is sent. *i.e.* choosing the nearest codeword is equivalent to choosing the most likely input message c given the received tuple r. This decoding strategy is known as maximum likelihood decoding.

We can then state the decoding problem in the following manner. Let U be the original message, X the encoded message and Y the message received after the noisy channel. This is schematized in the following figure.

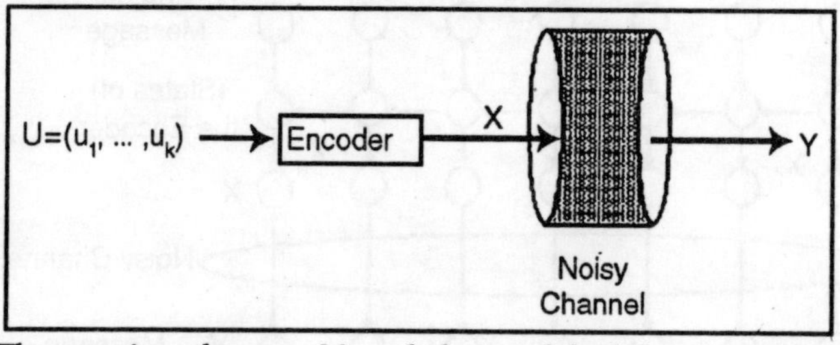

The receiver knows Y and the *model* of the encoder, *i.e.* is has a knowledge of how the original message was originally encoded. The problem now is finding the U that maximizes the probability that U was sent given that Y was received, *i.e.* the probability P(U | Y).

Having stated the decoding problem in probabilistic terms, we can take advantage of various methods that deal with probability estimations. A class of such methods is the class of graphical models. The simplest graphical model:

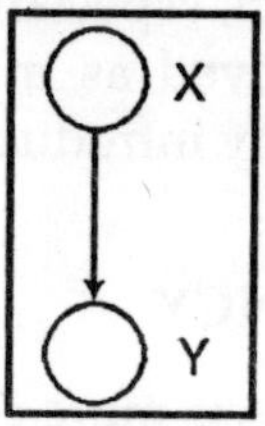

A classical problem of probability estimation is finding the probability distribution P(X | Y) where X and Y are 2 random variables. The graphical model framework allows for such probability estimations to be calculated in an efficient way. Note that the calculation of P(X | Y) from P(Y | X) and P(X) is just Bayes rule - P(X | Y) = P(Y | X)P(X)/P(Y) - and that graphical model inference algorithms can be viewed as generalizations of Bayes rule to arbitrary graphs.

Lets now see how we can view error correcting codes as graphical models. In the figure below, a convolution code as a graphical model. Let U be the original message, X the encoded message and Y the message received after the noisy channel.

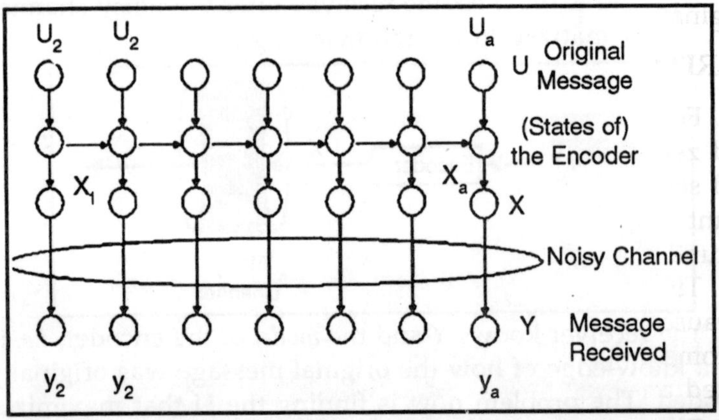

Now, the decoding problem of finding U that maximizes p(U|Y) can be tackled within the framework of graphical models.

ERROR CORRECTION METHOD

Errors introduced by communications faults, noise or other failures into valid data, especially compressed data were redudancy has been removed as much as possible, can be detected and/or corrected by introducing redundancy into the data stream.

SAFETY IN REDUNDANCY

More redundancy detects more errors, at the cost of more data transmitted. We could simply send each message 3 times, and discard any copy that disagrees with the other two. This is a simple example of a "perfect" code, although it is far from perfect, it is called that because it adds exactly enough redundancy to detect or correct some number of errors.

In this case, not that many. Note that although it is unlikely, it IS possible that the two identical copies both happened to have the exact same error, and the third copy is the correct one. If each copy arrived different in some way, we might have detected two errors. Error detection and correction systems are rated by how much redundancy they cost, and how many errors they can detect or correct. In this example three "symbols" are used, each is the length of the original message. It can detect two errors, and correct one.

PARITY

For example, if we send some specific sequence of ones and zeros, and then count the number of ones that we sent and send an extra 1 if that count is odd or an extra 0 if that count is even, then we have introduced a small amount of redundancy into the transmission.

The extra bit is called the parity bit, it is even parity because it makes the total number of 1's in the transmission become an even number, and is a simple example of what is called an "extended" code. The receiver can then count up the number of 1 bits they received, perform the same calculation, and if the result does not match the extra bit we sent them, they will know that an error occurred.

They have no way of knowing which bit was wrong, and if two bits were changed in value (a 1 to a 0 and a 0 to a 1) then the errors would pass undetected.

COST/BENEFIT

Our first example, sending a message three times, costs a lot more than our second example of even parity, and doesn't do much more. A slightly more complex parity system will give us the same advantages of the 3x repetition and for 'x' bits, cost only a few extra bits.

If we divide our bits up into rows and columns, which is pretty normal anyway, we can calculate a parity for each row, and for each column. Column parity is commonly referred to as an LRC.

When a single bit error occurs, we can tell which row it's in by checking the parity bit for that row, and the bit of that byte which is wrong will be shown by the incorrect parity of that column. For 8 bytes of data, the 64 bits have been protected against any 1 bit error, and a 2 bit error would be detectable, if not correctable. The cost is 8 column parity bits (one for each bit in a byte) and 9 row parity bits (one for each byte, and one more for the byte of column parity bits) for a total of 17 bits or 26% redundancy.

This would be written as [81,64,3] meaning that 81 bits are used to transmit 64 bits of data and changing any one bit in the data must change the extra error checking bits by at least 3. Note: Flipping 2 bits must cause the value to change by a value of at least three.

HAMMING CODES

IDEA

Hamming code is a set of error-correction code s that can be used to detect and correct bit errors that can occur when computer data is moved or stored. Hamming code is named for R.W. Hamming of Bell Labs.

Like other error-correction code, Hamming code makes use of the concept of parity and parity bit s, which are bits that are added to data so that the validity of the data can be checked when it is read or after it has been received in a data transmission. Using more than one parity bit, an error-correction code can not only identify a single bit error in the data unit, but also its location in the data unit.

In data transmission, the ability of a receiving station to correct errors in the received data is called forward error correction (FEC) and can increase throughput on a data link when there is a lot of noise present. To enable this, a transmitting station must add extra data (called *error correction bits*) to the transmission.

However, the correction may not always represent a cost saving over that of simply resending the information. Hamming codes make FEC less expensive to implement through the use of a *block parity* mechanism.

Computing parity involves counting the number of ones in a unit of data, and adding either a zero or a one (called a *parity bit*) to make the count odd (for odd parity) or even (for even parity). For example, 1001 is a 4-bit data unit containing two one bits; since that is an even number, a zero would be added to maintain even parity, or, if odd parity was being maintained, another one would be added. To calculate even parity, the XOR operator is used; to calculate odd parity, the XNOR operator is used. Single bit errors are detected when the parity count indicates that the number of ones is incorrect, indicating that a data bit has been flipped by noise in the line. Hamming codes detect two bit errors by using more than one parity bit, each of which is computed on different combinations of bits in the data. The number of parity bits required depends on the number of bits in the data transmission, and is calculated by the Hamming rule:

pd + p + 1 < = 2 (1)

Where *d* is the number of data bits and *p* is the number of parity bits. The total of the two is called the Hamming code word, which is generated by multiplying the data bits by a generator matrix .

DESCRIPTION

Hamming code is an error-detecting and error-correcting code, used in data transmission, that can (a) detect all single- and double-bit errors and which correct all single-bit errors. It was named after its inventor: Richard Hamming.

A Hamming code satisfies the relation $2^m \geq n+1$, where *n* is the total number of bits in the block, *k* is the number of information bits in the block, and *m* is the number of check bits in the block, where $m = n - k$.

Hamming Codes in Action

Let us examine the Hamming (7, 4) code.

We write a matrix

$$H = \begin{pmatrix} 0 & 0 & 0 & 1 & 1 & 1 & 1 \\ 0 & 1 & 1 & 0 & 0 & 1 & 1 \\ 1 & 0 & 1 & 0 & 1 & 0 & 1 \end{pmatrix}$$

(note each column is a binary digit) and we create a codeword vector:

$$c = (a \quad b \quad d_0 \quad c \quad d_1 \quad d_2 \quad d_3)^T$$

where *a, b,* and *c* are check digits, created by making the multiplication Hc=0.

Writing out the multiplication, we end up with

$a=d_0+d_1+d_3$,
$b=d_0+d_2+d_3$
$c=d_1+d_2+d_3$

and we send the codeword c with these values. On decoding, assume *one* error has occurred in the received codeword r. (this Hamming code cannot detect when more than one error has occurred).

If no error has occurred, we have constructed the codeword to be sent so Hc=0 so we can check this. Say an error has occurred in the *i*th place, so $r=c+e_i$ where e_i is a vector with a 1 in the *i*th place and zeroes otherwise.

Then

$Hr=Hc+He_i$

Now Hc=0, so

$Hr=0+He_i=He_i$

picking out the *i*th column of H, and thus since this column is a binary digit (say *k*), we can correct the error in the *k*th place of the received codeword.

CODE GENERATION

To illustrate what an error-correcting code (ECC) can do, I decided to implement a family of codes, the *Hamming codes,* which can correct one error per word, because these are exceedingly simple to encode and decode and they correspond to perfect sphere packings. The smallest interesting Hamming code is a (7, 4) linear code.

This means:

- The encoded words are seven bits long.
- The original message words are four bits long.
- Any two encoded words add up to a third encoded word.

This business about addition is a seemingly minor detail, and you can safely ignore it, but it is a key property to making the encoding and decoding very simple. The following table shows the entire (7, 4) Hamming code.

Message word	Encoded word
0000	0000 000
0001	0001 111
0010	0010 110
0011	0011 001
0100	0100 101
0101	0101 010
0110	0110 011
0111	0111 100
1000	1000 011
1001	1001 100
1010	1010 101
1011	1011 010
1100	1100 110
1101	1101 001
1110	1110 000
1111	1111 111

Formulas like this make it simple and quick to encode each block of four message bits. Technically, such formulas are maintained in data structures call "generator matrices." For decoding purposes, instead of one checksum, there are three.

In any valid encoded word:

- The sum of bits two through five must be zero. That is, there must be an even number of ones in places two through five.
- The sum of bits one, three, four, and six must be zero.
- The sum of bits one, two, four, and seven must be zero.

Technically, such checksums are maintained in data structures called "parity-check matrices." Now suppose one or more of these checksums is one.

Surely an error has occurred. We know it is possible to fix it (assuming only one bit of the seven was altered in the channel). But how do we figure it out? For the (7,4) Hamming code, we have three checksums, each of which is either zero or one. At least one of them is a one when an error has occurred. If we write the three checksums down in order, this gives seven possible sequences: 001, 010, 011, 100, 101, 110, and 111. Each of these can be read as a binary number, giving values ranging from 1 through 7. The binary value tells us the location of the bit that changed.

For example, suppose we want to transmit a 0110 block through the channel. It will be encoded as 0110001. Imagine that the fourth bit is changed during transmission from 0 to 1, so that 0111001 is received. The checksums are 1, 0, 0. In binary that's a four, telling us the fourth bit is incorrect. So we flip it back to a 0, drop the three check bits (they have done their job), and record a 0110 as having been received. Mission accomplished!

As I indicated earlier, there is more than one Hamming code. For every integer m >= 3, there is a (2^m–1, 2^m–1–m) Hamming code. The first three combinations are (7, 4), (15, 11), and (31, 26). The latter, for instance, adds five check bits to each block of 26 message bits, enabling detection of a single error in each sequence of 26 message bits. That's less protection against errors than the one-out-of-four for the (7, 4) Hamming code, but it's much more efficient, since messages expand in length only by 31/26 instead of by 7/4. As always, there is a trade-off between ability to correct errors and level of redundancy.

Constructing the Hamming codes is simple but difficult to describe without introducing specialized terminology from coding theory. If you are curious how it's done, check out the Avenue script Hamming. Make for creating generator and parity-check matrices for any Hamming code.

COMPUTER ORGANIZATION AND ARCHITECTURE

OVERVIEW

In describing computer system, a distinction is often made between computer architecture and computer organization. Computer architecture refers to those attributes of a system visible to a programmer, or put another way, those attributes that have a direct impact on the logical execution of a programme. Computer organization refers to the operational units and their interconnection that realise the architecture specification. Examples of architecture attributes include the instruction set, the number of bit to represent various data types (*e.g..*, numbers, and characters), I/O mechanisms, and technique for addressing memory.

Examples of organization attributes include those hardware details transparent to the programmer, such as control signals, interfaces between the computer and peripherals, and the memory technology used. As an example, it is an architectural design issue whether a computer will have a multiply instruction.

It is an organizational issue whether that instruction will be implemented by a special multiply unit or by a mechanism that makes repeated use of the add unit of the system. The organization decision may be bases on the anticipated frequency of use of the multiply instruction, the relative speed of the two approaches, and the cost and physical size of a special multiply unit.

Historically, and still today, the distinction between architecture and organization has been an important one. Many computer manufacturers offer a family of computer model, all with the same architecture but with differences in organization. Consequently, the different models in the family have different price and performance characteristics. Furthermore, an architecture may survive many years, but its organization changes with changing technology.

STRUCTURE AND FUNCTION

A computer is a complex system; contemporary computers contain million of elementary electronic components. How, then, can one clearly describe them? The key is to recognize the hierarchical nature of most complex system. A hierarchical system is a set of interrelated subsystem, each of the later, in turn, hierarchical in structure until we reach some lowest level of elementary subsystem.

The hierarchical nature of complex systems is essential to both their design and their description. The designer need only deal with a particular level of the system at a time. At each level, the system consists of a set of components and their interrelationships. The behaviour at each level depends only on a simplified, abstracted characterization of the system at the next lower level.

At each level, the designer is concerned with structure and function:

- *Structure*: The way in which the components are interrelated.
- *Function*: The operation of each individual component as part of the structure.

In term of description, we have two choices: starting at the bottom and building up to a complete description, or beginning with a top view and decomposing the system, describing their structure and function, and proceed to successively lower layer of the hierarchy. The approach taken in this course follows the latter.

Function

In general terms, there are four main functions of a computer:

- Data processing
- Data storage
- Data movement
- Control

It is also essential that a computer store data. Even if the computer is processing data on the fly (*i.e.*, data come in and get processed, and the results go out immediately), the computer must temporarily store at least those pieces of data that are being worked on at any given moment.

Thus, there is at least a short-term data storage function. Files of data are stored on the computer for subsequent retrieval and update. The computer must be able to move data between itself and the outside world.

The computer's operating environment consists of devices that serve as either sources or destinations of data. When data are received from or delivered to a device that is directly connected to the computer, the process is known as input-output (I/O), and the device is referred to as a peripheral. When data are moved over longer distances, to or from a remote device, the process is known as data communications.

Finally, there must be control of there three functions. Ultimately, this control is exercised by the individual who provides the computer with instructions. Within the computer system, a control unit manages the computer's resources and orchestrates the performance of its functional parts in response to those instructions. At this general level of discussion, the number of possible operations that can be performed is few. The figure depicts the four possible types of operations.

The computer can function as a data movement device as shown in Figure, simply transferring data from one peripheral or communications line to another. It can also function as a data storage device as shown in Figure, with data transferred from the external environment to computer storage (read) and vice versa (write). The final two diagrams show operations involving data processing, on data either in storage or in route between storage and the external environment.

Structure

The computer is an entity that interacts in some fashion with its external environment. In general, all of its linkages to the external environment can be classified as peripheral devices or communication lines.

We will have something to say about both types of linkages:

- *Central processing unit (CPU)*: Controls the operation of the computer and performs its data processing functions. Often simply referred to as processor.
- *Main memory*: Stores data.
- *I/O*: Moves data between the computer and its external environment.
- *System interconnection*: Some mechanism that provides for communication among CPU, main memory, and I/O.

There may be one or more of each of the above components. Traditionally, there has been just a single CPU. In recent years, there has been increasing use of multiple processors, in a single system. However, for our purpose, the most interesting and in some ways the most complex component is the CPU; its structure is depicted in Figure.

Its major structural components are:

- *Control unit (CU)*: Controls the operation of the CPU and hence the computer.
- *Arithmetic and logic unit (ALU)*: Performs computer's data processing functions.
- *Register*: Provides storage internal to the CPU.
- *CPU interconnection*: Some mechanism that provides for communication among the control unit, ALU, and register.

COMPUTER TYPES

Since the invention of computers from first generation and fourth generation computers, they have been classified according to their types and how they operate that is input, process and output information. Below you will get a brief discussion on various types of Computers we have Computer types can be divided into 3 categories according to electronic nature. Types of computers are classified according to how a particular Computer functions.

These computer types are:

- Analogue Computers
- Digital Computers
- Hybrid Computers

ANALOGUE COMPUTERS

Analogue types of Computer uses what is known as analogue signals that are represented by a continuous set of varying voltages and are used in scientific research centers, hospitals and flight centers. The analog computer is almost an extinct type of computer these days. It is different from a digital computer in respect that it can perform numerous mathematical operations simultaneously. It is also unique in terms of operation as it utilizes continuous variables for the purpose of mathematical computation. It utilizes mechanical, hydraulic, or electrical energy or operation. With analogue types of computer no values are represented by physical measurable quantities *e.g.* voltages. Analogue computer types programme arithmetic and logical operations by measuring physical changes *i.e.* temperatures or pressure.

DIGITAL COMPUTER TYPE

With these types of computers operation are on electrical input that can attain two inputs, states of ON=1 and state of OFF = 0. With digital type of computers data is represented by digital of 0 and 1 or off state and on state. Digital computer type recognizes data by counting discrete signal of (0 0r 1), they are high speed programmable; they compute values and stores results. After looking at the Digital computer type and how it functions will move to the third computer type as mentioned above.

HYBRID TYPE OF COMPUTER

Hybrid computer types are very unique, in the sense that they combined both analogue and digital features and operations. These types of computers are, as the name suggests, a combination of both Analog and Digital computers. The Digital computers which work on the principle of binary digit system of "0" and "1" can give very precise results.

But the problem is that they are too slow and incapable of large scale mathematical operation. In the hybrid types of computers the Digital counterparts convert the analog signals to perform Robotics and Process control. With Hybrid computers operate by using digital to analogue convertor and analogue to digital convertor. By linking the two types of computer above you come up with this new computer type called Hybrid.

OTHER TYPES

Supercomputer and Mainframe

Supercomputer is a broad term for one of the fastest computers currently available. Supercomputers are very expensive and are employed for specialized applications that require immense amounts of mathematical calculations (number crunching). For example, weather forecasting requires a supercomputer. Other uses of supercomputers scientific simulations, (animated) graphics, fluid dynamic calculations, nuclear energy research, electronic design, and analysis of geological data (*e.g.* in petrochemical prospecting). Perhaps the best known supercomputer manufacturer is Cray Research. Mainframe was a term originally referring to the cabinet containing the central processor unit or "main frame" of a room-filling Stone Age batch machine.

After the emergence of smaller "minicomputer" designs in the early 1970s, the traditional big iron machines were described as "mainframe computers" and eventually just as mainframes. Nowadays a Mainframe is a very large and expensive computer capable of supporting hundreds, or even thousands, of users simulta-neously. The chief difference between a supercomputer and a mainframe is that a supercomputer channels all its power into executing a few programmes as fast as possible, whereas a mainframe uses its power to execute many programmes concurrently.

In some ways, mainframes are more powerful than supercomputers because they support more simultaneous programmes. But supercomputers can execute a single programme faster than a mainframe. The distinction between small mainframes and minicomputers is vague, depending really on how the manufacturer wants to market its machines.

Minicomputer

It is a midsize computer. In the past decade, the distinction between large minicomputers and small mainframes has blurred, however, as has the distinction between small minicomputers and workstations. But in general, a minicomputer is a multiprocessing system capable of supporting from up to 200 users simultaneously.

Workstation

It is a type of computer used for engineering applications

(CAD/CAM), desktop publishing, software development, and other types of applications that require a moderate amount of computing power and relatively high quality graphics capabilities. Workstations generally come with a large, high-resolution graphics screen, at large amount of RAM, built-in network support, and a graphical user interface. Most workstations also have a mass storage device such as a disk drive, but a special type of workstation, called a diskless workstation, comes without a disk drive.

The most common operating systems for workstations are UNIX and Windows NT. Like personal computers, most workstations are single-user computers. However, workstations are typically linked together to form a local-area network, although they can also be used as stand-alone systems.

N.B.: In networking, workstation refers to any computer connected to a local-area network. It could be a workstation or a personal computer.

Personal Computer

It can be defined as a small, relatively inexpensive computer designed for an individual user. In price, personal computers range anywhere from a few hundred pounds to over five thousand pounds. All are based on the microprocessor technology that enables manufacturers to put an entire CPU on one chip.

Businesses use personal computers for word processing, accounting, desktop publishing, and for running spreadsheet and database management applications. At home, the most popular use for personal computers is for playing games and recently for surfing the Internet.

Personal computers first appeared in the late 1970s. One of the first and most popular personal computers was the Apple II, introduced in 1977 by Apple Computer. During the late 1970s and early 1980s, new models and competing operating systems seemed to appear daily. Then, in 1981, IBM entered the fray with its first personal computer, known as the IBM PC. The IBM PC quickly became the personal computer of choice, and most other personal computer manufacturers fell by the wayside. P.C. is short for personal computer or IBM PC. One of the few companies to survive IBM's onslaught was Apple Computer, which remains a major player in the personal computer marketplace. Other companies adjusted to IBM's dominance by building IBM clones, computers that were internally almost the same as the IBM PC, but that cost less.

Because IBM clones used the same microprocessors as IBM PCs, they were capable of running the same software. Over the years, IBM has lost much of its influence in directing the evolution of PCs. Therefore after the release of the first PC by IBM the term PC increasingly came to mean IBM or IBM-compatible personal computers, to the exclusion of other types of personal computers, such as Macintoshes.

In recent years, the term PC has become more and more difficult to pin down. In general, though, it applies to any personal computer based on an Intel microprocessor, or on an Intel-compatible microprocessor. For nearly every other component, including the operating system, there are several options, all of which fall under the rubric of PC. Today, the world of personal computers is basically divided between Apple Macintoshes and PCs. The principal characteristics of personal computers are that they are single-user systems and are based on microprocessors.

However, although personal computers are designed as single-user systems, it is common to link them together to form a network. In terms of power, there is great variety. At the high end, the distinction between personal computers and workstations has faded. High-end models of the Macintosh and PC offer the same computing power and graphics capability as low-end workstations by Sun Microsystems, Hewlett-Packard, and DEC.

Actual personal computers can be generally classified by size and chassis/case. The chassis or case is the metal frame that serves as the structural support for electronic components. Every computer system requires at least one chassis to house the circuit boards and wiring. The chassis also contains slots for expansion boards. If you want to insert more boards than there are slots, you will need an expansion chassis, which provides additional slots. There are two basic flavours of chassis designs–desktop models and tower models–but there are many variations on these two basic types. Then come the portable computers that are computers small enough to carry. Portable computers include notebook and sub notebook computers, hand-held computers, palmtops, and PDAs.

Tower Model

The term refers to a computer in which the power supply, motherboard, and mass storage devices are stacked on top of each other in a cabinet. This is in contrast to desktop models, in which these components are housed in a more compact box. The main advantage of tower models is that there are fewer space constraints, which makes installation of additional storage devices easier.

Desktop Model

A computer designed to fit comfortably on top of a desk, typically with the monitor sitting on top of the computer. Desktop model computers are broad and low, whereas tower model computers are narrow and tall. Because of their shape, desktop model computers are generally limited to three internal mass storage devices. Desktop models designed to be very small are sometimes referred to as slimline models.

Notebook Computer

An extremely lightweight personal computer. Notebook computers typically weigh less than 6 pounds and are small enough to fit easily in a briefcase. Aside from size, the principal difference between a notebook computer and a personal computer is the display screen. Notebook computers use a variety of techniques, known as flat-panel technologies, to produce a lightweight and non-bulky display screen. The quality of notebook display screens varies considerably. In terms of computing power, modern notebook computers are nearly equivalent to personal computers. They have the same CPUs, memory capacity, and disk drives. However, all this power in a small package is expensive. Notebook computers cost about twice as much as equivalent regular-sized computers.

Notebook computers come with battery packs that enable you to run them without plugging them in. However, the batteries need to be recharged every few hours.

Laptop Computer

A small, portable computer — small enough that it can sit on your lap. Nowadays, laptop computers are more frequently called notebook computers.

Sub Notebook Computer

A portable computer that is slightly lighter and smaller than a full-sized notebook computer. Typically, subnotebook computers have a smaller keyboard and screen, but are otherwise equivalent to notebook computers.

Hand-held Computer

A portable computer that is small enough to be held in one's hand. Although extremely convenient to carry, handheld computers have not replaced notebook computers because of their small keyboards and screens. The most popular hand-held computers are those that are specifically designed to provide PIM (personal information manager) functions, such as a calendar and address book.

Some manufacturers are trying to solve the small keyboard problem by replacing the keyboard with an electronic pen. However, these pen-based devices rely on handwriting recognition technologies, which are still in their infancy. Hand-held computers are also called PDAs, palmtops and pocket computers.

Palmtop

A small computer that literally fits in your palm. Compared to full-size computers, palmtops are severely limited, but they are practical for certain functions such as phone books and calendars. Palmtops that use a pen rather than a keyboard for input are often called hand-held computers or PDAs. Because of their small size, most palmtop computers do not include disk drives. However, many contain PCMCIA slots in which you can insert disk drives, modems, memory, and other devices. Palmtops are also called PDAs, hand-held computers and pocket computers.

PDA

Short for personal digital assistant, a handheld device that combines computing, telephone/fax, and networking features. A typical PDA can function as a cellular phone, fax sender, and personal organizer. Unlike portable computers, most PDAs are pen-based, using a stylus rather than a keyboard for input.

This means that they also incorporate handwriting recognition features. Some PDAs can also react to voice input by using voice recognition technologies. The field of PDA was pioneered by Apple Computer, which introduced the Newton MessagePad in 1993.

Shortly thereafter, several other manufacturers offered similar products. To date, PDAs have had only modest success in the marketplace, due to their high price tags and limited applications. However, many experts believe that PDAs will eventually become common gadgets. PDAs are also called palmtops, hand-held computers and pocket computers.

CLASSIFICATION OF COMPUTERS

Computers are classified according to their data processing speed, amount of data that they can hold and price. Generally, a computer with high processing speed and large internal storage is called a big computer. Due to rapidly improving technology, we are always confused among the categories of computers.

Depending upon their speed and memory size, computers are classified into following four main groups:

- Supercomputer.

- Mainframe computer.
- Mini computer.
- Microcomputer.

SUPERCOMPUTER

Supercomputer is the most powerful and fastest, and also very expensive. It was developed in 1980s. It is used to process large amount of data and to solve the complicated scientific problems. It can perform more than one trillions calculations per second. It has large number of processors connected parallel.

So parallel processing is done in this computer. In a single supercomputer thousands of users can be connected at the same time and the supercomputer handles the work of each user separately.

Supercomputer are mainly used for:

- Weather forecasting.
- Nuclear energy research.
- Aircraft design.
- Automotive design.
- Online banking.
- To control industrial units.

The supercomputers are used in large organizations, research laboratories, aerospace centers, large industrial units etc. Nuclear scientists use supercomputers to create and analyse models of nuclear fission and fusions, predicting the actions and reactions of millions of atoms as they interact. The examples of supercomputers are CRAY-1, CRAY-2, Control Data CYBER 205 and ETA A-10 etc.

MAINFRAME COMPUTERS

Mainframe computers are also large-scale computers but supercomputers are larger than mainframe. These are also very expensive. The mainframe computer specially requires a very large clean room with air-conditioner.

This makes it very expensive to buy and operate. It can support a large number of various equipments. It also has multiple processors. Large mainframe systems can handle the input and output requirements of several thousand of users. For example, IBM, S/390 mainframe can support 50,000 users simultaneously. The users often access then mainframe with terminals or personal computers. Tere are basically two types of terminals used with mainframe systems. These are:

Dumb Terminal

Dumb terminal does not have its own CPU and storage devices. This type of terminal uses the CPU and storage devices of mainframe system. Typically, a dumb terminal consists of monitor and a keyboard (or mouse).

Intelligent Terminal

Intelligent terminal has its own processor and can perform some processing operations. Usually, this type of terminal does not have its own storage. Typically, personal computrers are used as intelligent terminals. A personal computer as an intelligent terminal gives facility to access data and other services from mainframe system. It also enables to store and process data locally.

The mainframe computers are specially used as servers on the World Wide Web. The mainframe computers are used in large organizations such as Banks, Airlines and Universities etc. where many people (users) need frequent access to the same data, which is usually organized into one or more huge databases.

IBM is the major manufacturer of mainframe computers. The examples of mainframes are IBM S/390, Control Data CYBER 176 and Amdahl 580 etc.

MINICOMPUTERS

These are smaller in size, have lower processing speed and also have lower cost than mainframe. These computers are known as minicomputers because of their small size as compared to other computers at that time. The capabilities of a minicomputer are between mainframe and personal computer. These computers are also known as midrange computers. The minicomputers are used in business, education and many other government departments. Although some minicomputers are designed for a single user but most are designed to handle multiple terminals.

Minicomputers are commonly used as servers in network environment and hundreds of personal computers can be connected to the network with a minicomputer acting as server like mainframes, minicomputers are used as web servers. Single user minicomputers are used for sophisticated design tasks.

The first minicomputer was introduced in the mid-1960s by Digital Equipment Corporation (DEC). After this IBM Corporation (AS/400 computers) Data General Corporation and Prime Computer also designed the mini computers.

MICROCOMPUTER

The microcomputers are also known as personal computers or simply PCs. Microprocessor is used in this type of computer. These are very small in size and cost. The IBM's first microcomputer was designed in 1981 and was named as IBM-PC.

After this many computer hardware companies copied the design of IBM-PC. The term "PC-compatible" refers any personal computer based on the original IBM personal computer design. The most popular types of personal computers are the PC and the Apple. PC and PC-compatible computers have processors with different architectures than processors in Apple computers.

These two types of computers also use different operating systems. PC and PC-compatible computers use the Windows operating system while Apple computers use the Macintosh operating system (MacOS). The majority of microcomputers sold today are part of IBM-compatible. However the Apple computer is neither an IBM nor a compatible. It is another family of computers made by Apple computer. Personal computers are available in two models.

These are:

- Desktop PCs
- Tower PCs

A desktop personal computer is most popular model of personal computer. The system unit of the desktop personal computer can lie flat on the desk or table. In desktop personal computer, the monitor is usually placed on the system unit. Another model of the personal computer is known as tower personal computer.

The system unit of the tower PC is vertically placed on the desk of table. Usually the system unit of the tower model is placed on the floor to make desk space free and user can place other devices such as printer, scanner etc. on the desktop. Today computer tables are available which are specially designed for this purpose. The tower models are mostly used at homes and offices. Microcomputer are further divided into following categories.

- Laptop computer
- Workstation
- Network computer
- Handheld computer

Laptop Computer

Laptop computer is also known as notebook computer. It is small size (85-by-11 inch notebook computer and can fit inside a briefcase. The laptop computer is operated on a special battery and it does not have to be plugged in like desktop computer. The laptop computer is portable and fully functional microcomputer. It is mostly used during journey. It can be used on your lap in an airplane. It is because it is referred to as laptop computer.

The memory and storage capacity of laptop computer is almost equivalent to the PC or desktop computer. It also has the hard dist, floppy disk drive, Zip disk drive, CD-ROM drive, CD-writer etc. it has built-in keyboard and built-in trackball as pointing device. Laptop computer is also available with the same processing speed as the most powerful personal computer. It means that laptop computer has same features as personal computer. Laptop computers are more expensive than desktop computers. Normally these computers are frequently used in business travellers.

Workstations

Workstations are special single user computers having the same features as personal computer but have the processing speed equivalent to minicomputer or mainframe computer. A workstation computer can be fitted on a desktop. Scientists, engineers, architects and graphic designers mostly use these computers.

Workstation computers are expensive and powerful computers. These have advanced processors, more RAM and storage capacity than personal computers. These are usually used as single-user applications but these are used as servers on computer network and web servers as well.

Network Computers

Network computers are also version of personal computers having less processing power, memory and storage. These are specially designed as terminals for network environment. Some types of network computers have no storage.

The network computers are designed for network, Internet or Intranet for data entry or to access data on the network. The network computers depend upon the network's server for data storage and to use software. These computers also use the network's server to perform some processing tasks.

In the mid-1990s the concept of network computers became popular among some PC manufacturers. As a result several variations of the network computers quickly became available. In business, variations of the network computer are Windows terminals, NetPCs and diskless workstations. Some network computers are designed to access only the Internet or to an Intranet.

These devices are sometimes called Internet PCs, Internet boxes etc. In home some network computers do not include monitor. These are connected to home television, which serves as the output devices. A popular example of a home-based network computer is Web TV, which enables the user to connect a television to the Internet. The Web TV has a special set-top box used to connect to the Internet and also provides a set of simple controls which enable the user to navigate the Internet, send and receive e-mails and to perform other tasks on the network while watching television. Network computers are cheaper to purchase and to maintain than personal computers.

Handheld Computer

In the mid 1990s, many new types of small personal computing devices have been introduced and these are referred to as handheld computers. These computers are also referred to as Palmtop Computers.

The handheld computers sometimes called Mini-Notebook Computers. The type of computer is named as handheld computer because it can fit in one hand while you can operate it with the other hand. Because of its reduced size, the screen of handheld computer is quite small. Similarly it also has small keyboard.

The handheld computers are preferred by business traveller. Some handheld computers have a specialized keyboard. These computers are used by mobile employees, such as meter readers and parcel delivery people, whose jobs require them to move from place to place.

The examples of handheld computers are:

- Personal digital assistance
- Cellular telephones
- H/PC pro devices

Personal Digital Assistance (PDAs)

The PDA is one of the more popular lightweight mobile devices in use today. A PDA provides special functions such as taking notes, organizing telephone numbers and addresses. Most PDAs also offer a variety of other application software such as word processing, spreadsheet and games etc.

Some PDAs include electronic books that enable users to read a book on the PDA's screen. Many PDAs are web-based and users can send/receive e-mails and access the Internet. Similarly, some PDAs also provide telephone capabilities. The primary input device of a PDA is the stylus. A stylus is an electronic pen and looks like a small ballpoint pen. This input device is used to write notes and store in the PDA by touching the screen. Some PDAs also support voice input.

Cellular Phones

A cellular phone is a web-based telephone having features of analog and digital devices. It is also referred to as Smart Phone. In addition to basic phone capabilities, a cellular phone also provides the functions to receive and send e-mails and faxes and to access the Internet.

H/PC Pro Devices

H/PC Pro dive is new development in handheld technology. These systems are larger than PDAs but they are not quite as large as typical notebook PCs. These devices have features between PDAs and notebook PCs.

The H/PC Pro device includes a full-size keyboard but it does not include disk. These systems also have RAM with very low storage capacity and slow speed of processor.

FUNCTIONAL UNITS OF ACOMPUTER SYSTEM

Digital computer systems consist of three distinct units. *These units are as follows*:

Input unit

Central Processing unit

Output unit

These units are interconnected by electrical cables to permit communication between them. This allows the computer to function as a system.

INPUT UNIT

A computer must receive both data and programme statements to function properly and be able to solve problems. The method of feeding data and programmes to a computer is accomplished by an input device.

Computer input devices read data from a source, such as magnetic disks, and translate that data into electronic impulses for transfer into the CPU. Some typical input devices are a keyboard, a mouse, or a scanner.

CENTRAL PROCESSING UNIT

The brain of a computer system is the central processing unit (CPU). The CPU processes data transferred to it from one of the various input devices. It then transfers either an intermediate or final result of the CPU to one or more output devices. A central control section and work areas are required to perform calculations or manipulate data.

The CPU is the computing center of the system. It consists of a control section, an arithmetic-logic section as shown in fig, and an internal storage section (main memory). Each section within the CPU serves a specific function and has a particular relationship with the other sections within the

Cpu.Control Section

The control section directs the flow of traffic (operations) and data. It also maintains order within the computer. The flow of control is indicated by dotted arrows in figure. The control section selects one programme statement at a time from the programme storage area, interprets the statement, and sends the appropriate electronic impulses to the arithmetic-logic and storage sections so they can carryout the instructions.

The control section does not perform actual processing operations on the data. The control section instructs the input device on when to start and stop transferring data to the input storage area. It also tells the output device when to start and stop receiving data from the output storage area.

Arithmetic-Logic Section

The arithmetic-logic section performs arithmetic operations, such as addition, subtraction, multiplication, and division. Through internal logic capability, it tests various conditions encountered during processing and takes action based on the result.As indicated by the solid arrows in figure 3-1, data flows between the arithmetic-logic section and the internal storage section during processing. Specifically, data is transferred as needed from the storage section to the arithmetic-logic section, processed, and returned to internal storage.

At no time does processing take placein the storage section. Data maybe transferred back and forth between these two sections several times before processing is completed. The results are then transferred from internal storage to an output device, as indicated by the solid arrow in figure below.

The binary addition and multiplication tables are:

(
$0 + 0 = 0$
$0 + 1 = 1$
$1 + 1 = 10$
$1 + 0 = 1$
$0 \times 0 = 0$
$0 \times 1 = 0$
$1 \times 1 = 1$
$1 \times 0 = 0$
) (4)

Note that if carries are ignored,7 subtraction of two single-digit binary numbers yields the same bit as addition. Computers use high and low voltage values to express a bit, and an array of such voltages express numbers akin to positional notation. Logic circuits perform arithmetic operations.

Exercise: Add twenty-five and seven in base 2. Note the carries that might occur. Why is the result "nice"?

Solution: $25=11011_2$ and $7=111_2$. We find that $11001_2 + 111_2 = 100000_2=32$.

Also note that the logical operations of AND and OR are equivalent to binary addition (again if carries are ignored). The variables of logic indicate truth or falsehood. *AÂ"B*, the AND of *A* and *B*, represents a statement that both *A* and *B* must be true for the statement to be true. You use this kind of statement to tell search engines that you want to restrict hits to cases where both of the events *A* and *B* occur. *AÃ"B*, the OR of *A* and *B*, yields a value of truth if either is true. Note that if we represent truth by a "1" and falsehood by a "0," *binary multiplication corresponds to AND and addition (ignoring carries) to OR.*

The Irish mathematician George Boole discovered this equivalence in the mid-nineteenth century. It laid the foundation for what we now call Boolean algebra, which expresses as equations logical statements. More importantly, any computer using base-2 representations and arithmetic can also easily evaluate logical statements. This fact makes an integer-based computational device much more powerful than might be apparent.

Internal Storage Section

The internal storage section is sometimes called primary storage, main storage, or main memory, because this section functions similar to our own human memory. The storage section serves four purposes; three relate to retention (holding) of data during processing. First, as indicated by the solid arrow as shown in fig, data is transferred from an input device to the inputstorage area where it remains until the computers ready to process it.

Second, a workingstorage area ("scratch pad" memory) within the storage section holds both the data being processed and the intermediate results of the arithmetic-logic operations. Third, the storage section retains the processing results in the output storage area. From there the processing results can be transferred to an output device.

The fourth storage section, the programme storage area, contains the programme statements transferred from an input device to process the data. Please note that the four areas (input, working storage, output, and programme storage) are NOT famed in size or location but are determined by individual programme requirements.

OUTPUT UNIT

As programme statements and data are received by the

CPU from an input device, the results of the processed data are sent from the CPU to an OUTPUT DEVICE. These results are transferred from the output storage area onto an output medium, such as a floppy disk, hard drive, video display, printer, and so on.

BUSES AND ARCHITECTURE

BUS

A set of parallel conductors, which allow devices attached to it to communicate with the CPU.

The bus consists of three main parts:

Control lines
Address lines
Data lines

Control Lines

These allow the CPU to control which operations the devices attached should perform, *I.E.* read or write.

Address Lines

Allows the CPU to reference certain (Memory) locations within the device.

Data Lines

The meaningful data which is to be sent or retrieved from a device is placed on to these lines.

TYPES OF BUSES

EXPANSION BUS

Expansion buses (sometimes called *peripheral buses*) are buses that have connectors that allow you to add expansion cards (peripherals) to a computer.

There are different types of standard internal buses that are characterized by:

- Their shape
- The number of connector pins
- The type of signals (frequency, data, etc.)

ISA BUS

The original version of the ISA bus (*Industry Standard Architecture*) that appeared in 1981 with PC XT was an 8-bit bus with a clock speed of 4.77 MHz.

In 1984, with the appearance of PC AT (the *Intel 286* processor), the bit was expanded into a 16-bit bus and the clock speed went from 6 to 8 MHz and finally to 8.33 MHz, offering a maximum transfer rate of 16 Mb/s (in practice only 8 Mb/s because one cycle out of every two was used for addressing).

The ISA bus permitted bus mastering, *i.e.* it enabled controllers connected directly to the bus to communicate directly with the other peripherals without going through the processor. One of the consequences of *bus mastering* is direct memory access (DMA). However, the ISA bus only allows hardware to address the first 16 megabytes of RAM.

MCA BUS

The MCA bus (*Micro Channel Architecture*) is an improved proprietary bus designed by IBM in 1987 to be used in their PS/2 line of computer. This 16 to 32-bit bus was incompatible with the ISA bus and could reach a throughput of 20 Mb/s.

EISA BUS

The EISA bus (*Extended Industry Standard Architecture*) was developed in 1988 by a consortium of companies (AST, Compaq, Epson, Hewlett-Packard, NEC, Olivetti, Tandy, Wyse and Zenith) in order to compete with the MCA proprietary bus that was launched by IBM the previous year. The EISA bus used connectors that were the same size as the ISA connector but with 4 rows of contacts instead of 2, for 32-bit addressing.

The EISA connectors were deeper and the additional rows of contacts were placed below the rows of ISA contacts. Thus, it was possible to plug an ISA expansion board into an EISA connector. However, they did not plug as deep into the connector (because of the bezels) and thus only used the top rows (ISA) of contacts.

LOCAL BUS

Traditional I/O buses, such as ISA, MCA our EISA buses, are directly connected to the main bus and there are forced to work at the same frequency. However, some I/O peripherals need a very low bandwidth while other need higher bandwidths. Therefore there are bottlenecks on the bus. In order to solve this problem, the "local bus" architecture offers to take advantage of the system bus, or front side bus (*FSB*), by interfacing directly with it.

VLB BUS

In 1992, the VESA local bus (VLB) was developed by the *VESA* (*Video Electronics Standard Association*under the aegis of the company *NEC*) in order to offer a local bus dedicated to graphics systems.

REGISTERS

Registers are fast memory, almost always connected to circuitry that allows various arithmetic, logical, control, and other manipulations, as well as possibly setting internal flags. Most early computers had only one data register that could be used for arithmetic and logic instructions. Often there would be additional special purpose registers set aside either for temporary fast internal storage or assigned to logic circuits to implement certain instructions.

Some early computers had one or two address registers that pointed to a memory location for memory accesses (a pair of address registers typically would act as source and destination pointers for memory operations). Computers soon had multiple data registers, address registers, and sometimes other special purpose registers. Some computers have general purpose registers that can be used for both data and address operations. Every digital computer using a von Neumann architectuie has a register (called the programme counter) that points to the next executable instruction.

Many computers have additional control registers for implementing various control capabilities. Often some or all of the internal flags are combined into a flag or status register.

ACCUMULATORS

Accumulators are registers that can be used for arithmetic, logical, shift, rotate, or other similar operations. The first computers typically only had one accumulator. Many times there were related special purpose registers that contained the source data for an accumulator. Accumulators were replaced with data registers and general purpose registers.

DATA REGISTERS

Data registers are used for temporary scratch storage of data, as well as for data manipulations (arithmetic, logic, etc.). In some processors, all data registers act in the same manner, while in other processors different operations are performed are specific registers.

- *Mix*: One extension register; named X-register; five bytes plus sign; can be concatenated on the right hand side of the A-register (accumulator)
- *Motorola* 680 × 0, 68300: 8 long word (32 bit) data registers; named D0, D1, D2, D3, D4, D5, D6, and D7

ADDRESS REGISTERS

Address registers store the addresses of specific memory locations. Often many integer and logic operations can be performed on address registers directly (to allow for computation of addresses). Sometimes the contents of address register(s) are combined with other special purpose registers to compute the actual physical address. This allows for the hardware implementation of dynamic memory pages, virtual memory, and protected memory. The number of bits of an address register (possibly combined with information from other registers) limits the maximum amount of addressable memory. A 16-bit address register can address 64K of physical memory. A 24-bit address register can address address 16 MB of physical memory.

CONSTANT REGISTERS

Constant registers are special read-only registers that

store a constant. Attempts to write to a constant register are illegal or ignored. In some RISC processors, constant registers are used to store commonly used values (such as zero, one, or negative one) — for example, a constant register containing zero can be used in register to register data moves, providing the equivalent of a clear instruction without adding one to the instruction set.

Constant registers are also often used in floating point units to provide such value as pi or e with additional hidden bits for greater accuracy in computations.

FLOATING POINT REGISTERS

Floating point registers are special registers set aside for floating point math.

INDEX REGISTERS

Index registers are used to provide more flexibility in addressing modes, allowing the programmer to create a memory address by combining the contents of an address register with the contents of an index register (with displacements, increments, decrements, and other options).

In some processors, there are specific index registers (or just one index register) that can only be used only for that purpose. In some processors, any data register, address register, or general register (or some combination of the three) can be used as an index register.

- *IBM* 360/370: Any of the 16 general purpose registers may be used as an index register
- *Intel* 80 × 86: 7 of the 8 general purpose registers may be used as an index register (the ESP is the exception)
- *Mix*: Five index registers; named I-registers I1, I2, I3, I4, and I5; five bytes plus sign
- *Motorola* 680 ×.0, 68300: Any of the 8 data registers or the 8 address registers may be used as an index register

BASE REGISTERS

Base registers or segment registers are used to segment

memory. Effective addresses are computed by adding the contents of the base or segment register to the rest of the effective address computation. In some processors, any register can serve as a base register. In some processors, there are specific base or segment registers (one or more) that can only be used for that purpose.

CONTROL REGISTERS

Control registers control some aspect of processor operation. The most universal control register is the programme counter.

PROGRAMME COUNTER

Almost every digital computer ever made uses a programme counter. The programme counter points to the memory location that stores the next executable instruction. Branching is implemented by making changes to the programme counter.

Some processor designs allow software to directly change the programme counter, but usually software only indirectly changes the programme counter (for example, a JUMP instruction will insert the operand into the programme counter).

An assembler has a location counter, which is an internal pointer to the address (first byte) of the next location in storage (for instructions, data areas, constants, etc.) while the source code is being converted into object code. The VAX uses the 16th of 16 general purpose registers as the programme counter (PC).

Almost the entire instruction set can directly manipulate the programme counter, allowing a very rich set of possible kinds of branching. The programme counter in System/360 and 370 machines is contained in bits 40-63 of the programme status word (PSW), which is directly accessible by some instructions.

- *IBM* 360/370: Programme counter is bits 40-63 of the programme status word (PSW)
- *Intel* 8086/80286: 16-bit instruction pointer (IP)

- *Intel* 80386: 32-bit instruction pointer (EIP)
- *Motorola* 680 × 0, 68300: 32-bit programme counter (PC)

PROCESSOR FLAGS

Processor flags store information about specific processor functions. The processor flags are usually kept in a flag register or a general status register. This can include result flags that record the results of certain kinds of testing, information about data that is moved, certain kinds of information about the results of compations or transformations, and information about some processor states. Some conditions are determined by combining multiple flags. For example, if a processor has a negative flag and a zero flag, the equivalent of a positive flag is the case of both the negative and zero flags both simultaneously being cleared.

A few typical control flags (with processors that include them):

- Decimal overflow trap enable Set if decimal overflow occurs (or conversion error on a VAX). Used in Digital VAX [DV].
- Direction flag Determines the direction of string operations (set for autoincrement, cleared for autodecrement). Used in Intel 80x86 [DF].
- Floating underflow trap enable Set if floating underflow occurs. Used in Digital VAX [FU].
- Integer overflow trap enable Set if integer overflow occurs (or conversion error on a VAX). Used in Digital VAX [IV].
- Interupt enable Set if interrupts enabled. Used in Intel 80x86 [IF].
- i/o privilege level Used to control access to I/O instructions and hardware (thereby seperating control over I/O from other supervisor/user states). Two bits. Used in Intel 80x86 [IO PL].
- Nested task flag Used in Intel 80x86 [NF].
- Resume flag Used in Intel 80x86 [RF].
- Virtual 8086 mode Used to switch to virtual 8086 emulation. Used in Intel 80x86 [VM].

STACK POINTER

Stack pointers are used to implement a processor stack in memory. In many processors, address registers can be used as generic data stack pointers and queue pointers. A specific stack pointer or address register may be hardwired for certain instructions.

4

Programming and Data Structure

PROGRAMMING

Programming is a type in which programmers define not only the data type of a data structure, but also the types of operations (functions) that can be applied to the data structure. In this way, the data structure becomes an object that includes both data and functions. In addition, programmers can create relationships between one object and another. For example, objects can inherit characteristics from other objects.

One of the principal advantages of object-oriented programming techniques over procedural programming techniques is that they enable programmers to create modules that do not need to be changed when a new type of object is added. A programmer can simply create a new object that inherits many of its features from existing objects.

This makes object-oriented programmes easier to modify. To perform object-oriented programming, one needs an object-oriented programming language (OOPL). Java, C++ and Smalltalk are three of the more popular languages, and there are also object-oriented versions of Pascal.

OBJECTS

An object is a software bundle of related state and behaviour. Software objects are often used to model the real-world objects that you find in everyday life. This lesson explains how state and behaviour are represented within an object, introduces the concept of data encapsulation, and explains the benefits of designing your software in this manner.

CLASS

A class is a blueprint or prototype from which objects are created. This section defines a class that models the state and behaviour of a real-world object. It intentionally focuses on the basics, showing how even a simple class can cleanly model state and behaviour.

INHERITANCE

Inheritance provides a powerful and natural mechanism for organizing and structuring your software. This section explains how classes inherit state and behaviour from their superclasses, and explains how to derive one class from another using the simple syntax provided by the Java programming language.

INTERFACE

An interface is a contract between a class and the outside world. When a class implements an interface, it promises to provide the behaviour published by that interface. This section defines a simple interface and explains the necessary changes for any class that implements it.

PACKAGE

A package is a namespace for organizing classes and interfaces in a logical manner. Placing your code into packages makes large software projects easier to manage. This section explains why this is useful, and introduces you to the Application Programming Interface (API) provided by the Java platform.

Object-oriented programming (OOP) is a programming language model organized around "objects" rather than "actions" and data rather than logic. Historically, a programme has been viewed as a logical procedure that takes input data, processes it, and produces output data. The programming challenge was seen as how to write the logic, not how to define the data. Object-oriented programming takes the view that what we really care about are the objects we want to manipulate rather than the logic required to manipulate them. Examples of objects range from human beings (described by name, address, and so forth) to buildings and floors (whose properties can be described and managed) down to the little widgets on your computer desktop (such as buttons and scroll bars).

The first step in OOP is to identify all the objects you want to manipulate and how they relate to each other, an exercise often known as data modeling. Once you've identified an object, you generalize it as a class of objects (think of Plato's concept of the "ideal" chair that stands for all chairs) and define the kind of data it contains and any logic sequences that can manipulate it. Each distinct logic sequence is known as a method.

A real instance of a class is called (no surprise here) an "object" or, in some environments, an "instance of a class." The object or class instance is what you run in the computer. Its methods provide computer instructions and the class object characteristics provide relevant data. You communicate with objects - and they communicate with each other - with well-defined interfaces called messages. The concepts and rules used in object-oriented programming provide these important benefits: The concept of a data class makes it possible to define subclasses of data objects that share some or all of the main class characteristics.

Called inheritance, this property of OOP forces a more thorough data analysis, reduces development time, and ensures more accurate coding. Since a class defines only the data it needs to be concerned with, when an instance of that class (an object) is run, the code will not be able to accidentally access other programme data. This characteristic of data hiding provides greater system security

DEFINITION

The demand for businesses to deploy solutions across multiple servers is bound to increase. With the growth and acceptance of the Internet, businesses have come to think of their applications and information be connected and distributed across multiple servers from remote locations. Also data can be processed and accessed through the use of Web browsers and by user interfaces. But a number of problems stands on the way towards developing and deploying mission-critical business applications on several server systems.

These applications are named as distributed software applications. They are communication issues among different programming languages and platforms and security. There are a few promising technologies for promoting these critical applications. Microsoft has come out with a new technology called as Component Object Model (COM) that addresses these problems towards the goal of design of distributed software components.

COM

COM is an outgrowth of the OO technology. It is a specification that is based on a binary standard for reuse through interfaces.

That is, components, which are pre-compiled blocks of code, written for COM can be reused without any dependencies on the language in which they are coded. The programming language may be Visual Basic, C++ etc. COM uses system-level code that is implemented in the form of dynamic link libraries, which are collectively called COM library.

The COM library consists of several application programming interface (API) functions that are necessary for COM components to do various tasks. COM library is responsible for locating and activating server applications. With client applications, COM APIs contains the necessary functions for instantiating objects that the client want to use. Also the COM library provides locator services using the System Control Manager (SCM), which also provides transparent remote procedure calls when an object is executing out-of-process in a local or remote server.

COMPONENT-BASED DEVELOPMENT (CBD)

CBD came from OO software development methodology towards facilitating software reusability in larger scale. Suppose there is an object and we want to use that in an application. For that, we have to cut and paste the code in the application. If there is any changes made in the object, we have to search for all the object copies in the application to insert the relevant changes. This becomes cumbersome when there are more applications with more copies of the same object.

Here comes the idea of designing components as a robust solution. A component can be technically defined as a coarse-grained object. It is also defined as a reusable software module, which displays its services through interfaces for use by client software. On using a component, which is stored in a single place, applications can use the object directly from the component and get the same functionality. Thus both classes, where objects get derived from and components provide same type of services.

Classes pro! vide services to single applications because they can not communicate with other applications due to the differences in language and platform, while components provide services to numerous applications irrespective of the languages used. There came a number of architecture for developing both client-side and server-side components. They are OMG's CORBA, Sun's JaveBeans and Enterprise JavaBeans and Microsoft's COM.

Thus the world is full of software components, which in turn can be of greater use for hundreds of different applications. As both CORBA and COM supports language independence, a different software vendor can create components using different programming languages without any integration problems.

ADVANTAGES OF COM

1. COM promotes component-based software development - before component-based development came, software programmes have been coded using

procedural programming paradigm, which supports linear form of programme execution. But component-based programme development comes with a number of advantages, such as the ability to use pre-packaged components and tools from third party vendors into an application and support for code reusability in other parts of the same application.

2. COM promotes code reusability - standard classes are normally reused in the same application but not to be used easily in other applications. But COM components are designed to separate themselves from single applications and hence can be accessed and used by several different applications without any hassle.
3. COM promotes Object-oriented programming (OOP) - The primary characteristics of OOP are encapsulation, which allows the implementation details of an object to be hidden, polymorphism, which is the ability to exhibit multiple behaviours, and inheritance, which allows for the reuse of existing classes in order to design new and more specialized classes. Among these, encapsulation is one of COM's most important characteristics. Encapsulation helps to hide how an object has implemented a method internally. This ultimately helps to incorporate more vigourously implemented or advanced implementation into an object at later time without affecting the client which uses it.
4. COM comprises the necessary mechanisms for COM components to communicate with each other - In the normal case, two components coded using two different programming languages can not communicate with each other. But COM can make it possible for different language components, which adhere to the COM specification, to interact with each other and hence COM is language-independent.
5. COM helps to access components loaded in different machines on the network - COM component can

reside anywhere on our computer or even on another computer connected to a network. That is, applications using COM can access and share COM components regardless of their locations. Thus COM abstracts away the nitty-gritty of clients to locate COM components anywhere in the network. Thus COM provides location transparency and COM components are location independent.

COM INTERFACES

Components, especially server-side ones, are bound to have their own interfaces. An interface is simply a list of methods a COM component implements and makes them available to consumers. COM interface are immutable. That is, once a COM component has been released with an interface, this interface must never be manipulated. COM interfaces are the mechanisms by which a client contacts, connects and use components. If the client component is using a different language from the one a server component is coded, there will be language problem for interactions. In order to remove this barrier, COM interfaces provide an universal way so that components coded in different languages can communicate with each other. Thus every interface constitutes a binding contract between a COM object (no interface is attached with this) and a COM component with an interface. COM specification makes life easier by allowing a component to publish more than one interface at a time. New interfaces can! be incorporated to support new features of the components while keeping the original interface intact. We have to increment a version number for the new interface. A class module then would need to be implemented for both old and new interfaces in order to support both old clients that rely on the old interface and new clients that can take advantage of the new interface. Thus the immutability factor of COM interfaces can be overcome.

INTERFACE DEFINITION LANGUAGE (IDL)

To successfully make COM language-independent, the

COM interfaces have to coded using IDL. IDL is just a declaration language, not a programming language. The syntax for IDL is almost similar to C++ language. But IDL goes beyond what C++ can offer by being able to define functions that extend process boundaries. IDL provides many vital extensions that allow attributes such as type libraries, co-classes, interfaces, and method parameters to be specified quite elegantly. But if there is no language problem, it is not mandatory to use IDL for defining COM interfaces.

The QueryInterface method is the mechanism that a client uses to discover and navigate the interfaces of a component dynamically. It is the most significant method of all COM interfaces available for a component since this method allows run-time checking of all of these interfaces. When the QueryInterface method provides an interface pointer to a client, the QueryInterface calls the method AddRef. The only way to access a COM object is through a pointer to an interface.

An interface pointer is actually a pointer to a pointer in a virtual table that is implemented in memory. That is, for every class that contains public methods, a virtual table will be created and placed in memory at run time. Virtual tables are generated for each class and not for objects of that class. Each virtual table contains an array of function pointers whose elements contain the address of each specific function that an object can implement. At the top of every virtual table array will be three fundamental methods that make up this IUnknown interface.

The methods AddRef and Release manage reference counting. This reference count is an internal count of the number of clients using a particular COM object. It is possible for several clients to invoke the services available with a COM object at the same time. When a client begins a session with an object, it calls the AddRef method, which increments one to the existing count. Once the session is over, the corresponding Release method gets invoked to decrement one from the existing count.

The next line down is used to locate the definition for

the base interface IUnknown The next line identifies the interface method "SumofNumbers". This interface method is designed to return an HRESULT value. An HRESULT is used with COM to indicate whether a method call is successfully accomplished or not. Almost all COM interfaces return a special 32-bit code, called as HRESULT, from their methods to return status information.

It is actually the method COM utilizes to return errors to the caller of the method. The reason for this mechanism is due to the inability of COM to transmit error messages back to the client if there is anything wrong on the server side or on the way to the server. As components are being written using different programming languages and each language follows its own exception mechanisms, COM can not correctly pass on the error messages and hence HRESULT.

Following the HRESULT are three parameters for the interface method SumOfNumbers. The [in] in the first two parameters specifies that these parameters are input values to be passed to the interface method and the [out, retval] in the last parameter indicates that this parameter returns a value that will be ultimately passed to back to the client.

WINDOWS REGISTRY AND COMPONENTS ENVIRONMENT

COM components may be loaded in different address spaces in the same machine or machine connected with the network. Before an object can be created, the COM runtime must first locate the COM components. The COM runtime is able to locate COM components through the use of Windows registry.

COM components may be out-of-process or in-process. An out-of-process component can effectively be a separate programme containing objects. This type runs in its own process space and will thus be largely independent from any client programmes.

These components are often large applications themselves, and provide access to their objects to make it easy for other programmes to create macros or otherwise make use of existing functionality. This can be very beneficial, because the component developer can choose his own threading models. The drawback here is that the developer has to write the code for threading. This work can be handled by automatically COM+, the latest one from the COM family.

There is also a performance issue. Because the client application is communicating with objects which are in an entirely different process there is quite a bit of overhead. COM steps in between the client and the server and handles all the communication between them. Mainly out-of-process components are useful if we are trying to make use of the objects in a pre-existing application.

An in-process component is one where the objects run inside the client's process. Each client gets its own private copy of the component and hence a copy of all the objects in that component. An in-process component is often called COM DLLs or ActiveX DLLs. In-process component does not have a process of its own and it always runs within the context of another process.

Often this other process is the client application itself but may be run within the context of a different process entirely. In this case, we can get performance boost as the component is loaded in the client application itself.

There is almost no overhead when client interacts with an object that is running in the same process. The major advantages of having in-process components are stability and increased manageability

CREATING A COM OBJECT

There is a lot of communication that must occur behind the scenes in order for a COM object to be created. First of all, a client looking for an object has to make a call to an API function called CoCreate Instance with the CLSID for the class, which comprises the particular object.

The prefix Co in this function is a typical naming convention for COM runtime API functions. Co Create Instance in turn as a second step calls another API function called Co Get Class Object. Basically the function Co Create

Instance asks the SCM to search the Windows registry location, which is HKEY_CLASSES _ROOT\ CLSID. The function of SCM is to locate the requested class object by using the specified CLSID. The first place the SCM looks to locate the class object is within its own internal database. If the class is not located inside its database, the SCM turns to the system registry as a third step. As soon as the class object is found, the SCM immediately returns to COM an interface pointer referred to as IClass Factory.

Every COM class must have a factory object associated with it. The main purpose of these class objects is to implement the IClass Factory interface. Once the client gets the IClass Factory pointer, two things happen. One, by obtaining a pointer to the IClass Factory, Co Create Instance can call IClass Factory:: Create Instance in order to create the requested COM object. Once the object is created, a second step occurs: the interface pointer to the IClass Factory gets released.

The interface called IClass Factory's job is to talk to other class objects. Further, Co Get Class Object is a COM class object whose sole purpose is to create a new instance of a different class. Because this COM class creates class objects by implementing the IClass Factory interface, CoGet Class Object is referred to as a class factory.

LOCKSERVER

When an object is created it resides in memory. It is the client's job to notify the object when it is no longer needed. The Release method told above can decrement the reference count for the interface. If there are several interfaces for an object, it is possible that the object is still being accessed somewhere else.

The idea is that the reference count has to reach zero before the object is to be released from the memory. Releasing objects from memory usually improves performance. Some special clients constantly create and destroy objects, which normally affects the application's performance. The Lock Server method allows components to remain in memory by incrementing the reference count by one. Because LockServer keeps a count of one in the reference counter, the object will stay in memory even if it is not being accessed currently. Having the component reside in memory has the advantage of allowing the object to be called without having to go through the process of recre! ating it. But on the other hand, if objects are not destroyed when they are not in use, there will be reduction of system memory resources.

HIGH LEVEL LANGUAGE

C is sometimes referred to as a "high-level assembly language." Some people think that's an insult, but it's actually a deliberate and significant aspect of the language. If you have programmed in assembly language, you'll probably find C very natural and comfortable (although if you continue to focus too heavily on machine-level details, you'll probably end up with unnecessarily nonportable programmes).

If you haven't programmed in assembly language, you may be frustrated by C's lack of certain higher-level features. In either case, you should understand why C was designed this way: so that seemingly-simple constructions expressed in C would not expand to arbitrarily expensive (in time or space) machine language constructions when compiled.

If you write a C programme simply and succinctly, it is likely to result in a succinct, efficient machine language executable. If you find that the executable programme resulting from a C programme is not efficient, it's probably because of something silly you did, not because of something the compiler did behind your back which you have no control over. In any case, there's no point in complaining about C's low-level flavour: C is what it is.

A programming language is a tool, and no tool can perform every task unaided. If you're building a house, and I'm teaching you how to use a hammer, and you ask how to assemble rafters and trusses into gables, that's a legitimate question, but the answer has fallen out of the realm of "How do I use a hammer?" and into "How do I build a house?". In the same way, we'll see that C does not have built-in features to perform every function that we might ever need to do while programming. As mentioned above, C imposes relatively few built-in ways of doing things on the programmer. Some common tasks, such as manipulating strings, allocating memory, and doing input/output (I/O), are performed by calling on library functions.

Other tasks which you might want to do, such as creating or listing directories, or interacting with a mouse, or displaying windows or other user-interface elements, or doing colour graphics, are not defined by the C language at all. You can do these things from a C programme, of course, but you will be calling on services which are peculiar to your programming environment (compiler, processor, and operating system) and which are not defined by the C standard.

Since this course is about portable C programming, it will also be steering clear of facilities not provided in all C environments. Another aspect of C that's worth mentioning here is that it is, to put it bluntly, a bit dangerous. C does not, in general, try hard to protect a programmer from mistakes. If you write a piece of code which will (through some oversight of yours) do something wildly different from what you intended it to do, up to and including deleting your data or trashing your disk, and if it is possible for the compiler to compile it, it generally will.

You won't get warnings of the form "Do you really mean to...?" or "Are you sure you really want to...?". C is often compared to a sharp knife: it can do a surgically precise job on some exacting task you have in mind, but it can also do a surgically precise job of cutting off your finger. It's up to you to use it carefully.

This aspect of C is very widely criticized; it is also used (justifiably) to argue that C is not a good teaching language. C aficionados love this aspect of C because it means that C does not try to protect them from themselves: when they know what they're doing, even if it's risky or obscure, they can do it. Students of C hate this aspect of C because it often seems as if the language is some kind of a conspiracy specifically designed to lead them into booby traps. This is another aspect of the language which it's fairly pointless to complain about. If you take care and pay attention, you can avoid many of the pitfalls. These notes will point out many of the obvious (and not so obvious) trouble spots.

In general, a function may return a value to its caller, and main is no exception. When main returns (that is, reaches its end and stops functioning), the programme is at its end, and the return value from main tells the operating system (or whatever invoked the programme that main is the main function of) whether it succeeded or not. By convention, a return value of 0 indicates success.

This programme may look so absolutely trivial that it seems as if it's not even worth typing it in and trying to run it, but doing so may be a big (and is certainly a vital) first hurdle. On an unfamiliar computer, it can be arbitrarily difficult to figure out how to enter a text file containing programme source, or how to compile and link it, or how to invoke it, or what happened after (if?) it ran.

The most experienced C programmers immediately go back to this one, simple programme whenever they're trying out a new system or a new way of entering or building programmes or a new way of printing output from within programmes. As Kernighan and Ritchie say, everything else is comparatively easy. You may also have your choice of C compilers. On many Unix machines, the cc command is an older compiler which does not recognize modern, ANSI Standard C syntax.

An old compiler will accept the simple programmes we'll be starting with, but it will not accept most of our later programmes. If you find yourself getting baffling compilation errors on programmes which you've typed in exactly as they're shown, it probably indicates that you're using an older compiler.

On many machines, another compiler called acc or gcc is available, and you'll want to use it, instead. (Both acc and gcc are typically invoked the same as cc; that is, the above cc command would instead be typed, say, gcc -o hello hello.c .)

In an integrated or "visual" progamming environment, such as those on the Macintosh or under various versions of Microsoft Windows, the steps you take to enter, compile, and run a programme are somewhat different (and, theoretically, simpler). Typically, there is a way to open a new source window, type source code into it, give it a file name, and add it to the programme (or "project") you're building. If necessary, there will be a way to specify what other source files (or "modules") make up the programme.

Then, there's a button or menu selection which compiles and runs the programme, all from within the programming environment. (There will also be a way to create a standalone executable file which you can run from outside the environment.) In a PC-compatible environment, you may have to choose between creating DOS programmes or Windows programmes.

(If you have troubles pertaining to the printf function, try specifying a target environment of MS-DOS. Supposedly, some compilers which are targeted at Windows environments won't let you call printf, because until you call some fancier functions to request that a window be created, there's no window for printf to print to.) Again, check the introductory or tutorial manual that came with the programming package; it should walk you through the steps necessary to get your first programme running.

Finally, we have a call to the printf function, as before, but with several differences. First, the call to printf is within the *body* of the for loop. This means that control flow does not pass once through the printf call, but instead that the call is performed as many times as are dictated by the for loop. In this case, printfwill be called several times: once when i is 0, once when i is 1, once when i is 2, and so on until i is 9, for a total of 10 times.

A second difference in the printf call is that the string to be printed, "i is%d", contains a per cent sign. Whenever printf sees a per cent sign, it indicates thatprintf is not supposed to print the exact text of the string, but is instead supposed to read another one of its arguments to decide what to print. The letter after the per cent sign tells it what type of argument to expect and how to print it. In this case, the letter d indicates that printf is to expect an int, and to print it in decimal. Finally, we see that printf is in fact being called with another argument, for a total of two, separated by commas.

PROGRAMME STRUCTURE

We'll have more to say later about programme structure, but for now let's observe a few basics. A programme consists of one or more functions; it may also contain global variables. (Our two example programmes so far have contained one function apiece, and no global variables.)

At the top of a source file are typically a few boilerplate lines such as #include <stdio.h>, followed by the definitions (*i.e.* code) for the functions. (It's also possible to split up the several functions making up a larger programme into several source files, as we'll see in a later chapter.)

Each function is further composed of *declarations* and *statements,* in that order. When a sequence of statements should act as one (for example, when they should all serve together as the body of a loop) they can be enclosed in braces (just as for the outer body of the entire function). The simplest kind of statement is an *expression statement,* which is an expression (presumably performing some useful operation) followed by a semicolon. Expressions are further composed of *operators, objects*(variables), and *constants.*

C source code consists of several *lexical elements.* Some are words, such as for, return, main, and i, which are either *keywords* of the language (for, return) or *identifiers* (names) we've chosen for our own functions and variables (main, i). There are *constants* such as 1 and 10 which introduce new values into the programme.

There are *operators* such as =, +, and >, which manipulate variables and values. There are other punctuation characters (often called *delimiters*), such as parentheses and squiggly braces {}, which indicate how the other elements of the programme are grouped. Finally, all of the preceding elements can be separated by*whitespace*: spaces, tabs, and the "carriage returns" between lines. The source code for a C programme is, for the most part, "free form." This means that the compiler does not care how the code is arranged: how it is broken into lines, how the lines are indented, or whether whitespace is used between things like variable names and other punctuation.

Lines like #include <stdio.h> are an exception; they must appear alone on their own lines, generally unbroken. Only lines beginning with # are affected by this rule; we'll see other examples later. You can use whitespace, indentation, and appropriate line breaks to make your programmes more readable for yourself and other people (even though the compiler doesn't care).

You can place explanatory *comments* anywhere in your programme—any text between the characters /* and */ is ignored by the compiler. (In fact, the compiler pretends that all it saw was whitespace.) Though comments are ignored by the compiler, well-chosen comments can make a programme *much* easier to read.

The usage of whitespace is our first *style* issue. It's typical to leave a blank line between different parts of the programme, to leave a space on either side of operators such as + and =, and to *indent* the bodies of loops and other control flow constructs.

Typically, we arrange the indentation so that the subsidiary statements controlled by a loop statement (the "loop body," such as the printf call in our second example programme) are all aligned with each other and placed one tab stop (or some consistent number of spaces) to the right of the controlling statement.

This indentation (like all whitespace) is not required by the compiler, but it makes programs*much* easier to read. (However, it can also be misleading, if used incorrectly or in the face of inadvertent mistakes. The compiler will decide what "the body of the loop" is based on its own rules, not the indentation, so if the indentation does not match the compiler's interpretation, confusion is inevitable.) To drive home the point that the compiler doesn't care about indentation, line breaks, or other whitespace, here are a few (extreme) examples:

```
for(i = 0; i < 10; i = i + 1)
printf("%d\n", i);
```

and

```
for(i = 0; i < 10; i = i + 1) printf("%d\n",
i);
```

and

```
for(i=0;i<10;i=i+1)printf("%d\n",i);
```

and

```
for(i = 0; i < 10; i = i + 1)
printf("%d\n", i);
```

and

```
for( i
= 0;
i <10
; i=
i +1
) printf(
"%d\n" , i
) ;
```

and

```
for
(i=0;
i<10;i=
i+1)printf
("%d\n", i);
```

The fragments are all treated exactly the same way by the compiler. Some programmers argue forever over the best set of "rules" for indentation and other aspects of programming style, calling to mind the old philosopher's debates about the number of angels that could dance on the head of a pin.

Style issues (such as how a programme is laid out) *are* important, but they're not something to be too dogmatic about, and there are also other, deeper style issues besides mere layout and typography: Although C compilers do not care about how a programme looks, proper indentation and spacing are critical in making programmes easy for people to read. We recommend writing only one statement per line, and using blanks around operators to clarify grouping. The position of braces is less important, although people hold passionate beliefs. We have chosen one of several popular styles. Pick a style that suits you, then use it consistently.

TYPES

There are only a few basic data types in C. The first ones we'll be encountering and using are:

- Char a character
- Int an integer, in the range -32,767 to 32,767
- Long int a larger integer (up to +-2,147,483,647)
- Float a floating-point number
- Double a floating-point number, with more precision and perhaps greater range than float

If you can look at this list of basic types and say to yourself, "Oh, how simple, there are only a few types, I won't have to worry much about choosing among them," you'll have an easy time with declarations. (Some masochists wish that the type system were more complicated so that they could specify more things about each variable, but those of us who would rather not have to specify these extra things each time are glad that we don't have to.)

The ranges listed above for types int and long int are the guaranteed minimum ranges. On some systems, either of these types (or, indeed, any C type) may be able to hold larger values, but a programme that depends on extended ranges will not be as portable. Some programmers become obsessed with knowing exactly what the sizes of data objects will be in various situations, and go on to write programmes which depend on these exact sizes.

Determining or controlling the size of an object is occasionally important, but most of the time we can sidestep size issues and let the compiler do most of the worrying. (From the ranges listed above, we can determine that type int must be at least 16 bits, and that type long int must be at least 32 bits. But neither of these sizes is exact; many systens have 32-bit ints, and some systems have 64-bit long ints.) You might wonder how the computer stores characters. The answer involves a *character set*, which is simply a mapping between some set of characters and some set of small numeric codes.

Most machines today use the ASCII character set, in which the letter A is represented by the code 65, the ampersand and is represented by the code 38, the digit 1 is represented by the code 49, the space character is represented by the code 32, etc. (Most of the time, of course, you have *no* need to know or even worry about these particular code values; they're automatically translated into the right shapes on the screen or printer when characters are printed out, and they're automatically generated when you type characters on the keyboard.

Eventually, though, we'll appreciate, and even take some control over, exactly when these translations—from characters to their numeric codes—are performed.) Character codes are usually small—the largest code value in ASCII is 126, which is the ~ (tilde or circumflex) character. Characters usually fit in a byte, which is usually 8 bits. In C, type char is defined as occupying one byte, so it is usually 8 bits. Most of the simple variables in most programmes are of types int, long int, or double.

Typically, we'll use int anddouble for most purposes, and long int any time we need to hold integer values greater than 32,767. As we'll see, even when we're manipulating individual characters, we'll usually use an int variable, for reasons to be discussed later.

CONSTANTS

A *constant* is just an immediate, absolute value found in an expression. The simplest constants are decimal integers, *e.g.* 0,1, 2, 123 . Occasionally it is useful to specify constants in base 8 or base 16 (octal or hexadecimal); this is done by prefixing an extra 0 (zero) for octal, or 0x for hexadecimal: the constants 100, 0144, and 0x64 all represent the same number. (If you're not using these non-decimal constants, just remember not to use any leading zeroes. If you accidentally write 0123 intending to get one hundred and twenty three, you'll get 83 instead, which is 123 base 8.)

We write constants in decimal, octal, or hexadecimal for our convenience, not the compiler's. The compiler doesn't care; it always converts everything into binary internally, anyway. (There is, however, no good way to specify constants in source code in binary.)

A constant can be forced to be of type long int by suffixing it with the letter L (in upper or lower case, although upper case is strongly recommended, because a lower case l looks too much like the digit 1). A constant that contains a decimal point or the letter e (or both) is a floating-point constant: 3.14, 10.,.01, 123e4, 123.456e7 . The e indicates multiplication by a power of 10; 123.456e7 is 123.456 times 10 to the 7th, or 1,234,560,000. (Floating-point constants are of type double by default.)

We also have constants for specifying characters and strings. (Make sure you understand the difference between a character and a string: a character is exactly one character; a string is a set of zero or more characters; a string containing one character is distinct from a lone character.) A character constant is simply a single character between single quotes:'A', '.', '%'.

The numeric value of a character constant is, naturally enough, that character's value in the machine's character set. (In ASCII, for example, 'A' has the value 65.) A *string* is represented in C as a sequence or array of characters. (We'll have more to say about arrays in general, and strings in particular, later.) A string constant is a sequence of zero or more characters enclosed in double quotes: "apple","hello, world", "this is a test".

Within character and string constants, the backslash character \ is special, and is used to represent characters not easily typed on the keyboard or for various reasons not easily typed in constants.

The most common of these "character escapes" are:

\n a "newline" character

\b a backspace

\r a carriage return (without a line feed)

\' a single quote (*e.g.* in a character constant)

\" a double quote (*e.g.* in a string constant)

\\ a single backslash

For example, "he said \"hi\"" is a string constant which contains two double quotes, and '\'' is a character constant consisting of a (single) single quote. Notice once again that the character constant 'A' is very different from the string constant "A".

DECLARATIONS

Informally, a *variable* (also called an *object*) is a place you can store a value. So that you can refer to it unambiguously, a variable needs a name. You can think of the variables in your programme as a set of boxes or cubbyholes, each with a label giving its name; you might imagine that storing a value "in" a variable consists of writing the value on a slip of paper and placing it in the cubbyhole.

A *declaration* tells the compiler the name and type of a variable you'll be using in your programme. In its simplest form, a declaration consists of the type, the name of the variable, and a terminating semicolon:

```
char c;
int i;
float f;
```

You can also declare several variables of the same type in one declaration, separating them with commas:

```
int i1, i2;
```

Later we'll see that declarations may also contain *initializers, qualifiers* and *storage classes,* and that we can declare *arrays,functions, pointers,* and other kinds of data structures.

The placement of declarations is significant. You can't place them just anywhere (*i.e.* they cannot be interspersed with the other statements in your programme). They must either be placed at the beginning of a function, or at the beginning of a brace-enclosed block of statements (which we'll learn about in the next chapter), or outside of any function. Furthermore, the placement of a declaration, as well as its storage class, controls several things about its *visibility* and *lifetime*, You may wonder *why* variables must be declared before use.

There are two reasons:

- It makes things somewhat easier on the compiler; it knows right away what kind of storage to allocate and what code to emit to store and manipulate each variable; it doesn't have to try to intuit the programmer's intentions.
- It forces a bit of useful discipline on the programmer: you cannot introduce variables willy-nilly; you must think about them enough to pick appropriate types for them. (The compiler's error messages to you, telling you that you apparently forgot to declare a variable, are as often helpful as they are a nuisance: they're helpful when they tell you that you misspelled a variable, or forgot to think about exactly how you were going to use it.)

Although there are a few places where declarations can be omitted making use of these removes the advantages of reason 2 above, so I recommend always declaring everything explicitly. Most of the time, I recommend writing one declaration per line. For the most part, the compiler doesn't care what order declarations are in. You can order the declarations alphabetically, or in the order that they're used, or to put related declarations next to each other. Collecting all variables of the same type together on one line essentially orders declarations by type, which isn't a very useful order (it's only slightly more useful than random order). A declaration for a variable can also contain an initial value. This *initializer* consists of an equals sign and an expression, which is usually a single constant:

```
int i = 1;
int i1 = 10, i2 = 20;
```

VARIABLE NAMES

Within limits, you can give your variables and functions any names you want. These names consist of letters, numbers, and underscores. For our purposes, names must begin with a letter. Theoretically, names can be as long as you want, but extremely long ones get tedious to type after a while, and the compiler is not required to keep track of extremely long ones perfectly.

What this means is that if you were to name a variable, say, super calafragalistices pialidocious, the compiler might get lazy and pretend that you'd named it super calafragalisticespialidocio, such that if you later misspelled itsupercalafragalisticespialidociouz, the compiler wouldn't catch your mistake.

Nor would the compiler necessarily be able to tell the difference if for some perverse reason you *deliberately* declared a second variable namedsupercalafragalisticespialidociouz. The capitalization of names in C is significant: the variable names variable, Variable, and VARIABLE (as well as silly combinations like variable) are all distinct.

A final restriction on names is that you may not use *keywords* (the words such as int and for which are part of the syntax of the language) as the names of variables or functions (or as identifiers of any kind).

ARITHMETIC OPERATORS

The basic operators for performing arithmetic are the same in many computer languages:

+ addition
- subtraction
* multiplication
/ division
% modulus (remainder)

The - operator can be used in two ways: to subtract two numbers (as in a - b), or to negate one number (as in -a + bor a + -b). When applied to integers, the division operator /discards any remainder, so 1/2 is 0 and 7/4 is 1. But when either operand is a floating-point quantity (type float or double), the division operator yields a floating-point result, with a potentially nonzero fractional part. So 1/2.0 is 0.5, and 7.0/4.0 is 1.75. The *modulus* operator % gives you the remainder when two integers are divided: 1% 2 is 1; 7% 4 is 3. (The modulus operator can only be applied to integers.) An additional arithmetic operation you might be wondering about is exponentiation. Some languages have an exponentiation operator (typically ^ or **), but C doesn't. (To square or cube a number, just multiply it by itself.) Multiplication, division, and modulus all have higher *precedence* than addition and subtraction.

The term "precedence" refers to how "tightly" operators bind to their operands (that is, to the things they operate on). In mathematics, multiplication has higher precedence than addition, so 1 + 2 * 3 is 7, not 9. In other words, 1 + 2 * 3 is equivalent to1 + (2 * 3). C is the same way. All of these operators "group" from left to right, which means that when two or more of them have the same precedence and participate next to each other in an expression, the evaluation conceptually proceeds from left to right.

For example, 1 - 2 - 3 is equivalent to (1 - 2) - 3 and gives -4, not +2. ("Grouping" is sometimes called *associativity,* although the term is used somewhat differently in programming than it is in mathematics. Not all C operators group from left to right; a few group from right to left.) Whenever the default precedence or associativity doesn't give you the grouping you want, you can always use explicit parentheses. For example, if you wanted to add 1 to 2 and then multiply the result by 3, you could write (1 + 2) * 3. By the way, the word "arithmetic" as used in the title of this section is an adjective, not a noun, and it's pronounced differently than the noun: the accent is on the third syllable.

ASSIGNMENT OPERATORS

The assignment operator = assigns a value to a variable. For example,

x = 1

sets x to 1, and

a = b

sets a to whatever b's value is. The expression

i = i + 1

is, as we've mentioned elsewhere, the standard programming idiom for increasing a variable's value by 1: this expression takes i's old value, adds 1 to it, and stores it back into i. (C provides several "shortcut" operators for modifying variables in this and similar ways, which we'll meet later.)

We've called the = sign the "assignment operator" and referred to "assignment expressions" because, in fact, = *is* an operator just like + or -. C does not have "assignment statements"; instead, an assignment like a = b is an expression and can be used wherever any expression can appear. Since it's an expression, the assignment a = b has a value, namely, the same value that's assigned to a. This value can then be used in a larger expression; for example, we might write

c = a = b

which is equivalent to

c = (a = b)

and assigns b's value to both a and c. (The assignment operator, therefore, groups from right to left.). It's usually a matter of style whether you initialize a variable with an initializer in its declaration or with an assignment expression near where you first use it. That is, there's no particular difference between

```
int a = 10;
and
int a;
/* later... */
a = 10;
```

FUNCTION CALLS

We'll have much more to say about functions in a later chapter, but for now let's just look at how they're called.You call a function by mentioning its name followed by a pair of parentheses. If the function takes any arguments, you place the arguments between the parentheses, separated by commas. These are all function calls:

```
printf("Hello, world!\n")
```

```
printf("%d\n", i)
sqrt(144.)
getchar()
```

The arguments to a function can be arbitrary expressions. Therefore, you don't have to say things like

```
int sum = a + b + c;
printf("sum =%d\n", sum);
```

if you don't want to; you can instead collapse it to

```
printf("sum =%d\n", a + b + c);
```

Many functions return values, and when they do, you can embed calls to these functions within larger expressions:

```
c = sqrt(a * a + b * b)
x = r * cos(theta)
i = f1(f2(j))
```

The first expression squares a and b, computes the square root of the sum of the squares, and assigns the result to c. (In other words, it computes a * a + b * b, passes that number to the sqrt function, and assigns sqrt's return value toc.) The second expression passes the value of the variable theta to the cos (cosine) function, multiplies the result by r, and assigns the result to x. The third expression passes the value of the variable j to the function f2, passes the return value of f2 immediately to the function f1, and finally assigns f1's return value to the variable i.

ARRAYS

So far, we've been declaring simple variables: the declaration

int i;

declares a single variable, named i, of type int. It is also possible to declare an *array* of several elements. The declaration

int a[10];

declares an array, named a, consisting of ten elements, each of type int. Simply speaking, an array is a variable that can hold more than one value. You specify which of the several values you're referring to at any given time by using a numeric*subscript*. (Arrays in programming are similar to vectors or matrices in mathematics.)

We can represent the array a above with a picture like this:

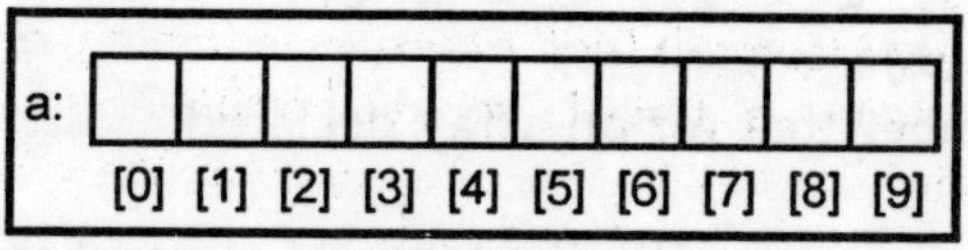

In C, arrays are *zero-based*: the ten elements of a 10-element array are numbered from 0 to 9. The subscript which specifies a single element of an array is simply an integer expression in square brackets. The first element of the array isa[0], the second element is a[1], etc. You can use these "array subscript expressions" anywhere you can use the name of a simple variable, for example:

```
a[0] = 10;
a[1] = 20;
a[2] = a[0] + a[1];
```

Notice that the subscripted array references (*i.e.* expressions such as a[0] and a[1]) can appear on either side of the assignment operator. The subscript does not have to be a constant like 0 or 1; it can be any integral expression. For example, it's common to loop over all elements of an array:

```
int i;
for(i = 0; i < 10; i = i + 1)
a[i] = 0;
```

This loop sets all ten elements of the array a to 0.

Arrays are a real convenience for many problems, but there is not a lot that C will do with them for you automatically. In particular, you can neither set all elements of an array at once nor assign one array to another; both of the assignments.

```
a = 0; /* WRONG */
and
int b[10];
b = a; /* WRONG */PP
```

are illegal.

To set all of the elements of an array to some value, you must do so one by one, as in the loop example above. To copy the contents of one array to another, you must again do so one by one:

```
int b[10];
for(i = 0; i < 10; i = i + 1)
b[i] = a[i];
```

Remember that for an array declared

int a[10];

there is no element a[10]; the topmost element is a[9]. This is one reason that zero-based loops are also common in C.

Note that the for loop

for(i = 0; i < 10; i = i + 1)

...

does just what you want in this case: it starts at 0, the number 10 suggests (correctly) that it goes through 10 iterations, but the less-than comparison means that the last trip through the loop has i set to 9. (The comparison i <= 9 would also work, but it would be less clear and therefore poorer style.) In the little examples so far, we've always looped over all 10 elements of the sample array a. It's common, however, to use an array that's bigger than necessarily needed, and to use a second variable to keep track of how many elements of the array are currently in use. For example, we might have an integer variable

int na;/* number of elements of a[] in use */

Then, when we wanted to do something with a (such as print it out), the loop would run from 0 to na, not 10 (or whatevera's size was):

for(i = 0; i < na; i = i + 1)

printf("%d\n", a[i]);

Naturally, we would have to ensure ensure that na's value was always less than or equal to the number of elements actually declared in a. Arrays are not limited to type int; you can have arrays of char or double or any other type. Here is a slightly larger example of the use of arrays.

Suppose we want to investigate the behaviour of rolling a pair of dice. The total roll can be anywhere from 2 to 12, and we want to count how often each roll comes up. We will use an array to keep track of the counts: a[2] will count how many times we've rolled 2, etc. We'll simulate the roll of a die by calling C's random number generation function, rand().

Each time you call rand(), it returns a different, pseudo-random integer. The values that rand() returns typically span a large range, so we'll use C'*smodulus* (or "remainder") operator % to produce random numbers in the range we want. The expression rand()% 6produces random numbers in the range 0 to 5, and rand()% 6 + 1 produces random numbers in the range 1 to 6.

Here is the programme:

```
#include <stdio.h>
#include <stdlib.h>
main()
{
int i;
int d1, d2;
int a[13]; /* uses [2..12] */
for(i = 2; i <= 12; i = i + 1)
a[i] = 0;
for(i = 0; i < 100; i = i + 1)
{
d1 = rand()% 6 + 1;
d2 = rand()% 6 + 1;
a[d1 + d2] = a[d1 + d2] + 1;
}
for(i = 2; i <= 12; i = i + 1)
printf("%d:%d\n", i, a[i]);
return 0;
}
```

We include the header <stdlib.h> because it contains the necessary declarations for the rand() function. We declare the array of size 13 so that its highest element will be a[12].

We're wasting a[0] and a[1]; this is no great loss. The variables d1 and d2 contain the rolls of the two individual dice; we add them together to decide which cell of the array to increment, in the line

a[d1 + d2] = a[d1 + d2] + 1;

After 100 rolls, we print the array out. Typically (as craps players well know), we'll see mostly 7's, and relatively few 2's and 12's. (By the way, it turns out that using the % operator to reduce the range of the rand function is *not* always a good idea. We'll say more about this problem in an exercise.)

ARRAY INITIALIZATION

Although it is not possible to assign to all elements of an array at once using an assignment expression, it is possible to initialize some or all elements of an array when the array is defined. The syntax looks like this:

```
int a[10] = {0, 1, 2, 3, 4, 5, 6, 7, 8, 9};
```

The list of values, enclosed in braces {}, separated by commas, provides the initial values for successive elements of the array. (Under older, pre-ANSI C compilers, you could not always supply initializers for "local" arrays inside functions; you could only initialize "global" arrays, those outside of any function. Those compilers are now rare, so you shouldn't have to worry about this distinction any more. We'll talk more about local and global variables later in this chapter.) If there are fewer initializers than elements in the array, the remaining elements are automatically initialized to 0.

For example,

```
int a[10] = {0, 1, 2, 3, 4, 5, 6};
```

would initialize a[7], a[8], and a[9] to 0. When an array definition includes an initializer, the array dimension may be omitted, and the compiler will infer the dimension from the number of initializers.

For example,

```
int b[] = {10, 11, 12, 13, 14};
```

would declare, define, and initialize an array b of 5 elements (*i.e.* just as if you'd typed int b[5]). Only the dimension is omitted; the brackets [] remain to indicate that b is in fact an array.

In the case of arrays of char, the initializer may be a string constant:

```
char s1[7] = "Hello,";
char s2[10] = "there,";
char s3[] = "world!";
```

As before, if the dimension is omitted, it is inferred from the size of the string initializer. (We haven't covered strings in detail yet—we'll do so in chapter 8—but it turns out that all strings in C are terminated by a special character with the value 0. Therefore, the array s3 will be of size 7, and the explicitly-sized s1 does need to be of size at least 7. For s2, the last 4 characters in the array will all end up being this zero-value character.)

MULTIDIMENSIONAL ARRAYS

When we said that "Arrays are not limited to type int; you can have arrays of... any other type," we meant that more literally than you might have guessed. If you have an "array of int," it means that you have an array each of whose elements is of type int. But you can have an array each of whose elements is of type *x*, where *x* is any type you choose. In particular, you can have an array each of whose elements is another array! We can use these arrays of arrays for the same sorts of tasks as we'd use multidimensional arrays in other computer languages (or matrices in mathematics).

Naturally, we are not limited to arrays of arrays, either; we could have an array of arrays of arrays, which would act like a 3-dimensional array, etc.

The declaration of an array of arrays looks like this:

int a2[5][7];

You have to read complicated declarations like these "inside out." What this one says is that a2 is an array of 5 somethings, and that each of the somethings is an array of 7 ints. More briefly, "a2 is an array of 5 arrays of 7 ints," or, "a2 is an array of array of int." In the declaration of a2, the brackets closest to the identifier a2 tell you what a2 first and foremost is. That's how you know it's an array of 5 arrays of size 7, not the other way around.

You can think of a2 as having 5 "rows" and 7 "columns," although this interpretation is not mandatory. (You could also treat the "first" or inner subscript as "x" and the second as "y." Unless you're doing something fancy, all you have to worry about is that the subscripts when you access the array match those that you used when you declared it, as in the examples below.) To illustrate the use of multidimensional arrays, we might fill in the elements of the above array a2 using this piece of code:

```
int i, j;
for(i = 0; i < 5; i = i + 1)
{
for(j = 0; j < 7; j = j + 1)
a2[i][j] = 10 * i + j;
}
```

This pair of nested loops sets a[1][2] to 12, a[4][1] to 41, etc. Since the first dimension of a2 is 5, the first subscripting index variable, i, runs from 0 to 4. Similarly, the second subscript varies from 0 to 6. We could print a2 out with a similar pair of nested loops:

```
for(i = 0; i < 5; i = i + 1)
{
for(j = 0; j < 7; j = j + 1)
printf("%d\t", a2[i][j]);
printf("\n");
}
```

(The character \t in the printf string is the tab character.)

Just to see more clearly what's going on, we could make the "row" and "column" subscripts explicit by printing them, too:

```
for(j = 0; j < 7; j = j + 1)
printf("\t%d:", j);
printf("\n");
for(i = 0; i < 5; i = i + 1)
{
printf("%d:", i);
for(j = 0; j < 7; j = j + 1)
printf("\t%d", a2[i][j]);
printf("\n");
}
```

This last fragment would print

```
0: 1: 2: 3: 4: 5: 6:
0: 0 1 2 3 4 5 6
1: 10 11 12 13 14 15 16
2: 20 21 22 23 24 25 26
```

```
3: 30 31 32 33 34 35 36
4: 40 41 42 43 44 45 46
```

Finally, there's no reason we have to loop over the "rows" first and the "columns" second; depending on what we wanted to do, we could interchange the two loops, like this:

```
for(j = 0; j < 7; j = j + 1)
{
for(i = 0; i < 5; i = i + 1)
printf("%d\t", a2[i][j]);
printf("\n");
}
```

Notice that i is still the first subscript and it still runs from 0 to 4, and j is still the second subscript and it still runs from 0 to 6.

VISIBILITY

We haven't said so explicitly, but variables are channels of communication within a programme. You set a variable to a value at one point in a programme, and at another point you read the value out again. The two points may be in adjoining statements, or they may be in widely separated parts of the programme. How long does a variable last? How widely separated can the setting and fetching parts of the programme be, and how long after a variable is set does it persist? Depending on the variable and how you're using it, you might want different answers to these questions.

The *visibility* of a variable determines how much of the rest of the programme can access that variable. You can arrange that a variable is visible only within one part of one function, or in one function, or in one source file, or anywhere in the programme. Why would you want to limit the visibility of a variable? For maximum flexibility, wouldn't it be handy if all variables were potentially visible everywhere? As it happens, that arrangement would be *too* flexible: everywhere in the programme, you would have to keep track of the names of all the variables declared anywhere else in the programme, so that you didn't accidentally re-use one. Whenever a variable had the wrong value by mistake, you'd have to search the entire programme for the bug, because any statement in the entire programme could potentially have modified that variable. You would constantly be stepping all over yourself by using a common variable name like i in two parts of your programme, and having one snippet of code accidentally overwrite the values being used by another part of the code. The communication would be sort of like an old party line—you'd always be accidentally interrupting other conversations, or having your conversations interrupted. To avoid this confusion, we generally give variables the narrowest or smallest visibility they need. A variable declared within the braces {} of a function is visible only within that function; variables declared within functions are called *local variables*. If another function somewhere else declares a local variable with the same name, it's a different variable entirely, and the two don't clash with each other.

On the other hand, a variable declared outside of any function is a *global variable*, and it is potentially visible anywhere within the programme. You use global variables when you *do* want the communications path to be able to travel to any part of the programme. When you declare a global variable, you will usually give it a longer, more descriptive name so that whenever you use it you will remember that it's the same variable everywhere. Another word for the visibility of variables is *scope*. How long do variables last? By default, local variables (those declared within a function) have *automatic duration*: they spring into existence when the function is called, and they disappear when the function returns.

Global variables, on the other hand, have *static duration*: they last, and the values stored in them persist, for as long as the programme does. Finally, it is possible to split a function up into several source files, for easier maintenance. When several source files are combined into one programme (we'll be seeing how in the next chapter) the compiler must have a way of correlating the global variables which might be used to communicate between the several source files.

Bibliography

Arora, Ashok: *Foundations of Computer Science*, India: John Wiley and Sons, 2002.

Baeza-Yates, Ricardo: *Foundations of information technology in the era of network*, New Jersey: Engelwood Cliffs, 2000.

Barta, B. Z.: *Information technology in educational management*, New Delhi: Oxford University Press, 2001.

Basu, Ron: *Information systems foundations: constructing and criticizing*, California: University of California, 2007.

Colin, Baker: *Foundations of bilingual education and bilingualism*, UK: Addison–Wesley Publishing Company, 2004.

Dana, J.: *Australian national bibliography: Volume 1*, New York: Prentice Hall, 2007.

Dennis, N.: *The Utility Business Architecture: Designing for Change*, New Jersey: Engelwood Cliffs, 2000.

Dianne, P. O: *The mathematics of information coding, extraction, and distribution*, UK: Addison–Wesley Publishing Company, 2004.

Donald, M.: *The foundations of vacuum coating technology*, New York: McGraw–Hill, 2003.

Fredrick, Nafukho: *Foundations of adult education in Africa*, New Jersey: Engelwood Cliffs, 2000.

James, A.: *Management information systems: a managerial end user perspective*, New York: McGraw–Hill, 2003.

Jorma, Rissanen: *Journal of the American Society for Information Science: Volume 48*, UK: Addison–Wesley Publishing Company, 2004.

Kathleen, A.: *Physical therapy professional foundations: keys to success,* New Jersey: Engelwood Cliffs, 2000.

Khosrowpour, Mehdi: *Advanced topics in information resources management: Volume 2,* India: John Wiley and Sons, 2002.

Koohang, Alex: *Knowledge Management: Theoretical Foundations,* New York: McGraw–Hill, 2003.

Kumar, Rakesh: *Foundations to information technology,* India: John Wiley and Sons, 2002.

Lucia, Faravelli: *Proceedings of the US-Europe workshop on sensors,* New Jersey: Engelwood Cliffs, 2000.

Michael, A.: *Durability of Building Materials and Components 8: Information,* UK: Addison–Wesley Publishing Company, 2004.

Rangarajan, Ramesh: *Foundations of Web technology,* New Delhi: Oxford University Press, 2001.

Richard, Baskerville: *Business agility and information technology diffusion: IFIP,* New Jersey: Engelwood Cliffs, 2000.

Ruth, Nabwala : *Fostering research on the economic and social impacts,* New York: Prentice Hall, 1997.

Singh, Sumit: *Negotiating via information technology: theory and application,* New Delhi: Oxford University Press, 2001.

Yadav, D. S.: *Foundations of Information Technology,* New Delhi: Oxford University Press, 2006.

Index